The First-Year Experience
Monograph Series No. 36

Involvement in Campus Activities and the Retention of First-Year College Students

Tracy L. Skipper
Roxanne Argo

Editors

educational gains

program assessment

improving education

creating connections

transforming culture

developing community
research

leadership courses

campus activities

student success

student retention
educational attainment

providing alternatives

NATIONAL RESOURCE CENTER
THE FIRST-YEAR EXPERIENCE
& STUDENTS IN TRANSITION
University of South Carolina, 2003

naca
National Association for Campus Activities

#5138909Y

Cite as:

Skipper, T. L., & Argo, R. (Eds.). (2003). *Involvement in campus activities and the retention of first-year college students* (Monograph No. 36). Columbia, SC: University of South Carolina, National Resource Center for The First-Year Experience and Students in Transition.

Sample Chapter Citation:

Schroeder, C. C. (2003). Meeting the changing needs of students. In T. L. Skipper, & R. Argo (Eds.), *Involvement in campus activities and the retention of first-year college students* (Monograph No. 36) (pp. 19-34). Columbia, SC: University of South Carolina, National Resource Center for The First-Year Experience and Students in Transition.

The Freshman Year Experience® and The First-Year Experience® are service marks of the University of South Carolina. A license may be granted upon written request to use the terms The Freshman Year Experience and The First-Year Experience. This license is not transferrable without written approval of the University of South Carolina.

Additional copies of this monograph may be obtained from the National Resource Center for The First-Year Experience and Students in Transition, University of South Carolina, 1629 Pendleton Street, Columbia, SC 29208. Telephone (803) 777-6029. Telefax (803) 777-4699.

Involvement in campus activities and the retention of first-year college students/ Tracy L. Skipper and Roxanne Argo, editors.
     p.cm. -- (First-year experience monograph series; no. 36)
Includes bibliographical references.
ISBN 1-889271-40-3
1. College freshman--United States. 2. Student Activities--United States. 3. College attendance--United States. I. Skipper, Tracy L. (Tracy Lynn) II. Argo, Roxanne. III. Series

LB2343.32.I59 2003
378.1'98--dc21   2003000341

Acknowledgments

Any joint effort between two national centers takes a good bit of organization and cooperation— and many talented and dedicated individuals who work to ensure a high-quality outcome from that collaboration. The staffs of the National Resource Center and the National Association for Campus Activities wish to thank the following individuals for their guidance and assistance with this publication.

Dawn Thomas, Director of Research and Educational Program Services at NACA, for development of the initial plan for this volume and for assistance with content editing.

Jean Henscheid, former Associate Director of the National Resource Center and currently the Manager of Publishing for the College of Agricultural and Life Sciences at the University of Idaho, for her guidance in developing the initial plan for this volume and for her assistance in revising the introduction.

Barbara Tobolowsky, Associate Director of the National Resource Center, and Amy Murray and Holli Armstrong, Editorial Assistants, for copy editing and proofreading assistance.

Kylie Cafiero, Editorial Assistant at the National Resource Center, for design and layout of the volume.

Laura Bestler-Wilcox, Assistant Director of Student Activities at Iowa State University, for proofreading assistance.

Contents

Foreword

Alan B. Davis
National Association for Campus Activities
Mary Stuart Hunter
*National Resource Center for The
First-Year Experience and Students in Transition*

Involvement in Campus Activities and the Retention of First-Year College Students represents the culmination of many months of engaged collaboration between the National Resource Center for The First-Year Experience and Students in Transition and the National Association for Campus Activities. This monograph follows a half dozen published by the National Resource Center in collaboration with other professional associations: The Association of College and University Housing Officers-International in 1991, the National Orientation Directors Association and the Association of Deans and Directors of University Colleges and Undergraduate Divisions in 1993, the National Academic Advising Association in 1995, the National Student Employment Association in 1996, and the National Association for Developmental Education in 1998. Each of these earlier monographs provided a quality academic publication to the organizations' memberships and, just as important, shone a spotlight on the vital work of those associations for the higher education community at large. As these partnerships so well demonstrate, attention to the success of first-year students and students in transition at all levels of the undergraduate experience can be achieved by educators in a wide variety of settings within higher education.

We know that first-year students make critical decisions about how they spend their discretionary hours soon after they arrive on our campuses. We also know that the institution has a critical role to play in helping students make these decisions. This monograph offers insight into educationally purposeful out-of-class activities and the impact they have on the student experience. It also provides future direction for the campus activities field and identifies ways to improve the educational experience of first-year students in order to enhance their scholarly experience and, ultimately, increase persistence to graduation. More specifically, the authors propose a broader view of student activities, one that ties together more closely the curricular and social aspects of the institution. We believe that faculty, campus activities and student affairs professionals, and academic personnel will find this monograph to be a valuable resource that enriches the underlying philosophy of their work.

As with each of the other monographs published by the National Resource Center for The First-Year Experience and Students in Transition, this volume would not have been possible without the efforts of the contributing authors, their valuable insight and diverse perspectives on the field of campus activities, and their day-to-day experiences as champions of the campus activities profession. The editors, Tracy L. Skipper and Roxanne Argo, were also instrumental in shaping a monograph with the potential to provide a nexus for attention to meaningful campus activities, one that may be the catalyst to bring this topic to the center of campus dialogue. The editors and the chapter authors realize that the most valuable and successful educational environments are those that combine traditional academic curriculum with campus and community activities. This, in fact, is education. We anticipate that after you read this monograph, you will embrace this belief as well.

Shifting Our Focus on Retaining First-Year Students and Campus Activities: An Introduction

Tracy L. Skipper
University of South Carolina
Roxanne Argo
National Association for Campus Activities

The first year is a critical moment in the retention of college students, because 40% of students who start a four-year degree program leave college before graduation, and nearly 57% of those who leave four-year institutions do so before the beginning of the second year (Tinto, n.d.). Students leave college for a variety of reasons, some of which are involuntary (e.g., academic suspension). While comprehensive retention strategies include academic support structures, most efforts target voluntary departures. For example, retention efforts designed to reach first-year students often focus on their lives outside the classroom; therefore, campus activities programs are frequently designed with the intent of helping students connect to the campus community and increase their desire to remain within that community. The retention goals associated with campus activities programs are closely related to what Whipple (1996) suggests are the primary objectives of such programs— to "enhance learning outside the classroom, provide for relationship and community building . . . and promote a value-based developmental experience" (p. 303). In light of this, colleges and universities traditionally have offered a wide range of campus activities through a variety of administrative offices. These activities include concerts, lectures, films, health awareness programs, social functions, and late-night programs, to name just a few.

The literature on student retention, as reviewed below, clearly suggests that as involvement in co-curricular experiences during the academic career increases, students are more likely to feel satisfied, experience academic success, and persist toward graduation (Berger & Milem, 1999; Peltier, Laden, & Matranga, 1999; Upcraft, 1985, 1989). In fact, this relationship may be recursive—students who are involved are more likely to have contacts with faculty and other students related to their academic work, leading to increased learning (Tinto, 1993). Such engagement in learning may lead to feelings of satisfaction and increase the likelihood that students will remain enrolled at the institution.

Although each higher education institution has a unique history, tradition, personality, academic environment, and student culture, most institutions strive for a successful campus activities program that benefits both the student body and the larger campus community. Participation in these programs can not only contribute to a student's social and intellectual development, it can also offer opportunities for the interchange of ideas and opinions, and can involve students in diverse cultural experiences. Because such factors as being closed to new ideas and experiences, failing to see the relevance or value of coursework, feeling alienated and socially isolated are common risk factors for departure (Fries-Britt, Gardner, Low, & Tinto, 2002), co-curricular experiences that provide students with an opportunity to explore a range of ideas, cultures, beliefs, and art forms may increase the likelihood of student persistence. Further, leadership and social activities can add to the overall development of a skill-set that prepares students for success after college and helps them develop mature interpersonal relationships with others on campus (Kuh, Schuh, Whitt, & Associates, 1991). As a result, institutions may experience a renewed emphasis on institutional mission, a thriving campus community, and increasing graduation rates.

Thus, a strong campus activities program can be invaluable. While campus activities programs and academic curriculum overlap in numerous ways, together they can form a critical mixture that shapes each student's perception of her college years and the institution as a whole, affecting academic success and persistence and perhaps a life-long commitment to the institution. Unfortunately, while the link between retention and involvement in campus activities is clear, the American higher education community continues to be plagued by what Upcraft (1985, 1989) calls a "lack of specificity." While the focus may be on those activities that require institutional planning and support, many activities in which students engage happen spontaneously, making it difficult to ascertain which activities have the most impact on retention and success (Upcraft 1985, 1989). Further, research suggests that while involvement in some social activities and peer relationships may increase the likelihood of persistence, they may decrease the likelihood of intellectual development and academic success (Kuh et al., 1991; Peltier et al., 1999). This would suggest that institutions need to focus on providing a balanced offering of out-of-class experiences as well as seeking to create environments where the spontaneous activities in which students engage increase the likelihood of persistence while supporting their learning and success.

The Connection Between Campus Activities and Retention

Collectively, the authors of this monograph will argue that a combination of intellectually rich, socially positive, and personally engaging formal and informal campus activities will yield the greatest retention results. This alchemy of campus activities is richly supported in the body of research reviewed here. The research on campus involvement suggests that a number of activities influence retention, including general participation in extra-curricular activities, establishing close friendships, belonging to student organizations, participation in orientation, involvement in social and cultural activities, attending lectures, and using campus facilities (Upcraft 1985, 1989). As will be described in this volume, educationally purposeful campus activities can offer opportunities for involvement for a variety of students in the social and intellectual life of the institution. As the following review suggests, this kind of involvement is central to student persistence beyond the first year. This first section focuses on involvement on campus, social integration, and the intersections between social integration and academic integration as they relate to student persistence. Throughout this monograph, chapter authors provide a research-based argument for and examples of successful programs that engage students in learning and focus on their cognitive and affective needs—two characteristics of successful retention efforts (Fries-Britt et al., 2002). We begin our review of the literature by summarizing two widely recognized models related to student retention.

Models of Student Departure

Astin's theory of student involvement. Drawing on Freud's concept of cathexis and the concept of time-on-task from learning theorists, Astin (1999/1984) proposes that student involvement is "the amount of physical and psychological energy that a student devotes to the academic experience" (p. 518). For Astin, the academic experience comprised both the formal classroom environment and the larger, informal environment of the campus as a whole. He also suggested that such an investment is primarily behavioral (focused on the activity rather than the intention of the student), occurs along a continuum, and can be described in terms of its quantity and quality. Moreover, he theorized that learning and personal development are "directly proportional to the quality and quantity of student involvement" (p. 519). The implication of this theory for practitioners, Astin suggested, is that we can judge the effectiveness of any program or practice by the extent to which that program or practice contributes to student involvement. To the extent that learning and involvement are related, one might also measure program effectiveness in relation to its ability to enhance learning.

The theory of student involvement grew out of a longitudinal study of college dropouts. In attempting to identify the factors associated with college departure, Astin (1999/1984) discovered that every significant trend could be explained by involvement: Positive aspects of the environment (or those elements that increased the likelihood of persistence) led to increased involvement, while negative aspects (those things leading to attrition) led to decreased involvement. Living on campus is one of the most significant environmental factors contributing to involvement, as residential students simply have more time and opportunity to join student organizations and participate in campus activities. Further, those students in Astin's (1999/1984) study who joined social fraternities or sororities or participated in extracurricular activities were less likely to drop out than their non-involved peers.

Tinto's model of student departure. In *Leaving College,* Tinto (1993) draws on anthropological studies of rites of passage and sociological studies of suicide to create a model of student departure. In short, the model suggests that students who persist through the first year of college separate from their communities of origin, make the transition to the academic environment, and become incorporated into the college community. While students leave for a variety of reasons, many will make the decision to leave the institution because they have failed to establish a strong, satisfying membership within the college or university community. His longitudinal model of student departure is stepwise, suggesting that students move through these stages in time, but explorations of Tinto's model and his own discussions of the cyclical nature of involvement argue in favor of a more recursive process, making the picture more complex. Tinto suggests that the adoption of norms and behaviors necessary for success in the college community "requires some degree of transformation and perhaps rejection of the norms of past communities" (p. 95). However, the extent to which a student separates from past communities may depend on the student's age, residential status, family or work commitments, and a host of other factors. While attempting to meet the demands of multiple communities may increase the likelihood of departure for some students, "social support from family . . . moderates, or reduces, the adverse effects of negative school events" on academic performance (Napoli & Wortman, 1998, p. 447; Christie & Dinham, 1991; Elkins, Braxton, & James, 2000). Moreover, conventional wisdom suggests that those students of traditional college age who maintain close connections with high school friends will be less likely to become integrated into the social network of the campus. However, "students with high-school friends who shared their commitment toward college made more progress toward transition from high-school to college friendships" (Christie & Dinham, 1991, p. 426). Only when close contact is maintained with friends not enrolled in college do negative effects on college social transitions appear. Thus, separation from past communities is not a necessary precursor to persistence, and in some cases, maintaining connections may actually provide the support students need to remain in college.

While students do not need to make a complete break with the past community to succeed in college, integration into the campus culture is an important factor in persistence. Drawing on studies of suicide, Tinto suggests that students are most likely to leave college when they hold values that are at odds with those of the institution or when they have "insufficient personal affiliation" with other community members (p. 102). As noted above, students may not adopt the norms of the institution, but Tinto believes it critical that those students "locate at least one community in which to find membership and the support membership provides" (p. 105). Moreover, the likelihood of persistence increases when the communities in which students are members are central rather than peripheral. In other words, strong local affiliations do not necessarily result in strong affiliation to the institution and may interfere with a student's ability to respond to the academic demands of the culture (see for example, Milem & Berger, 1997; Pascarella & Terenzini, 1991; Tinto & Goodsell, 1994). Thus, it is not enough for student affairs professionals and faculty members to encourage students to make friends and get involved on campus; they must also ensure that the communities which students form and in which they situate themselves are closely connected to the goals and values of the dominant institutional community. Moreover, educators need to ensure that a wide range of communities exist on campus so that students have the opportunity "to play out a multiplicity of roles and satisfy a range of needs that no one community may be able to fulfill" (Tinto, 1993, p. 122). Tinto (1993) also suggested "the intriguing possibility that student persistence, and quite possibly social and intellectual growth, involves, perhaps requires, a changing mix of social and academic memberships over time" (p. 126). Therefore, while this monograph focuses primarily on the first year of college, it is important to remember that students should be constantly re-engaged in the campus community through a flexible and responsive program of out-of-class activities. Arminio and Loflin explore this issue in greater depth in Chapter 3.

Involvement on Campus

Peltier et al. (1999) reviewed the literature on student persistence in college, noting that full-time students will spend approximately 15 hours per week in formal classroom settings. That said, an abundance of time exists for students to become engaged in the academic and social environments of the campus. Whether that engagement comes through informal social interactions with peers, participation in traditional campus activities, interactions with faculty, or on-campus work, the bottom line is that the more time and energy students devote to activities outside of class the more likely they are to persist at the institution. Of course, Astin's emphasis on the quality of involvement cannot be overlooked. Over-involvement in activities or participation in certain types of activities can be counterproductive for some students. For example, Peltier et al. (1999) describe several studies finding negative indications for learning and success for students in White Greek organizations. To the extent that involvement in Greek organizations connects students to a community at the institution, such organizations may also appear to aid in retention. Ultimately, Tinto suggests these local communities may have negative implications for retention if they are not committed or connected to the larger educational mission of the institution. Light (2001) underscores the importance of quality in extra-curricular involvement when he suggests that *substantial* commitment to *one or two* activities can lead to increased satisfaction. While such involvement has little impact on grades, according to Light, the increased satisfaction students experience may contribute positively to persistence.

Student Characteristics

Person-environment fit models of student retention (e.g., Tinto and Astin) suggest that pre-entry characteristics play a large role in persistence. In some cases, students may change pre-entry values, beliefs, or behaviors to ensure a better fit with the new environment. However, many pre-entry characteristics are beyond the student's control. In these cases, the institution may need to reexamine structures, policies, and environmental conditions that deter persistence. In this volume, Kuh, Palmer, and Kish (Chapter 1) and Arminio and Loflin (Chapter 3) review literature highlighting the differential impact of involvement in co-curricular and leadership experiences for special populations of students. In Chapter 2, Schroeder examines the implications of changing student populations for the design and delivery of educationally purposeful activities. Some of the student characteristics most frequently examined in the retention literature are discussed below.

Race/ethnicity. According to Berger and Milem (1999), "being black is the third largest negative predictor of persistence" (p. 657). African-American students report lower levels of institutional support during the fall semester and are more likely to report involvement in activist behaviors in the fall (Milem & Berger, 1997). Activist behaviors may have a negative impact on retention because while White students are engaging in traditional social activities that help them focus on and build relationships within the institution, African-American students' attention may be focused outside the institution. Moreover, engaging in activist behaviors may put African-American students in conflict with the campus community, making the establishment of early connections more difficult.

Strategies for increasing persistence for racial and ethnic minority students include building "welcoming, supportive and culturally" relevant communities for all students and providing opportunities for successful leadership experiences for students of color (Peltier et al., 1999, p. 363). Students of color also need help building self-confidence, developing strategies for dealing with racism, and identifying campus support structures (Peltier et al., 1999).

Gender. Interactions with peers and developing close personal relationships are related to persistence for both men and women (Nora, Cabrera, Hagedorn, & Pascarella, 1996), but women may have an easier time or be more adept at developing such relationships. Milem and Berger (1997) identified a direct positive path between being a woman and social integration. For example, they found that women reported higher levels of early peer involvement and higher levels of perceived institutional and peer support than their male counterparts. Women also report greater initial goal commit-ment than men (Napoli & Wortman, 1998). While women may have the advantage in peer relationships, male students may be more likely to have early contact with faculty (Milem & Berger, 1997). Because of the importance of social interactions to persistence, Nora et al. (1996) suggest institutions should encourage students to join student organizations, participate in campus activities, and form study groups. Creating more opportunities for interactions with faculty, especially for women, may also be important.

Academic achievement. Because students with higher levels of academic achievement may be less likely to participate in traditional campus activities, student affairs professionals need to design activities that bridge the academic and social environments of the campus to ensure that these students have adequate opportunities to form important peer and faculty/staff relationships. Such students are more likely to be involved in organized activities (e.g., volunteer work, student clubs or organizations, residence hall programs or activities, religious services or meetings) in the fall semester, but those activities are less likely to be traditional social activities (e.g., Greek social activities, dating, drinking alcohol). A higher high school GPA is also predictive of less involvement in organized activities in the spring semester (Milem & Berger, 1997). These findings suggest that students with a greater academic orientation at the time of enrollment may remain academically focused.

Residents versus commuters. In their review of college persistence literature, Peltier et al. (1999) discuss the characteristics of residents and commuter students. They cite a study (Velez, 1985) that found a positive correlation between living on campus and persistence. Proposed explanations for this finding include the fact that residents may work fewer hours (particularly hours off campus, a negative indicator of involvement and persistence according to Astin) than non-residents, that the friends of resident students tend to be more academically oriented (in that they are more likely to be other college students) than those of commuters, and that these students are more likely to be integrated into the life of the campus. Christie and Dinham (1991) found that living on campus enhanced social integration in four ways: (a) helping students meet other students, (b) facilitating the development of friendships, (c) providing greater access to information about the social activities on campus, and (d) decreasing the reliance on high school friends. Other characteristics of resident students suggest that they are more likely to be women, come from families with high levels of formal education, have high levels of academic aptitude, and may have been more involved in secondary school extra-curricular activities (Pascarella, 1985 as cited in Peltier et al., 1999). Commuter students, who are most likely to be female, may have lower socio-economic status and report less frequent attendance at organized campus events than resident students (Santana & Nonnamaker, 1992 as cited in Peltier et al., 1999).

Involvement and Integration

Many researchers have examined the relationship between involvement on campus and integration into the campus community. Milem and Berger (1997) suggest that this connection is cyclical—behaviors contribute to perceptions and those perceptions shape future behaviors. For example, they suggest that involvement on campus influences perceptions of peer and institutional support, which in turn affects subsequent levels of involvement and persistence. Summarizing the research on involvement, Berger and Milem (1999) note, "student involvement leads to greater integration in the social and academic systems of the college and promotes institutional commitment" (p. 644). Therefore, involvement affects levels of institutional commitment, a key component in student departure decisions. Further, early non-involvement has negative implications for a number of areas: Students are more likely to stay uninvolved, less likely to perceive their institution and peers as supportive, less likely to become integrated, and less likely to persist (Berger & Milem, 1999). Other research suggests that graduates have higher rates of extra-curricular participation than non-persisters (Daly & Breegle, 1989 as cited in Peltier et al., 1999).

One strategy for increasing involvement on campus is to increase the interactions among students and faculty early in students' college careers. Early involvement with faculty is a predictor of involvement with organized activities and traditional social activities (Milem & Berger, 1997). Because of the importance of involvement to integration and persistence, institutions should do a better job helping students make early connections with faculty members and matching student needs to programs and services offered on campus (Berger & Milem, 1999). For example, Murray and Hall (2001) propose using Holland's model as a referral system designed to improve student retention. Students can be directed toward activities that not only match their personal values and interest but also tie to future career goals.

Intersection Between Social Integration and Academic Integration

Tinto (1993) identifies a critical link between learning and leaving, suggesting that "the more students are involved in the social and intellectual life of a college, the more frequently they make contact with faculty and other students about learning issues, especially outside the class, the more students are likely to learn" (p. 69). Such involvement leads to satisfaction. In a study of Harvard undergraduates, Light (2001) found that the students who were the happiest and most academically successful were those who worked with faculty and other students outside of class to accomplish substantive academic work.

Other researchers have examined the link between active learning and social integration, suggesting that active learning may actually be a precursor to social integration (Braxton, Milem, & Sullivan, 2000; Milem & Berger, 1997):

> Thus, students who frequently encounter active learning in their courses perceive themselves gaining knowledge and understanding from their course work. As a consequence, such students may be more likely to view their collegiate experience as personally rewarding. Because their classes

are judged to be rewarding, students may invest the psychological energy needed to establish membership in the social communities of their college or university. (Braxton et al., 2000, p. 572)

For example, students whose classes employ active learning strategies (e.g., class discussion, group work, and higher-order thinking activities) may feel they need to spend less time out of class preparing and studying, and, thus, feel they "have more time available for participation in collegiate social communities" (Braxton et al., 2000, p. 572). Such courses may also help them establish a network of peer support and develop friendships. According to Tinto and Goodsell (1994), this is also one of the strong selling points of learning communities—they allow students to pursue academic and social goals at the same time. Tinto (1997) also emphasizes the social aspect of learning central to linked course structures, suggesting that students "get to know each other quickly and fairly intimately, in a way that is part and parcel of their academic experience" (p. 54).

Braxton et al. (2000) suggest that the social implications of active learning strategies are likely to be amplified when courses are linked to living/learning programs designed for first-year students. Membership in such academic/social communities is also more likely to deter students from less positive activities, because these communities are more closely aligned to the central mission of the institution than more peripheral and purely social ones. The design of such communities may be important for institutions that are trying to influence the informal activities in which students engage outside the classroom. Kuh et al. (1991) remind us that peers may have a negative influence on learning:

> . . .spending time with friends whose orientation to learning is incompatible with the educational purposes of the institution may reinforce inappropriate behaviors. The peer group, rather than challenging old attitudes and behaviors, may allow a student to rely

on comfortable, perhaps anti-intellectual behavior patterns. (pp. 12-13)

As discussed earlier, decreased learning may mean decreased satisfaction for some students. Moreover, negative peer influence may also lead to other problems that contribute to early departure from college (e.g., substance abuse, academic failure). For example, Schroeder (2002) interviewed three fellow educators on the impact of living/learning programs on student drinking behaviors. At the University of Wisconsin-Madison, students in learning communities drink just as much as their peers, but those students enrolled in living/learning programs experience fewer negative effects from drinking than their peers living elsewhere on campus (Schroeder, 2002). Zeller hypothesizes that the reason for the difference is that the relationships among students in an academic/social community is fundamentally different than the relationships among students in a purely social community:

> Although alcohol is still being used in these interactions, it may not be the primary focus of the relationship. I suspect that the academic link helps create different types of conversations and interactions that promote healthier and more mature drinking behaviors. Conversely, when there is not an academic link in the peer group, drinking may become the focus of interactions, thus promoting binge behaviors. (qtd. in Schroeder, 2002, p. 5).

Echoing Zeller, a senior reflecting on a sophomore tutorial at Harvard University demonstrates how academic connections transform social relationships among students:

> And the difference between these friends and all my other friends is that a significant part of our friendship is based around substantive discussions about ideas. None of us feels hesitant about initiating a discussion

or question about Freud or whomever. After all, we did it every week for a whole year together in a room where we live, right down the hall. And we certainly learned a lot about each other, and from each other (qtd. in Light, 2001, p. 214)

The students in this tutorial were among this senior's closest friends as he prepared to graduate from Harvard. He credits this, in part, to their willingness to confront each other on tough issues, especially those surrounding diversity—conversations that began in the classroom and spilled over into the residence hall where they lived. Gray, Lang, and Collins's case study of West Virginia University in Chapter 7 further demonstrates the importance of academic-social connections in transforming the campus community.

Tinto (1997) and others note that learning communities are natural points of collaboration for student affairs and academic affairs. Because student affairs professionals frequently use active learning strategies in their programming and student development work, Braxton et al. (2000) suggest that they can play an important role in encouraging and training faculty to use active learning strategies. But the academic-social connection is not uni-directional. In other words, embedding the social community within the academic community is not the only effective way to merge academic and social integration and improve the possibility of persistence. Kuh, Douglas, Lund, and Ramin-Gyurnek (1994) suggest that student affairs professionals can and should develop strategies that encourage students to bring classroom knowledge to bear on traditional campus activities. The simulations and role-playing activities, described by Dadabhoy in Chapter 5 on distance learning, provide good examples of such points of connection.

Integration and Involvement on Two-Year and Commuter Campuses

Living on campus is often cited as one of the most important predictors of involvement, which, as noted above, increases the likelihood of persistence. For example, Astin (1999/1984) noted that campus residents were more likely to achieve in leadership and athletics than commuters were. He suggests that involvement for students on two-year campuses is at best minimal, and that these students are more likely to drop out than their four-year counterparts. Given the relationship between involvement and integration, it might follow that students who live on campus are also more likely to enjoy high levels of academic and social integration and, thus, greater persistence. Commuters and students on two-year campuses, on the other hand, because of lower levels of involvement, would be less integrated into the community and less likely to persist. However, research on academic and social integration does not present clear patterns of connection between integration and persistence for commuters or students on two-year campuses. For example, some research suggests that social integration may be a liability for commuter students (Pascarella & Terenzini, 1991), while other research suggests that it has little effect on persistence or that positive effects may be limited to short-term persistence (Napoli & Wortman, 1996, 1998). Given that commuter students are now the norm on campuses and that the average age of undergraduates continues to rise, institutions must be increasingly sensitive to the external commitments (e.g., work, family, friends) that compete with the academic community for students' time and attention. Educationally purposeful activities that help students make connections among their academic work, career aspirations, and current reality may be more beneficial to them (and lead to greater satisfaction with the entire educational experience) than those designed to simply bond them more closely to the academic community of the college. In short, campus activities programs must begin to encompass the whole range of communities—both internal and external to the college-in which students operate.

In one study of academic and social integration among community college students (Borglum & Kubala, 2000), researchers found that while students did not participate in extracurricular activities, they did spend time talking or studying with friends. Moreover, these students frequently had no opinion concerning workshops, extra-curricular activities, and cultural programs offered by the college, but they were nonetheless satisfied with their academic and social experiences. Specifically, the study found that approximately half of the students had no desire to engage in campus activities, nor did they want to spend more time on campus. Their disinterest in organized activities suggests that, at least on some campuses, educators may be better served to devote their efforts to designing environments where students can engage in informal, yet educationally purposeful conversations and activities with other students rather than attempting to create a range of formal campus activities.

A Developmental Approach to Campus Activities in the First College Year

Given that involvement in the formal academic community, both in and out of the classroom, is important to student retention, how should colleges and universities approach campus activities programming for first-year students? Obviously, programs must be of interest to students; they must be well-advertised and accessible. Upcraft (1989) suggests that programs for first-year students should be "some combination of what [they] think they need and what we know they need, based on developmental research" (p. 153). For example, he, along with other researchers, identified six major developmental issues that students must address in their college careers (Upcraft, 1985). While the developmental work suggested by these issues spans the entire college career (and in some cases, a lifetime), higher educators should help students navigate these issues early on—especially since many of them may have important implications for persistence and college success. Upcraft (1989) outlines a series of campus activities that can be used to address each of these developmental issues:

1. *Developing intellectual and academic competence.* Study skills sessions and tutoring; cultural programs; and exploration of moral, ethical, and spiritual issues

2. *Establishing and maintaining interpersonal relationships.* Traditional social activities, support groups for marginalized or at-risk groups of students, and workshops on diversity issues

3. *Developing sex-role identity and sexuality.* Men's and women's consciousness-raising groups, seminars on changing sex roles, support groups, programs on sexually transmitted infections and safer sex behaviors, discussions about sexual orientation, and explorations of sexual morality

4. *Deciding on career and lifestyle.* Seminars for undecided students; career fairs; and workshops on decision making and problem solving, resume writing, interview skills, or for special student populations

5. *Maintaining personal health and wellness.* Programs and services on campus designed to help students learn about and adopt healthy physical, emotional, and spiritual behaviors.

6. *Formulating an integrated philosophy of life.* Values clarification exercises and discussions about religious beliefs and faith development, morality, philosophy, and major social issues

While these are important developmental tasks for students that can be addressed outside of the classroom, Upcraft argues for the active participation of faculty in many of these programs. The authors of this monograph frequently echo Upcraft in their call for the collaboration among faculty and academic and student affairs professionals in the design and implementation of educationally purposeful campus activities.

The Case for a Taking a Broad View of Campus Activities

While the authors of this volume, and numerous researchers and practitioners elsewhere, make a strong case for the value of campus activities for retaining students, frequently this aspect of the college experience has been viewed as separate and distinct from the academic life of students.

Commonly used terminology reflects this distinction. "Extra-curricular activities" suggests those experiences that occur outside of the formal curriculum and, thus, offer a tenuous connection to that curriculum. For example, Morrell and Morrell (1986) present a rather traditional, if limiting, view of the value of campus activities, suggesting that the "learning experiences best provided through student activities have to do primarily with interpersonal skills development and abilities to work effectively within organizational settings" (p. 77). But according to Kuh et al. (1994), fewer students today are participating in formal extra-curricular activities, suggesting that they may be seeking different kinds of experiences outside the classroom.

On the other hand, the term "co-curricular" suggests activities that occur alongside the formal curriculum. Because the two occur in tandem, a more robust connection may exist between them. Interpersonal development still takes place but it does so in concert with intellectual development. Moreover, "most students perceive in-class and out-of-class experiences to be seamless" (Kuh et al., 1991, p. 184). Because learning in college is not neatly subdivided into friendships, membership in organizations, participation in classes, social activities, and out-of-class assignments (Kuh et al., 1991), the term co-curricular may more appropriately describe the out-of-class experiences of students. However, these terms are frequently used interchangeably; and while extra-curricular involvement helps students make important connections to the campus community and gains in personal development, the authors in this monograph suggest that co-curricular experiences are most powerful in producing positive gains in student learning and contributing to student persistence. Thus, while chapter authors use both terms, our emphasis in this monograph is on the co-curricular or the educationally purposeful out-of-class activity.

Volume Overview

The authors of this volume collectively argue that to become truly successful in retaining first-year students, institutions should seek to engage students intellectually as well as socially. Further, these contributors posit that colleges and universities must recognize that as the student population and its expectations for educational experience change, the kinds of out-of-class experiences offered must also evolve.

The monograph opens with George Kuh, Megan Palmer, and Kelly Kish, who argue that because the types of activities in which students are engaged has changed, campus activities should be more broadly defined. They explore the outcomes associated with participation in activities, including educational and developmental gains. The implications section of their chapter addresses the institutional benefits of activities, the need for assessment, and the need for collaboration between academic and student affairs to design educationally purposeful campus activities programs.

Charles Schroeder follows with a chapter examining how changes in American society since the 1960s are reflected in today's student population in terms of expectations, attitudes, values, beliefs, and academic needs. He explores how these changes have influenced higher education and the student experience on our campuses. Like Kuh, Palmer, and Kish, he advocates taking a broader view of student activities and highlights ways that information on the changing student population can be used to address their educational needs and promote learning and success.

In Chapter 3, Jan Arminio and Stephen Loflin examine student involvement over the course of a student's college career. They seek to answer a number of important questions, including (a) Does early involvement shape later involvement? (b) Once belonging needs have been met, do students seek out activities that involve greater risk-taking? What other needs do students seek to fulfill? and (c) How does personal development shape involvement, and does involvement change over the course of the college career along developmental constructs?

Chapters 4 and 5 address two important issues in higher education today. The first is persistent—how do we build inclusive and involving communities on our campuses? —while the second is emergent-how do we connect distance students to a campus community traditionally located in a single physical space and time?

Nancy King and Brian Wooten tie the importance of developing community to research on student retention. They also examine challenges to developing community, identify critical opportunities, and describe the advantages for students of being connected to campus community. Zav Dadabhoy argues that the increasing focus on distance learning requires a paradigm shift for both academic and student affairs administrators. Rather than simply viewing distance programs as cash cows, we must seek innovative strategies for enhancing the learning and development of students not physically studying on our campuses.

Jonathan Dooley and Kathy Shellogg take up the issues related to student leadership programs in Chapter 6. They provide a model for assessing, planning, and implementing curricular and co-curricular leadership programs and examine barriers to implementing such programs. The chapter also includes descriptions of several exemplary leadership programs.

Chapter 7 is an illustration from one campus of many of the concepts described in this volume. Kenneth Gray, Gerald Lang, and Mary Collins describe a campus transformation in their case study on West Virginia University. In their discussion of a renewed emphasis on the first year and on finding alternatives to less positive activities, they exemplify the overriding theme of this monograph—that educationally purposeful out-of-class activities improve retention.

Increasingly, institutions and programs are being asked to justify their existence, to demonstrate that what they do matters. In Chapter 8, Michael Siegel discusses strategies for assessing co-curricular experiences in the first college year.

In the concluding chapter, Carolyn Haynes and Dennis Roberts provide an integrative summary of several models for improving the educational experiences of first-year students and summarize salient points from earlier chapters and recent literature that point to future directions for the student affairs field and the first-year experience movement.

In essence, we strive to make the point that has long been made about campus activities—that they are an important part of any success-ful retention effort. But the authors also hope to move beyond that to suggest that activities must do more than simply entertain students or increase their satisfaction with campus social life. To the extent that learning is related to student retention, campus activities programs must also seek to engage students intellectually. In many ways, this monograph makes a philosophical argument, but the authors have also attempted to ground that argument in the practical. In each of these chapters, the reader will find inspiring examples of educationally purposeful out-of-class activities. The contributors hope that these, along with the philosophical grounding provided by the monograph as a whole, help you transform the nature of campus activities—and of student learning and success—on your campus.

References

Astin, A. W. (1999). Student involvement: A developmental theory for higher education. *Journal of College Student Development, 40*(5), 518-29. (Original work published in 1984).

Berger, J. B., & Milem, J. F. (1999). The role of student involvement and perceptions of integration in a causal model of student persistence. *Research in Higher Education, 40*(6), 641-64.

Borglum, K., & Kubala, T. (2000). Academic and social integration of community college students: A case study. *Community College Journal of Research and Practice, 24,* 567-76.

Braxton, J. M., Milem, J. F., & Sullivan, A. S. (2000). The influence of active learning on the college student departure process: Toward a revision of Tinto's theory. *The Journal of Higher Education, 71*(5), 569-590.

Christie, N. G., & Dinham, S. M. (1991). Institutional and external influences on social integration in the freshman year. *Journal of Higher Education, 62*(4), 412-436.

Elkins, S. A., Braxton, J. M., & James, G. W. (2000). Tinto's separation stage and its influence on first-semester college student persistence. *Research in Higher Education, 41*(2), 251-68.

Fries-Britt, S., Gardner, J. N., Low, L., & Tinto, V. (2002, March 7). *Retaining students: New questions and fresh perspectives* [Video Teleconference Print Resource Packet]. Columbia, SC:

University of South Carolina, National Resource Center for The First-Year Experience and Students in Transition.

Kuh, G. D., Douglas, K. B., Lund, J. P., & Ramin-Gyurnek, J. (1994). *Student learning outside the classroom: Transcending artificial boundaries*. ASHE-ERIC Higher Education Reports, No. 8. Washington, DC: The George Washington University, Clearinghouse on Higher Education.

Kuh, G. D., Schuh, J. H., Whitt, E. J., & Associates (1991). *Involving colleges: Successful approaches to fostering student learning and development outside the classroom*. San Francisco: Jossey-Bass.

Light, R. J. (2001). *Making the most of college: Students speak their minds*. Cambridge, MA: Harvard University Press.

Milem, J. F., & Berger, J. B. (1997). A modified model of college student persistence: Exploring the relationship between Astin's Theory of Involvement and Tinto's Theory of Student Departure. *Journal of College Student Development, 38*(4), 387-400.

Morrell, S. A., & Morrell, R. C. (1986). Learning through student activities. In *Managing programs for learning outside the classroom*. New Directions for Higher Education, No. 56 (pp. 77-87). San Francisco: Jossey-Bass.

Murray, J. L., & Hall, P. M. (2001). The Student Activities Interest Questionnaire: Relating Holland's vocational theory to student involvement. *Journal of College Student Retention, 2*(4), 355-365.

Napoli, A. R., & Wortman, P. M. (1996, Fall). A meta-analysis of the impact of academic and social integration on persistence of community college students, *Journal of Applied Research in the Community Colleges*, 5-21.

Napoli, A. R., & Wortman, P. M. (1998). Psychosocial factors related to retention and early departure of two-year community college students. *Research in Higher Education, 39*(4), 419-56.

Nora, A., Cabrera, A., Hagedorn, L. S., & Pascarella, E. (1996). Differential impacts of academic and social experiences on college-related behavioral outcomes across different ethnic and gender groups at four-year institutions. *Research in Higher Education, 37*(4), 427-51.

Pascarella, E. T., & Terenzini, P. T. (1991). *How college affects students*. San Francisco: Jossey-Bass.

Peltier, G. L., Laden, R., & Matranga, M. (1999). Student persistence in college: A review of research. *Journal of College Student Retention, 1*(4), 357-75.

Schroeder, C. (2002). Do learning communities discourage binge drinking? [Interview with A. M. Brower, K. A. Bruffee, & W. Zeller]. *About Campus, 7*(2), 5-13.

Tinto, V. (1993). *Leaving college: Rethinking the causes and cures of student attrition* (2nd ed.). Chicago: University of Chicago Press.

Tinto, V. (1997). Enhancing learning via community. *Thought and Action, 13*(1), 53-58.

Tinto, V. (n.d.). *Rethinking the first year of college*. Syracuse, NY: Syracuse University. Retrieved February 15, 2002 from http://soeweb.syr.edu/departments/hed/resources.htm

Tinto, V., & Goodsell, A. (1994). Freshman interest groups and the first-year experience: Constructing student communities in a large university. *Journal of The Freshman Year Experience, 6*(1), 7-28.

Upcraft, M. L. (1985). Residence halls and student activities. In L. Noel, R. Levitz, D. Saluri, & Associates (Ed.), *Student retention: Effective programs and practices for reducing the dropout rate* (pp. 319-344). San Francisco: Jossey-Bass.

Upcraft, M. L. (1989). Residence halls and campus activities. In M. L. Upcraft, J. N. Gardner, & Associates (Eds.), *The freshman year experience: Helping students survive and succeed in college.* (pp. 142-155). San Francisco: Jossey-Bass.

Whipple, E. G. (1996). Student activities. In Rentz, A. L. & Associates (Eds.), *Student affairs practice in higher education* (2nd ed). (pp. 298-333). Springfield, IL: Charles C. Thomas.

The Value of Educationally Purposeful Out-of-Class Experiences

George Kuh
Megan Palmer
Kelly Kish
Indiana University

One thing about the college student experience is certain: Students learn more when they are engaged at reasonably high levels in a variety of educationally purposeful activities, inside and outside the classroom, over an extended period of time (Astin, 1984; Kuh, Douglas, Lund, & Ramin-Gyurnek, 1994; Kuh, Schuh, Whitt, & Associates, 1991; Pascarella & Terenzini, 1991; Tinto, 1987). That is, neither classroom nor co-curricular experiences alone offer the range of learning opportunities that will enable students to acquire the skills and competencies required to survive and thrive in our rapidly changing, increasingly complex world. Fortunately, evidence is accumulating that student affairs—in partnership with faculty members and academic administrators—"can intentionally create the conditions that enhance student learning and personal development" (American College Personnel Association, 1994, p. 1).

To create this seamless learning environment, we must design and implement educationally effective policies and practices that will integrate in-class and out-of-class experiences (Kuh, 1996). To do this, student affairs professionals must be knowledgeable about the out-of-class experiences that positively contribute to student development.

This chapter summarizes the contributions of out-of-class experiences to desired outcomes of college and offers implications for campus programming and institutional policy and practice. We emphasize out-of-class experiences typically associated with the formal co-curriculum, such as leadership positions in student government and membership in campus organizations as well as activities that may be an extension of class experiences but occur outside the classroom, such as service-learning and internships. Recent trends indicate that students are less involved in traditional forms of activities and are more involved in activities such as academic clubs, service-learning, work, undergraduate research, and community service. Thus, we cast a broad net to include out-of-class experiences, on- and off-campus, that are either social and academic in orientation or a combination of the two components. The variety of educationally purposeful out-of-class activities that positively contribute to persistence and educational attainment will be discussed more extensively in later chapters.

What We Know About Out-of-Class Experiences and Student Development

Our review of the literature uses Kuh's (1993) typology to categorize outcomes and student engagement in activities beyond the classroom that are linked to growth and development. The outcome categories are cognitive complexity, knowledge acquisition and application, humanitarianism, inter- and intrapersonal communication, and practical competence. We emphasize research published since 1995 because Kuh et al. (1994) summarized the literature up to that point in the ASHE-ERIC Report, *Student Learning Outside the Classroom: Transcending Artificial Boundaries*. For each of the outcome categories we briefly summarize major findings from the literature before 1995 before discussing some of the more important research published since that time. The contributions of various types of out-of-class activities to each outcome domain are summarized in a table. We used a "weight of the evidence" approach to determine whether the experience is generally related positively or negatively to the outcome. Cases where the research is inconclusive are represented by "none," or no relationship. In some instances the findings are "mixed," meaning that some studies have found positive relationships between participating in the activity and others have found the experience to be negatively related to gains in the particular outcome domain.

Cognitive Complexity

This outcome domain represents critical thinking, quantitative reasoning, reflective judgment, and intellectual flexibility. In discussing the relationship between out-of-class-activities and cognitive complexity, Kuh et al. (1994) concluded that "when gains in cognitive development are linked to out-of-class experiences, they tend to be related to the amount of effort students expend in educationally purposeful activities" (p. 25). Previous studies on cognitive complexity have provided mixed evidence of the effects of out-of-class experiences. Hood, Craig, and Ferguson (1992) found no relationship between residence, employment, and campus involvement and cognitive complexity. However, evidence suggests that gains in this area largely depend on whether the activity induces students to integrate their class learning with experiences outside the classroom (Chickering, 1974; Frost, 1991; Kuh, 1995; Pace, 1990; Pascarella & Terenzini, 1991; Pike, 1999, 2000). Specific activities that have been shown to influence growth in cognitive ability include student-faculty interaction (Baxter Magolda, 1992; Terenzini & Pascarella, 1980); living in residences organized around educational themes (Pascarella & Terenzini, 1980); and interactions with peers, especially those who are from different backgrounds and have different political, social, and religious views (Pace, 1987, 1990). Table 1 is based on the research reviewed by Kuh et al. (1994) and recently published studies; the latter are discussed in some detail.

Fraternity and sorority membership. Most studies show that Greek affiliation is generally

Table 1

Out-of-Class Activities Associated With Gains in Cognitive Complexity

Activity	Impact
Fraternity membership for African-American men	Positive
Fraternity membership for White men	Negative
Sorority membership for White women and women of color	Mixed
Living in academic theme residences/living-learning communities	Positive
Living on-campus	Mixed
Participation in intercollegiate athletics	Negative to none
Service-learning and volunteering	Positive
Tutoring	Positive to none
Work	Positive
Membership in honor societies	Positive
Membership in service organizations	Positive
Undergraduate research	Positive
Student-faculty interaction	Positive
Diversity experiences	Positive

antithetical to gains in areas related to cognitive complexity. Specifically, Greek affiliation during the first-year of college appears to have a negative impact on critical thinking, especially for men (Pascarella, Edison, Whitt, et al., 1996; Pascarella, Flowers, & Whitt, 2001). The results are particularly troubling for first-year White male fraternity members; though for Black men Greek affiliation seems to have a modest positive influence. (Pascarella, Edison, Whitt, et al., 1996; Pascarella et al., 2001). However, these differences do not seem to pertain to White women and women of color who join Greek membership groups (Pascarella, Edison, Whitt et al., 1996). In fact, sorority membership generally has less of a dampening influence on cognitive complexity (Pascarella, Flowers, et al., 2001). Other studies reveal similar patterns (Pascarella, Flowers et al., 2001; Terenzini, Pascarella, & Blimling, 1996; Wilder & McKeegan, 1997). Though the bulk of the evidence seems to support the commonly held belief that the values of White Greek-letter organizations are counter to those of the academy, one recent study concluded that Greek students' self-reported gains in thinking critically and analytically were significantly higher than non-members (Hayek, Carini, O'Day, & Kuh, 2002).

Residence. Students living in a residential learning community (RLC) tend to report greater gains in general education compared with their counterparts who live in a traditional residence hall (TRH) (Pike, 1999). The effects of living in an RLC on learning and intellectual development gains are indirect, suggesting that it is not necessarily the fact that students live there that is important but what they do while living there. For example, RLC students tend to interact more with faculty members and have a wider variety and more frequent conversations with peers, which are also strongly associated with intellectual development. These findings are similar to others, in that students who live in RLCs tend to not only be more academically focused but also experience greater cognitive gains than do TRH students (Terenzini et al., 1996). Similarly, MacGregor (1993) reported that students involved in coordinated studies communities generally made significant gains in intellectual de-

velopment during their learning community experience. However, Inman and Pascarella (1998) found no significant contribution of living in a campus residence to critical thinking ability; moreover, there were no differences between campus residents and commuter students on critical thinking measures. Taken together, these studies suggest that the type of campus housing is more important to gains in cognitive complexity than simply living on campus.

Intercollegiate athletics. Participation in intercollegiate athletics has little impact on learning for self-understanding, preferring higher order cognitive activities and motivation for academic success learning orientation (Wolniak, Pierson, & Pascarella, 2001). Specifically, athletes (in both revenue and non-revenue generating sports) were nearly equal to their non-athlete peers in making gains in self-understanding, internal locus of control toward academic success, and using higher order cognitive skills in completing exams and assignments. In similar studies, no differences were found between athletes and non-athletes with regard to cognitive development (Pascarella, Bohr, Nora, & Terenzini, 1995; Terenzini et al., 1996). However, McBride and Reed (1998) found that athletes scored significantly lower on two tests of critical thinking ability and predisposition when compared to non-athletes, perhaps because the rigid, autocratic nature of college athletics (e.g., strict coaches and practice schedules, detailed predetermined training schedules, required meal times and study times) discourages independent thinking and inquisitiveness.

Service-learning and volunteering. Service-learning and volunteering appear to positively affect critical thinking (Astin & Sax, 1998) and other dimensions of cognitive complexity, such as understanding complicated material, problem analysis, and cognitive development (Eyler, Giles, Stenson, & Gray, 2001).

Tutoring. Tutoring provides opportunities for students to exercise responsibility and also

> "Most studies show that Greek affiliation is generally antithetical to gains in areas related to cognitive complexity."

promotes cognitive development by inducing student tutors to move away from egocentric perspectives into more decentered perspectives that value multiple points of view (Mann, 1994). Students who served as tutors were also more able to understand interpersonal dimensions of tutoring, resolving conflicts, and problem solving (Mann, 1994).

Work. Pascarella, Bohr, Nora, Desler, and Zusman (1994) found that the amount of on- and off-campus work had little impact on first-year critical thinking. This study seems to contradict other previous claims that too much work and working off campus can have negative effects on retention and attainment (Astin, 1975; Ehrenberg & Sherman, 1987), finding that work may not be interfering with knowledge acquisition and cognitive gains to the extent widely believed (Pascarella et al., 1994). In fact, there is only "modest and inconsistent evidence to suggest that...work seriously inhibits students' learning or cognitive development" (Inman & Pascarella, 1998, p. 567).

Campus activities. Membership in collegiate organizations seems to be consistent with the goals of a liberal arts education such as thinking and communicating clearly, understanding the physical universe, awareness of the intrinsic value of thought and learning, and independent action, among others (McNamara & Cover, 1999). For example, serving as a peer advisor or student government leader (Kuh & Lund, 1994) and studying abroad were found to increase cognitive outcomes (Kuh, 1995). Highly involved students reported greater commitment to the goals of a liberal arts education including cognitive complexity (McNamara & Cover, 1999).

Inman and Pascarella (1998) found that extra-curricular involvement positively influenced cognitive development while involvement in athletics and attending athletic events seemed to have a negative effect. Additionally, higher levels of library use negatively affect cognitive development during the first-year, perhaps because libraries serve as a social, rather than an academic, environment for first-year students (Inman & Pascarella, 1998).

Student-faculty interaction. Substantive interactions with faculty members outside the classroom are positively related to student self-reported intellectual development. Doing research with a faculty member also has positive effects on students' ability to master scientific concepts, practice critical thinking (Kuh, 1995; Volkwein, King, & Terenzini, 1986), solve problems, and make effective decisions (Eddins, Williams, Bushek, & Porter, 1997).

Diversity experiences. Students' exposure to diversity experiences (e.g., discussions with different students, courses, cultural awareness workshops) generally have been shown to have a positive relationship with the development of critical thinking, analytical, and problem-solving skills (Astin, 1993a; Hu & Kuh, 2001; Kuh, 1995; Pascarella, Palmer, Moye, & Pierson, 2001; Terenzini, Springer, Pascarella, & Nora, 1994). White students appear to benefit more from exposure to people from diverse backgrounds compared with students of color (Hu & Kuh, 2001; Pascarella, Palmer, et al., 2001; Whitt, Edison, Pascarella, Terenzini, & Nora, 2001).

Knowledge Acquisition and Application

In this section we discuss the out-of-class experiences that contribute to knowledge acquisition and application, or the ability to understand knowledge from a variety of disciplines and realities (e.g., physical, geographic, economic, political, cultural, and religious), and to relate knowledge to daily life including integrating and synthesizing information from several courses (Kuh, 1993).

Earlier studies indicated that knowledge acquisition and application are positively related to community service (Serow & Dreyden, 1990), holding leadership positions, and tutoring other students (Astin, 1993b). Too much socializing with other students may discourage deepening one's commitment to learning (Terenzini, Springer, Pascarella, & Nora, 1995). Involvement in Greek-letter organizations provided mixed results (Center for the Study of the College Fraternity, 1992; Pike & Askew, 1990). More recent studies tend to support these conclusions regarding the impact of extra-curricular experiences on knowledge acquisition and application (Table 2).

Fraternity and sorority membership. Pascarella

4

et al. (1996) found that Greek-affiliated first-year male students had significantly lower reading comprehension, mathematics, and composite achievement scores compared with their non-affiliated counterparts. Fraternity membership had a strong, negative influence on these outcomes for White men, but a slight positive impact for men of color (Pascarella, Edison, Whitt, et al., 1996). For women, the effects of joining a sorority in the first-year were also negative for reading comprehension and composite achievement. Pascarella, Flowers, et al. (2001) reported that being a male member of a fraternity tended to negatively affect some aspects of knowledge acquisition, though the effects were much less pronounced during the second and third years of college. These findings appear to support the idea that, "any major negative learning consequences of Greek affiliation occur primarily when students pledge a fraternity or sorority in the first-year of college" (Pascarella, Flowers, et al., 2001, p. 297).

Residence. Pike, Schroeder, and Berry (1997) found that being in a residential Freshman Interest Group did not directly contribute to academic achievement and persistence. However, a subsequent study discovered that living in a residential learning community was linked to high levels of integrating course information (Pike, 1999). In another study of living-learning centers, academic achievement was significantly affected by involvement in the community (Edwards & McKelfresh, 2002). Finally, compared with commuter students, students who live on campus report greater gains in writing, speaking, and analytical skills (Kuh, Gonyea, & Palmer, 2001).

Intercollegiate athletics. No significant difference exists in grades between athletes and non-athletes when controlling for gender, ethnicity, and academic aptitude test scores nor does athletics affect academic achievement during the first-year (Hood et al., 1992) or the amount of time athletes spend studying or attending class compared with non-athletes (Richards & Aries, 1999). Schroeder's (2000) study of NCAA Division III basketball players at a small, private, liberal arts college revealed that athletes were highly engaged in their academics, spending an average of 15 hours per week studying with the majority earning GPAs exceeding 3.0.

Richards and Aries (1999) found no significant difference in GPA between athletes and non-athletes despite the fact that athletes entered college with significantly lower SAT scores. Pascarella et al. (1995) reported that male football and basketball players scored lower on reading comprehension and mathematics than non-athletes and male athletes in other sports. There was

Table 2
Out-of-Class Activities Associated With Gains in Knowledge Acquisition and Application

Activity	Impact
Fraternity membership for men of color	Positive
Fraternity or sorority membership for White students	Negative
Living on campus	Positive or none
Participation in intercollegiate athletics	Mixed or none
Service-learning and volunteering	Positive
Study abroad	Positive
Work	Positive or none
Involvement in clubs and organizations	Mixed
Involvement in clubs and organizations for adult students	Positive
Peer education participation	Positive
Recreational sports participation	Positive
Tutoring	Positive
Undergraduate research	Positive

parity between male non-athletes and male athletes in nonrevenue generating sports in both reading and math. Female athletes had lower reading comprehension scores than non-athletes, although the two groups were essentially the same in math measurements. However, women who entered college with higher levels of ability were affected less by their athletic participation. Overall, it seems that participating in athletics may negatively affect gains in reading and math knowledge during the first-year of college (Pascarella et al., 1995).

Service-learning and volunteering. Service-learning appears to enhance knowledge acquisition and application as reflected by higher grades, aspirations for future educational degrees, increase in general knowledge, increase in field or discipline knowledge, preparation for graduate school, heightened academic self-concept, increased time devoted to studying or homework, doing extra work for class, and increased contact with faculty (Astin & Sax, 1998; Astin, Vogelgesang, Ikeda, & Yee, 2000; Sax & Astin, 1997). Service-learning also positively affects students' ability to connect learning with the "real world" (Astin et al., 2000; Eyler et al., 2001) and appears to have both direct and indirect effects on post-college outcomes such as attending graduate school (Astin, Sax, & Avalos, 1999). Others, however, reported that students in courses with a service-learning component do not differ from their counterparts in the same courses without a service-learning component in the areas of academic competencies (writing ability, disciplinary knowledge) and professional skill development (career preparation, confidence in major choice) (Gray, Ondaatje, Fricker, & Geschwind, 2000).

Study abroad. In an analysis of study abroad experiences, Day-Vines, Barker, and Exum (1998) concluded that students' travel experience inspired them to learn more about history, culture, and heritage and motivated them to work harder in their classes. Further, the experience of studying abroad helped students link experiences with the past and real life in order to better understand themselves (Day-Vines et al., 1998). Study abroad also is related to increased language proficiency and knowledge about different cultures and multinational issues (Gray, Murdock, & Stebbins, 2002; Kuh, 1995).

Work. Pascarella et al. (1994) found that even though the amount of on- and off-campus work tended to reduce the amount of time spent studying per week, work had little negative impact on first-year reading or mathematics comprehension. Thus, while working many hours may negatively influence persistence and educational attainment, it may not dampen knowledge acquisition.

Campus activities. Involvement in campus organizations has mixed effects on knowledge acquisition and use. For example, participating in student clubs, organizations, college sports, and doing group projects for class were negatively associated with verbal skills development (Anaya, 1996). However, others reported that student government members reported gains in knowledge and academic skills (Kuh, 1995; Kuh & Lund, 1994).

Tutoring, participating in independent research projects, and paraprofessional experience appear to contribute to student learning (Anaya, 1996; Badura, Millard, Peluso, & Ortman, 2000). Undergraduate research may also have a positive influence on knowledge acquisition since content knowledge and information accumulates during the research process (Eddins et al., 1997). Doing research with a faculty member promotes learning, especially when undergraduate research internships require presentations of findings (Kuh, 1995).

Though understudied, another area of campus activity that appears to affect knowledge acquisitions is recreational sports. Specifically, frequency of use of a student recreational center by first-year students was positively associated with higher first-semester grades, cumulative grade point average, and a greater number of credit hours completed (Belch, Gebel, & Maas, 2001).

Similar relationships between involvement in campus organizations hold for older students. Graham and Gisi (2000) found no significant interaction effects of age when examining work, course-related activities, and involvement in clubs and organizations. However, adults who reported more involvement also reported greater gains, especially in scientific reasoning and intellectual development. It appears that the net effects of involvement tend to be greater for older students as contrasted with traditional age students (Graham & Gisi, 2000).

Humanitarianism

It is increasingly important that students acquire the skills and competencies needed to function effectively in a variety of settings and with individuals from a wide range of backgrounds and perspectives. Among the out-of-class activities associated with gains in humanitarianism are discussing racial or ethnic issues (Astin, 1993a; Kuh, 1995), attending workshops on race and culture (Astin, 1993a, 1993b), studying abroad (Baxter Magolda, 1992; Kauffmann & Kuh, 1985), holding a part-time job on campus (Astin, 1993b), and socializing with a wide range of people (Baxter Magolda, 1992). Fraternity or sorority membership has a negative effect on students' openness to diversity (Pascarella, Edison, Nora, Hagedorn, & Terenzini, 1996).

As with the previous sections, the information reported in Table 3 includes both the studies reported in Kuh et al. (1994) as well as studies published more recently.

Fraternity and sorority membership. Belonging to a Greek organization has modest, but sta-

tistically significant negative effects on openness to diversity (Pascarella, Edison, Nora, et al., 1996), especially for White students. Other studies show similar findings, with Greek members over time becoming less open to diversity and less liberal minded in general (Wolniak et al., 2001). Black Greek men and women have significantly higher scores on liberalism and social conscience compared with their White Greek peers (Whipple, Baier, & Grady, 1991).

Intercollegiate athletics. Athletes interact effectively with people from diverse backgrounds because "broad exposure to difference is almost a given in athletics, as athletes compete with and against people from socioeconomic, racial and ethnic, and religious backgrounds other than theirs" (Wolf-Wendel, Toma, & Morphew, 2001, p. 385).

Service-learning and volunteering. Service-learning and volunteering have positive effects on being willing to help others, promoting racial understanding, serving the community, doing volunteer work, and getting along with people of difference races and cultures (Astin & Sax, 1998; Astin et al., 1999; Pike, 2000). Service-learning experiences also help to reduce stereotypes and promote cultural understanding, social responsibility, and cultivation of citizenship skills (Eyler et al., 2001). The more time

Table 3
Out-of-Class Activities Associated With Gains in Humanitarianism

Activity	Impact
Fraternity or sorority membership by White students	Negative
Participation in intercollegiate athletics	Positive
Service-learning and volunteering	Positive
Study abroad	Positive
Interacting with peers	Positive
Leadership experiences	Positive
Living on campus	Positive
Participation in a cultural awareness workshop	Positive
Participation in religious services and activities	Positive
Social interaction with people from a variety of racial and ethnic backgrounds	Positive
Work	Positive
Participation in group projects	Positive
Internships	Positive
Diversity experiences	Positive

students spend volunteering, the more likely they are to become familiar with multicultural and community issues and to exercise civic responsibility (Cress, Astin, Zimmerman-Oster, & Burkhardt, 2001). Volunteer experience also contributes to a belief that people can make a difference, to understanding the importance of community service, and to a commitment to perform volunteer service in the future (Cress et al., 2001; Gray et. al, 2000).

Study abroad. Visiting other countries dispels myths and promotes intercultural sensitivity (Day-Vines et al., 1998). Also, students develop the ability to empathize with non-native English speakers (Gray et al., 2002)

Living on campus and campus activities. Living on campus contributes to openness to diversity (Hu & Kuh, 2001; Pascarella, Edison, Nora, et al., 1996; Pascarella, Palmer, et al., 2001; Pike, 2000). Women student leaders increase their interest in performing community service as a result of holding leadership positions (Romano, 1996). Participation in leadership training activities, group class projects, and internships positively influence acceptance of others from different races and cultures and understanding of community problems (Cress et al., 2001). In addition, serving as a peer advisor increases an appreciation for issues that underrepresented racial and ethnic groups contend with on predominantly White campuses (Kuh, 1995).

Diversity experiences. Hurtado, Milem, Clayton-Pedersen, and Allen (1999) found that interacting with diverse peers improved intergroup relations and mutual understanding. Students who interacted frequently with peers with different views or from different racial and ethnic backgrounds and those who participated in a racial or cultural awareness workshop were more open and appreciative of human diversity (Hu & Kuh, 2001; Pascarella, Edison, Nora, et al., 1996; Whitt et al., 2001).

Interpersonal and Intrapersonal Competence

Interpersonal and intrapersonal competence represents the integration of personal attributes and skills in a manner that allows one to perform in a variety of situations with competence and confidence (Kuh, 1993). Personal attributes include identity development, self-esteem, self-efficacy, confidence, integrity, and an appreciation for the aesthetic and spiritual qualities of life. Personal skills can be defined as the ability to work with people different than oneself and the ability to be a team member. Among the more powerful out-of-class experiences in terms of self-confidence, self-awareness, and communication skills are holding a leadership position in a student group or serving as a paraprofessional such as a resident advisor (Astin, 1977; Kuh, 1995; Pascarella, Smart, Ethington, & Nettles, 1987). Other activities that contribute to this domain are contacts with faculty members, living on campus, living in academic theme-based campus residences (Astin, 1993b; Pace, 1984), participating in intercollegiate athletics (Pascarella et al., 1987), peer education training (Badura et al., 2000), study abroad (Baxter Magolda, 1992; Kauffmann & Kuh, 1985), and being in an honors program (King, 1973).

In general, research studies published since the mid-1990s confirm these same relationships (Table 4).

Fraternity and sorority membership. Overall, involvement in the Greek system has a mixed impact on developing interpersonal and intrapersonal competence for White students, though membership appears to benefit students of color. For example, Kimbrough (1995) and Kimbrough and Hutcheson (1999) found that members of a Black Greek-letter organization reported higher levels of self-confidence, gains they attributed to increased opportunities to hold leadership positions since joining the group (Kimbrough, 1995; Kimbrough & Hutcheson, 1999). Such self-reported benefits may be because involvement in same-race groups, whether Greek-affiliated or not, provides opportunities to explore cultural identity that is lacking in predominantly White groups (Arminio et al., 2000).

Brand and Dodd (1998) found that male Greek members had significantly higher self-esteem ratings compared with non-Greeks; however, input variables were not controlled in this study and previous research indicates such variables could account for these differences (Atlas & Morier, 1994; Wilder, Hoyt, Surbeck, & Wilder, 1986). Other studies show that Greek membership is positively related to establishing and clarifying purpose, developing mature relationships, establishing trusting relationships (Hunt & Rentz, 1994) and greater gains than non-members in working effectively with others and self understanding (Hayek et al., 2002).

Residence. Living in a residential learning community is linked to increased social integration (Pike et al., 1997) and higher levels of interaction with faculty and peers compared with students who live in other settings (Pike, 1999). Compared with commuter students, residential students report greater gains in ethical development, understanding of self, community awareness, and getting along with others (Kuh et al., 2001).

Intercollegiate athletics. Participating in intercollegiate athletics may lead to social isolation (Riemer, Beal, & Schroeder, 2000; Wolf-Wendel et al., 2001). For example, spending time with teammates may strengthen bonds among team members, while at the same time limiting interaction with non-athletes (Wolf-Wendel et al., 2001). Wolniak et al. (2001) reported that participating in intercollegiate athletics had negative, direct effects on self-understanding and openness to diversity of male athletes. In one instance, however, Schroeder (2000) found that basketball players created a social learning community that did not necessarily isolate them from non-athletes.

Service-learning and volunteering. Service-learning enhances life skill development including social self-confidence, conflict resolution skills, interpersonal skills, and the ability to work cooperatively and get along with others (Astin & Sax, 1998; Eyler et al., 2001). Apparently, the more time students spend volunteering the more likely they are to deepen their understanding of personal and social values (Cress et al., 2001).

Work. Students who work on campus gain teamwork skills (Broughton & Otto, 1999) and the ability to deal with people from different backgrounds (Baxter Magolda, 1992). Working either on or off campus may contribute to openness to diversity (Wolniak et al., 2001). But the amount of time one works is important. Students who work off campus more than 30 hours per week were significantly less involved in campus activities and had less interaction with faculty than students without a job, those who worked on campus, and those who worked off campus less than 30 hours per week (Furr & Elling, 2000). Thus, the influence of work on interpersonal competence is mixed.

Campus activities. Involvement in student organizations was related to an increase in the

Table 4
Out-of-Class Activities Associated With Gains in Interpersonal and Intrapersonal Competence

Activity	Impact
Fraternity or sorority membership	Mixed
Living on campus	Mixed
Participation in intercollegiate athletics	Mixed
Service-learning and volunteering	Positive
Work	Mixed
Interacting with peers	Positive
Internships	Positive
Involvement in clubs and organizations	Positive
Involvement in ethnic clubs and organizations	Positive
Leadership experiences	Positive
Participation in African-American student organization for African Americans	Positive
Participation in group projects	Positive
Study abroad	Positive
Undergraduate research	Positive
Diversity experiences	Positive

clarity of life's purpose, life management skills, and communication skills (Baxter Magolda, 1992; Cooper, Healy, & Simpson, 1994; Kuh, 1995). Students with leadership experience in student organizations gained more in these areas than other members. Women student leaders also acquired interpersonal communication skills, increased self-awareness, self-confidence, and a heightened awareness of their values and needs from holding leadership positions (Romano, 1996). Students of color who were involved in ethnic student organizations benefit in similar ways, with increased self-awareness, self-esteem, and positive adjustment to college (Moran, Yengo, & Algier, 1994; Taylor & Howard-Hamilton, 1995).

Other campus activities that affect inter- and intrapersonal competence include study abroad, participation in recreational sports, and service as a student government leader (Kuh & Lund, 1994). Specifically, study abroad experiences influence students' self-awareness and contribute to personal development by encouraging students to examine their opinions and perceptions about their own culture (Gray et al., 2002; Kuh, 1995). Participating in recreational sports seems to be positively related to high-quality relationships with others and an enhanced ability to live a self-directed life (Cornelius, 1995). Cress et al. (2001) found that participating in class group projects led to gains in students' understanding of their own personal and social values. Other activities that promote character development include participating in religious services and activities and participating in leadership education or training (Astin & Antonio, 2000).

Diversity experiences. Character development is related to engaging in social activities with students from a variety of racial and ethnic backgrounds (Astin & Antonio, 2000). Blimling (2001) concluded that students attending diverse institutions develop greater self-confidence, interpersonal competencies, and hold fewer prejudices. Hu and Kuh (2001) found that diversity experiences had substantial, uniformly positive effects on virtually all areas of personal development including a "diversity competence" measure they constructed

to indicate student's knowledge of different cultures as well as the ability to get along with different kinds of people. Moreover, this general finding held for all students (i.e., White students and students of color) at all types of institutions.

Student-faculty interaction. In terms of undergraduate research internships Eddins et al. (1997) found that students' collaboration with faculty on research projects empowered students to improve their overall educational experience and their communication skills. However, Kuh and Hu (2001a) found that the net effects of student-faculty interaction on personal development gains were negative, perhaps because the nature of many of the interactions were not necessarily related to positive experiences, such as discussing criticisms of written work.

Practical Competence

Success during and after college requires practical competence—the ability to identify and solve problems, manage time effectively, and make good decisions. Practical competence is a broad area that includes the above-mentioned attributes as well as leadership development and career choice (Kuh et al., 1994).

Student-faculty contact and involvement in a wide range of co-curricular activities can, given the purpose and intensity of the activity, lead to gains in practical competence (Astin, 1993b; Ethington, Smart, & Pascarella, 1988; Kuh, 1995; Kuh et al., 1994). Living on campus and being involved in organizations positively influenced one's ability to manage everyday responsibilities (Baxter Magolda, 1992). Studies prior to 1995 are mixed in terms of the relationships between development of practical competencies and participation in intercollegiate athletics (DuBois, 1978; Howard, 1986; Pascarella & Smart, 1991; Pascarella & Terenzini, 1991), employment (Kuh, 1995; Pascarella & Terenzini, 1991), and general co-curricular involvement (Pascarella & Smart, 1991; Schuh & Laverty, 1983). Table 5 summarizes findings related to practical competence outcomes from prior studies and more current research.

10

Fraternity or sorority membership. Membership in Black Greek-letter organizations increases members' reported gains in leadership skill development and self-confidence. Fraternity members indicate that their leadership skills increase in Black organizations because there are more opportunities to hold leadership positions than in traditional White organizations (Kimbrough, 1995; Kimbrough & Hutcheson, 1999).

Residence. Compared with commuters, students who live on campus tend to report greater gains in computer and information technology, quantitative, and job-related skills and knowledge needed for work (Kuh et al., 2001).

Intercollegiate athletics. Student athletes devote significantly more time to extra-curricular activities than do members of other groups and learn critical time management skills through their involvement (Richards & Aries, 1999). Also, participating in recreational sports seems to be positively related to effective time management (Cornelius, 1995).

Service-learning and volunteering. Students with community service experience gain more in terms of learning to work productively with others (Astin & Sax, 1998; Eyler et al., 2001). Further, students enrolled in service-learning courses made significant gains in life skills (Gray et al., 2000) including self-rated leadership abilities (Astin et al., 2000).

Work. Students who work on campus gain in the areas of leadership, teamwork, and such skills as creating a calendar to track work schedules, giving new employees a tour of the department, and planning a special activity for the department (Broughton & Otto, 1999).

Campus activities. Cress et al. (2001) compared student leaders to participants in leadership training activities and found that student leaders gained more in terms of understanding leadership theories and encouraging others to take on leadership roles. Similar benefits accrued for students who participated in class group projects or who had an internship (Cress et al., 2001). Female student leaders also have gained public-speaking skills, a better understanding of the workings of bureaucracies, conflict management skills, and heightened awareness of their chosen career path (Romano, 1996).

Peer education training appears to contribute to significant gains in time management, goal setting, and public speaking skills (Badura et al., 2000; Kuh, 1995). Compared with non-members, members of student organizations reported greater growth in career planning, lifestyle planning, and

Table 5
Out-of-Class Activities Associated With Gains in Practical Competence

Activity	Impact
Fraternity or sorority membership	Positive
Living on campus	Positive
Participation in intercollegiate athletics	Mixed or none
Service-learning and volunteering	Positive
Work	Positive
Internships	Positive
Involvement in clubs and organizations	Positive
Leadership experiences	Positive
Membership in service organizations	Positive
Participation in group projects	Positive
Peer education participation	Positive
Recreational sports participation	Positive
Undergraduate research	Positive
Student-faculty interaction	Positive or none
Diversity experiences	Positive

life management (Cooper et al., 1994). Further, students who held leadership positions in student groups also showed significant growth in these areas over a three-year period when compared with members who did not have such roles.

Student-faculty interaction. Doing research with a faculty member has positive effects on problem solving and decision-making ability (Eddins et al., 1997; Kuh, 1995; Volkwein et al., 1986). These and other substantive contacts with faculty members also positively shape practical competence (Kuh & Hu, 2001a). In a study of undergraduate research internships with McNair Scholars, Nnadozie, Ishiyama, and Chon (2001) concluded that learning how to develop research interests, articulate a research design, write a research proposal, and complete a manuscript for presentation and publication are all competencies that are associated with gaining admission to graduate school, obtaining funding for graduate study, and completing a graduate degree. Undergraduate research also leads to the development of teamwork skills, self-reflection, self-evaluation, leadership, planning and organizing, and adapting to change (Eddins et al., 1997).

Diversity experiences. Students who frequently studied with individuals different from themselves (in terms of race and ethnicity) reported growth in problem-solving skills, critical thinking, and ability to work cooperatively, suggesting that "diverse peers are important factors in the learning environment and key educational outcomes related to skills for living in a complex, pluralistic society" (Hurtado et al., 1999, p. 54).

Summary and Implications

This review of the literature leads us to five conclusions about the relationships between out-of-class experiences and desired outcomes of college.

1. *Life outside the classroom is replete with opportunities that can enrich the undergraduate experience.* The array of desired outcomes associated with out-of-class experiences summarized in this chapter clearly demonstrates that engaging students in educationally purposeful activities out-

side the classroom enhances student learning and contributes to student success, broadly defined to include student satisfaction, persistence, and educational attainment. Because many of the studies published since the mid-1990s controlled for entering student characteristics, we can be more confident today than a decade ago about the important contributions out-of-class experiences make to these desired outcomes of college. Students of all backgrounds seem to benefit from out-of-class experiences, though the benefits "do not always accrue equally to all students" (Pascarella, Edison, Nora, et al., 1996, p. 192). This is especially true of diversity experiences, where although interactions with students from different racial and ethnic backgrounds have positive effects across the board, White students tend to benefit more than students of color from such interactions (Hu & Kuh, 2001).

2. *With few exceptions, recent studies generally corroborate the trends reported in earlier reviews of the literature* (Kuh et al., 1994; Pascarella & Terenzini, 1991; Terenzini et al. 1996). Students benefit more in desired ways when they live in campus residences organized by educational themes (such as a Freshman Interest Group), participate in service-learning, study abroad, complete an internship, perform leadership roles in organizations on and off campus, and engage in purposeful interactions with a wide variety of peers from diverse backgrounds and with faculty members, especially on research projects. Working on campus a few hours a week also has positive effects overall; in fact, working a reasonable number of hours does not appear to have deleterious effects on learning, though working too much is positively related to premature departure from college. Areas where the findings are mixed include being a member of a social fraternity and participating in intercollegiate athletics; particularly in revenue sports at the Division I level. These trends in the research on students' out-of-class experiences have been consistent for several decades, though recent studies underscore the importance of such activities as service-learning. Also, primarily social contacts with faculty members do not have the magnitude of positive effects that substantive contacts do.

3. *Peers remain a key variable in whether out-of-class experiences have educational value.* Most of the time students spend outside of the classroom is in the company of peers, whether on or off campus and no matter the age of the student. Peers can be a positive influence, or a negative influence. Though this is not a new insight (see Astin, 1977, 1993; Feldman & Newcomb, 1969; Pascarella & Terenzini, 1991), it is sometimes overlooked or undervalued when considering how to improve learning environments.

4. *The positive effects of out-of-class experiences on desired learning and personal development outcomes could be enhanced through partnerships between academic and student affairs that induce students to engage more frequently in educationally purposeful activities.* At too many institutions, student affairs professionals are exclusively charged with managing students and their out-of-class experiences. The weight of the literature suggests that out-of-class experiences that influence the broadest array of outcomes and have the deepest effects tend to be those connected directly or indirectly to the academic mission of the institution (Kuh et al., 1991). Service-learning, living-learning centers and other forms of educational theme housing, undergraduate research, internships, and study abroad are good examples. When academic affairs and student affairs work together to encourage student involvement in these types of activities, the results are almost uniformly positive (Schuh & Whitt, 1999). Collaborative relationships might evolve into unified policy positions on such matters as, for example, requiring all students to live on campus for at least the first, and maybe second, year (where demographics and institutional mission are compatible), completion of two service-linked courses (one general education and one in the major), and an internship either on or off campus.

5. *Additional research and assessment efforts are needed to inform institutional improvement efforts that address students' out-of-class experiences.* Too little is known about the out-of-class experiences of certain types of students in certain types of institutions. While the research base has grown substantially during the past decade, we still know much more about the out-of-class experiences of traditional-aged students at residential campuses than we do about commuter, part-time, and older students. Inasmuch as the latter categories of students compose the majority of undergraduates, more attention must be given to these groups. Despite pleas over the last decade, the studies summarized here remain dominated by White, traditional-aged, full-time students attending four-year, residential institutions. To advance our understanding of the impact of student engagement on the contemporary cohort of undergraduates, more research is needed into the experiences of historically underrepresented groups.

In addition, very little is known about traditional-aged students who leave their home communities to attend college, live on campus for a short period of time (usually only the first-year), and then live off campus the rest of the time. These students essentially are residential commuters; they've become more or less independent of their families but are not exposed to the same degree to diversity experiences or cultural performances that campuses provide. In the same vein, assessments of the quality of students' out-of-class experiences must be linked to other existing data and find their way into campus policy decisions. Tools appropriate to the task can be found on the web site of the Policy Center on the First Year of College (www.brevard.edu/fyc/resources/list.htm).

We also need to learn more about promising developments such as service-learning and mentoring programs, as well as understudied but expanding areas of student interest such as a capella groups, recreational and club sports, undergraduate research, study abroad, honors programs, and those organizations that integrate both academic and social experiences such as business student associations and debate clubs. Also worthy of assessment efforts are new academic initiatives that draw on out-of-class experiences and are consistent with holistic student development values, such as portfolio assessment, active and collaborative group problem-solving tasks, and the use and impact of technology on how students spend their time outside the classroom. With regard to the latter, the early results are promising (Kuh & Hu, 2001b) but much more must be learned.

Concluding Thoughts

A great deal is known about the contributions of out-of-class experiences to desired outcomes of college, particularly cognitive complexity, knowledge acquisition, interpersonal communication, practical competence, humanitarianism, and retention. As subsequent chapters indicate, persistence and educational attainment also are positively linked with participation in educationally purposeful out-of-class experiences. At the same time we should be open to the prospect that there are experiences and outcomes to which studies up to now have overlooked. The typology (Kuh, 1993) used to organize our synthesis of the literature is a case in point. It may be insensitive to emerging areas of skills and competencies. Additional qualitative inquiries might open up new areas of understanding. For example, students may be better able to identify and help us understand the values of their experiences as student organization members, their rationale for getting involved in such groups, and the effects of service-learning if they can explain these matters in their own words. Perhaps when students are free to explore the boundaries of their experiences unfettered by predetermined survey response sets we may discover other developmentally powerful out-of-class experiences and valued outcomes.

Students grow and develop holistically. Changes in one domain of student development almost always are accompanied by changes in other areas (Terenzini et al., 1996). And it's rare that any single experience has a profound effect. Desired outcomes are usually a product of multiple, often diverse, and mutually shaping experiences or conditions. For these reasons, it really does take a whole campus to educate a student. Moreover, to focus and coordinate institutional resources in a way that induces students to take advantage of out-of-class learning opportunities, strong, collaborative efforts are needed on the part of the educators who work with students both inside and outside the classroom.

References

American College Personnel Association. (1994). *The student learning imperative: Implications for student affairs*. Washington, DC: Author.

Anaya, G. (1996). College experiences and student learning: The influence of active learning, college environments, and cocurricular activities. *Journal of College Student Development*, 37(6), 611-622.

Arminio, J. L., Carter, S., Jones, S. E., Kruger, K., Lucas, N., Washington, J., Young, N., & Scott, A. (2000). Leadership experiences of students of color. *NASPA Journal*, 37(3), 496-510.

Astin, A. W. (1975). *Preventing students from dropping out*. San Francisco: Jossey-Bass.

Astin, A. W. (1977). *Four critical years: The effects of college on beliefs, attitudes, and knowledge*. San Francisco: Jossey-Bass.

Astin, A. W. (1984). Student involvement: A developmental theory for higher education. *Journal of College Student Personnel*, 25, 297-308.

Astin, A. W. (1993a). Diversity and multiculturalism on campus: How are students affected? *Change*, 25, 44-49.

Astin, A. W. (1993b). *What matters in college: Four critical years revisited*. San Francisco: Jossey-Bass.

Astin, A. W., & Sax, L. J. (1998). How undergraduates are affected by service participation. *Journal of College Student Development*, 39(3), 251-263.

Astin, A. W., Sax, L. J., & Avalos, J. (1999). Long-term effects of volunteerism during the undergraduate years. *Review of Higher Education*, 22(2), 187-202.

Astin, A. W., Vogelgesang, L. J., Ikeda, E. K., & Yee, J. A. (2000). *How service-learning affects students*. Higher Education Research Institute: University of California, Los Angeles.

Astin, H. S., & Antonio, A. L. (November-December, 2000). Building character in college. *About Campus*, 5, 3-7.

Atlas, G., & Morier, D. (1994). The sorority rush process: Self-selection, acceptance criteria, and the effect of rejection. *Journal of College Student Development*, 35, 346-353.

Badura, A. S., Millard, M., Peluso, E. A., & Ortman, N. (2000). Effects of peer education training on peer educators: Leadership, self-esteem, health knowledge, and health behaviors. *Journal of College Student Development, 41*(5), 471-478.

Baxter Magolda, M. B. (1992). Cocurricular influences on college students' intellectual development. *Journal of College Student Development, 33*, 203-213.

Belch, H. A., Gebel, M., & Maas, G. M. (2001). Relationship between student recreation complex use, academic performance, and persistence of first-time freshmen. *NASPA Journal, 38*(2), 254-268.

Blimling, G. S. (2001). Diversity makes you smarter. *Journal of College Student Development, 42*(6), 517-519.

Brand, J. A., & Dodd, D. K. (1998). Self-esteem among college men as a function of Greek affiliation and year in college. *Journal of College Student Development, 39*(6), 611-615.

Broughton, E. A., & Otto, S. K. (1999). On-campus student employment: Intentional learning outcomes. *Journal of College Student Development, 40*(1), 87-88.

Center for the Study of the College Fraternity. (1992). *Survey of fraternity advisors.* Bloomington, IN: Indiana University.

Chickering, A. (1974). *Commuting versus residential students: Overcoming educational inequities of living off campus.* San Francisco: Jossey-Bass.

Cooper, D. L., Healy, M. A., & Simpson, J. (1994). Student development through involvement: Specific changes over time. *Journal of College Student Development, 35*, 98-102.

Cornelius, A. (1995). The relationship between athletic identity, peer and faculty socialization, and college student development. *Journal of College Student Development, 36*(6), 560-573.

Cress, C. M., Astin, H. S., Zimmerman-Oster, K., & Burkhardt, J. C. (2001). Developmental outcomes of college students' involvement in leadership activities. *Journal of College Student Development, 42*(1), 15-27.

Day-Vines, N., Barker, J. M., & Exum, H. A. (1998). Impact of diasporic travel on ethnic identity development of African American college students. *College Student Journal, 32*(3), 463-471.

DuBois, P. (1978). Participation in sports and occupations attainment: A comparative study. *Research Quarterly, 49*(1), 28-37.

Eddins, S. G. N., Williams, D. F., Bushek, D., & Porter, D. (1997). Searching for a prominent role of research in undergraduate education: Project interface. *Journal on Excellence in College Teaching, 8*(1), 69-81.

Edwards, K. E., & McKelfresh, D. A. (2002). The impact of a living learning center on students' academic success and persistence. *Journal of College Student Development, 43*(3), 395-401.

Ehrenberg, R. G., & Sherman, D. (1987). Employment while in college, academic achievement, and postcollege outcomes: A summary of results. *Journal of Human Resources, 22*(1), 1-23.

Ethington, C., Smart, J., & Pascarella, E. (1988). Influences on women's entry into male-dominated occupations. *Higher Education, 17*(5), 545-562.

Eyler, J., Giles, D. E., Stenson, C. M., & Gray, C. J. (2001). *At a glance: What we know about the effects of service-learning on students, faculty, institutions, and communities, 1993-2000.* Nashville, TN: Vanderbilt University.

Feldman, K. A., & Newcomb, T. M. (1969). *The impact of college on students.* San Francisco: Jossey-Bass Publishers.

Frost, S. H. (1991). Fostering the critical thinking of college women through academic advising and faculty contact. *Journal of College Student Development, 32*(4), 359-366.

Furr, S. R., & Elling, T. W. (2000). The influence of work on college student development. *NASPA Journal, 37*(2), 454-470.

Graham, S., & Gisi, S. L. (2000). Adult undergraduate students: What role does college involvement play? *NASPA Journal, 38*(1), 99-121.

Gray, K. S., Murdock, G. K., & Stebbins, C. D. (2002). Assessing study abroad's effect on an international mission. *Change, 34*(3), 45-51.

Gray, M. J., Ondaatje, E. H., Fricker, R. D., & Geschwind, S. A. (2000). Assessing service-learning: Results from a survey of "Learn and Serve America, Higher Education." *Change, 32*(2), 30-39.

Hayek, J. C., Carini, R. M., O'Day, P. T., & Kuh, G. D. (2002). Triumph or tragedy: Comparing student engagement levels of members of

Greek-letter organizations and other students. *Journal of College Student Development, 43*(5), 643-663.

Hood, A. B., Craig, A. F., & Ferguson, B. W. (1992). The impact of athletics, part-time employment, and other activities on academic achievement. *Journal of College Student Development, 33*, 447-453.

Howard, A. (1986). College experiences and managerial performance. *Journal of Applied Psychology Monographs, 71*(3), 530-552.

Hu, S., & Kuh, G. D. (2001, November). *The effects of interactional diversity on selected self-reported learning and personal development outcomes.* Presented at the annual meeting of the Association for the Study of Higher Education, Richmond.

Hunt, S., & Rentz, A. L. (1994). Greek-letter social group members' involvement and psychosocial development. *Journal of College Student Development, 35*, 289-295.

Hurtado, S., Milem, J. F., Clayton-Pederson, A. R., & Allen, W. R. (1999). *Enacting diverse learning environments: Improving the climate for racial ethnic diversity in higher education.* ASHE/ERIC Higher Education Report, No. 8. Washington, DC: George Washington University.

Inman, P., & Pascarella, E. T. (1998). The impact of college residence on the development of critical thinking skills in college freshmen. *Journal of College Student Development, 39*(6), 557-568.

Kauffmann, N., & Kuh, G. D. (1985). The impact of study abroad on personal development of college students. *Journal of International Student Personnel, 2*(2), 6-10.

Kimbrough, W. M. (1995). Self-assessment, participation, and value of leadership skills, activities, and experiences for Black students relative to their membership in historically Black fraternities and sororities. *Journal of Negro Education, 64*(1), 63-74.

Kimbrough, W. M., & Hutcheson, P. A. (1999). The impact of membership in black Greek-letter organizations on black students' involvement in collegiate activities and their development of leadership skills. *Journal of Negro Education, 67*(2), 96-105.

King, S. (1973). *Five lives at Harvard: Personality change during college.* Cambridge, MA: Harvard University Press.

Kuh, G. D. (1993). In their own words: What students learn outside the classroom. *American Educational Research Journal, 30*(2), 277-304.

Kuh, G. D. (1995). The other curriculum: Out-of-class experiences associated with student learning and personal development. *Journal of Higher Education, 66*(2), 123-155.

Kuh, G. D. (1996). Guiding principles for creating seamless learning environments for undergraduates. *Journal of College Student Development, 37*, 135-148.

Kuh, G. D., Douglas, K. B., Lund, J. P., & Ramin-Gyurnek, J. (1994). *Student learning outside the classroom: Transcending artificial boundaries* (8). Washington, DC: George Washington University Graduate School of Education.

Kuh, G. D., Gonyea, R. M., & Palmer, M. (2001). The disengaged commuter students: Fact of fiction? *Commuter Perspectives, 27*(1), 2-5.

Kuh, G. D., & Hu, S. (2001a). The effects of student-faculty interaction in the 1990s. *The Review of Higher Education, 24*, 309-332.

Kuh, G. D., & Hu, S. (2001b). The relationships between computer and information technology use, student learning, and other college experiences. *Journal of College Student Development, 42*, 217-232.

Kuh, G. D., & Lund, J. (1994). What students gain from participating in student government. In M. Terrell, & M. Cuyjet (Eds.), Developing student government leadership, *New Directions for Student Services, No. 66.* San Francisco: Jossey-Bass.

Kuh, G. D., Schuh, J. H., Whitt, E. J., & Associates (1991). *Involving colleges: Successful approaches to fostering learning and personal development outside the classroom.* San Francisco: Jossey-Bass.

MacGregor, J. (1993). *Student self-evaluation: Fostering reflective learning.* Unpublished manuscript, San Francisco.

Mann, A. F. (1994). College peer tutoring journals: Maps of development. *Journal of College Student Development, 35*, 164-169.

McBride, R. E., & Reed, J. (1998). Thinking and college athletes—are they predisposed to critical thinking? *College Student Journal, 32*(3), 443-450.

McNamara, K. M., & Cover, J. D. (1999). An

assessment of extramural activities that encourage support for the liberal arts. *College Student Journal, 33*(4), 594-607.

Moran, J. J., Yengo, L., & Algier, A. (1994). Participation in minority oriented cocurricular organizations. *Journal of College Student Development, 35,* 143.

Nnadozie, E., Ishiyama, J., & Chon, J. (2001). Undergraduate research internships and graduate school success. *Journal of College Student Development, 42*(2), 145-156.

Pace, C. R. (1984). *Measuring the quality of college student experiences.* Los Angeles: University of California-Los Angeles, Center for the Study of Evaluation.

Pace, C. R. (1987). *Good things go together.* Los Angeles, CA: University of California-Los Angeles Center for the Study of Evaluation.

Pace, C. R. (1990). *The undergraduates: A report of their activities and progress in college in the 1980s.* Los Angeles, CA: University of California-Los Angeles Center for Study of Evaluation.

Pascarella, E. T., Bohr, L., Nora, A., Desler, M., & Zusman, B. (1994). Impacts of on-campus and off-campus work on first-year cognitive outcomes. *Journal of College Student Development, 35,* 364-370.

Pascarella, E. T., Bohr, L., Nora, A., & Terenzini, P. T. (1995). Intercollegiate athletic participation and freshmen-year cognitive outcomes. *Journal of Higher Education, 66*(4), 369-387.

Pascarella, E. T., Edison, M., Nora, A., Hagedorn, L. S., & Terenzini, P. T. (1996). Influences on students' openness to diversity and challenge in the first-year of college. *Journal of Higher Education, 67*(2), 174-195.

Pascarella, E. T., Edison, M., Whitt, E. J., Nora, A., Hagedorn, L. S., & Terenzini, P. T. (1996). Cognitive effects of Greek affiliation during the first-year of college. *NASPA Journal, 33,* 254-259.

Pascarella, E. T., Flowers, L., & Whitt, E. J. (2001). Cognitive effects of Greek affiliation in college: Additional evidence. *NASPA Journal, 38*(3), 280-301.

Pascarella, E. T., Palmer, B., Moye, M., & Pierson, C. T. (2001). Do diversity experiences influence the development of critical thinking? *Journal of College Student Development, 42*(3), 257-271.

Pascarella, E. T., & Smart, J. (1991). Impact of intercollegiate athletic participation for African American and Caucasian men: Some further evidence. *Journal of College Student Development, 32,* 123-130.

Pascarella, E. T., Smart, J. C., Ethington, C., & Nettles, M. (1987). The influence of college on self-concept: A consideration of race and gender differences. *American Educational Research Journal, 70*(1), 35-41.

Pascarella, E., & Terenzini, P. T. (1980). Student-faculty and student-peer relationships as mediators of the structural effects of undergraduate residence arrangement. *Journal of Educational Research, 2*(73), 344-353.

Pascarella, E. T., & Terenzini, P. T. (1991). *How college affects students.* San Francisco: Jossey-Bass.

Pike, G. R. (1999). The effects of residential learning communities and the traditional living arrangements on educational gains during the first-year of college. *Journal of College Student Development, 40*(3), 269-284.

Pike, G. R. (2000). The influence of fraternity or sorority membership on students' college experiences and cognitive development. *Research in Higher Education, 41,* 117-139.

Pike, G. R., & Askew, J. W. (1990). The impact of fraternity or sorority membership on academic involvement and learning outcomes. *NASPA Journal, 28*(1), 13-19.

Pike, G. R., Schroeder, C. C., & Berry, T. R. (1997). Enhancing the educational impact of residence halls: The relationship between residential learning communities and first-year college experiences and persistence. *Journal of College Student Development, 38*(6), 609-621.

Richards, S., & Aries, E. (1999). The Division III student-athlete: Academic performance, campus involvement, and growth. *Journal of College Student Development, 40*(3), 211-218.

Riemer, B. A., Beal, B., & Schroeder, P. (2000). The influences of peer and university culture on female student athletes' perceptions of career termination, professionalization, and social isolation. *Journal of Sport Behavior, 23*(4), 364-378.

Romano, C. R. (1996). A qualitative study of women student leaders. *Journal of College Student Development, 37*(6), 676-683.

Sax, L. J., & Astin, A. W. (1997). The Benefits of Service: Evidence from Undergraduates. *Educational Record, 78*(3-4), 25-32.

Schroeder, P. J. (2000). An assessment of student involvement among selected NCAA Division III basketball players. *Journal of College Student Development, 41*(6), 616-626.

Schuh, J. H., & Laverty, M. (1983). The perceived long-term influence of holding a significant student leadership position. *Journal of College Student Personnel, 24*(1), 28-32.

Schuh, J. H., & Whitt, E. J. (Eds.). (1999). Creating successful partnerships between academic and student affairs. *New Directions for Student Services, No. 87.* San Francisco: Jossey-Bass.

Serow, R. C., & Dreyden, J. I. (1990). Community service among college and university students: Individual and institutional relationships. *Adolescence, 25*(99), 553-566.

Taylor, C. M., & Howard-Hamilton, M. F. (1995). Student involvement and racial identity attitudes among African American males. *Journal of College Student Development, 36*(4), 330-336.

Terenzini, P. T., & Pascarella, E. (1980). Student/faculty relationships and freshman year educational outcomes: A further investigation. *Journal of College Student Personnel, 21*(6), 521-528.

Terenzini, P. T., Pascarella, E. T., & Blimling, G. S. (1996). Students' out-of-classroom experiences and their influence on learning and cognitive development: A literature review. *Journal of College Student Development, 37*(2), 149-162.

Terenzini, P. T., Springer, L., Pascarella, E., & Nora, A. (1994). *The multiple influences on college students' critical thinking skills.* Paper presented at the meeting of the Association for Study of Higher Education, Tucson, AZ.

Terenzini, P. T., Springer, L., Pascarella, E. T., & Nora, A. (1995). In and out-of-class influences affecting the development of students' intellectual orientations. *Review of Higher Education, 19*(1), 23-44.

Tinto, V. (1987). *Leaving college: Rethinking the causes and cures of student attrition.* Chicago: University of Chicago Press.

Volkwein, J., King, M., & Terenzini, P. T. (1986). Student-faculty relationships and intellectual growth among transfer students. *Journal of Higher Education, 57*(4), 413-430.

Whipple, E. G., Baier, J. L., & Grady, D. L. (1991). A comparison of black and white Greeks at a predominantly white university. *NASPA Journal, 28*(2).

Whitt, E. J., Edison, M. I., Pascarella, E. T., Terenzini, P. T., & Nora, A. (2001). Influences on students' openness to diversity and challenge in the second and third years of college. *Journal of Higher Education, 72,* 172-204.

Wilder, D. H., Hoyt, A. E., Surbeck, B. S., & Wilder, J. C. (1986). Greek affiliation and attitude change in college students. *Journal of College Student Development, 27,* 510-519.

Wilder, D. H., & McKeegan, H. F. (1997). Greek-letter social organizations in higher education: A review of research. *Handbook of Higher Education Research and Practice, XIV,* 317-366.

Wolf-Wendel, L. E., Toma, J. D., & Morphew, C. C. (2001). There's no "I" in "Team": Lessons from athletes on community building. *The Review of Higher Education, 24*(4), 369-396.

Wolniak, G. C., Pierson, C. T., & Pascarella, E. T. (2001). Effects of intercollegiate athletics participation on male orientations toward learning. *Journal of College Student Development, 42*(6), 604-624.

Meeting the Changing Needs of Students

Charles C. Schroeder
University of Missouri-Columbia

Educators committed to designing responsive, intentional, and effective first-year experiences must clearly understand today's college students and ways to meet their needs. Understanding the expectations, attitudes, and behaviors of any individual student is a complex task, and attempting to understand the collective dynamics of a generation of students is even more daunting. So how do we understand contemporary students? This chapter attempts to answer that question from multiple perspectives. For example, using the 1960s as a benchmark, how has society changed and what impact have these changes had on student characteristics and higher education? What do we know about current students—their expectations, attitudes, values, academic needs, and social patterns? How do these characteristics influence their college experience and the learning outcomes prized by their institutions? How can educators use this knowledge to create activities and experiences that address their educational needs, promote their learning, and foster their academic and social success? And, finally, what new strategies and best practices can be employed to respond effectively to these changing needs?

Returning to the Past to Better Understand the Present

Using the early 1960s as a benchmark provides a relatively easy way to describe how dramatically college students and their undergraduate experiences have changed in a short period of time. In 1963, I entered a small, selective liberal arts college of approximately 1,100 students in Texas. My memories of my first-college year center on the rules, which seemed to outnumber the students. First-year students, who were often referred to as "rats," were required to wear beanies during the first six weeks, and everyone attended compulsory Saturday classes. New students were not allowed to have cars on campus, and house mothers routinely conducted bed checks to ensure that all women complied with the curfews. Administrators believed that the best way to control men was to force women into their own residence halls by 11:00 p.m. Sunday through Thursday, and by 1:00 a.m. on Friday and Saturday. The rules against kissing your boyfriend or girlfriend goodnight on the dorm steps were clear, and no one ever dreamed of co-ed dorms. By 1967, the college allowed men and women to entertain members of the opposite sex in their rooms on Sunday afternoon. There was one catch: Your door had to be open at least a book's length; enterprising students used a matchbook to meet the requirement.

Students' use of technology was relatively primitive. Although my dorm had a TV lounge, no one had a television set in his room and only the more affluent students could afford cabinet-style stereos. The campus had a mainframe computer that ran on data cards; however, the only way students could use it was by taking a three-credit course on computer languages such as Fortran or Cobol. Since handheld, electronic calculators had not been invented, students used mechanical calculating machines as computational tools in various courses. And, due to the limited number of personal electrical devices (e.g., radio, clock), two electrical outlets per room were more than adequate.

Because more than 95% of students lived on campus, social life generally occurred within the boundaries of the institution. The student union was not only the place where students ate three meals a day, it was also the center of informal campus activities and occasional weekend dances chaperoned by administrators and a few faculty. Expectations about student conduct were clearly communicated during first-year orientation, and the dean of men and dean of women consistently enforced campus rules, including dress codes for women! They acted *in loco parentis*, a doctrine that made explicit the institution's right to assume parental control with regard to student conduct. In this way, the institution attempted to foster students' character development.

Although many male students consumed alcohol, the college had stringent regulations and expectations concerning drinking on campus. Students caught drinking or keeping alcohol in their rooms would be immediately suspended. Significant gender differences in drinking patterns were evident—female students were rarely intoxicated.

My classmates were a relatively privileged, homogeneous lot—White, middle class, generally well-prepared for college-level work, and moderately ambitious. Very few students held outside jobs, and even fewer worked to pay for college. Credit cards were just beginning to appear, but they were not available to college students. Everyone I knew took a full course load every semester and graduated in four years. Most faculty on my campus were eager to spend time with students inside and outside the classroom. To this day, I recall strong personal relationships with faculty members willing to provide additional assistance in difficult courses, to discuss moral and philosophical issues, and to listen to my personal concerns and career aspirations.

In the early 60s, diversity on my campus was defined not in racial or ethnic terms but by the occasional out-of-state student from Arkansas and Louisiana. Only one of my peers was Black, and he was an exchange student from South Africa. Very few students were from divorced families; in fact, in 1963 only 8% of first-year students entering college nationwide came from divorced families.

Finally, students of my generation were the first to participate in the National Freshman Survey sponsored by the Higher Education Research Institute at UCLA. Surveys of students who entered school at that time showed that the number one reason for going to college was to develop a meaningful philosophy of life; being financially secure ranked ninth in order of importance (Astin, Parrott, Korn, & Sax, 1997). Results from this survey also indicated that males clearly outnumbered females on my campus and throughout the nation. Gender differences in choice of majors were also quite apparent, with women over-represented in education, nursing, home economics, and social work.

In the early 60s, three major events—the Civil Rights Movement, the Vietnam War, and the Women's Movement—significantly influenced campus life across the country. Although many students became politically active and even engaged in demonstrations, none of this occurred on my campus, with the exception of one two-hour candlelight vigil involving eight students. Few opportunities to participate in community service were available on my campus, and service-learning as a pedagogy had not been introduced there or elsewhere.

20

Although the decade of the 60s was a period of dramatic change, it was but a precursor to the major social, demographic, economic, technological, and global changes that would occur in the next 40 years. Some of the most radical changes have been the fundamental shifts in family life, which have been documented extensively by Keller (2001a & 2001b). He indicates, for example, that in the early 60s, 90% of children grew up in homes with a mother and a father and the vast majority of mothers with children below school age did not work. Since that time, the nuclear family has crumbled, with the divorce rate more than doubling between 1960 and 1998 and the percentage of children born to unmarried persons jumping from 6% to 32%. Finally, the proportion of married mothers with young children working full-time climbed from 19% in the early 60s to over 70% in the late 90s (Keller, 2001b).

With the passage of the 1965 Immigration and Nationalization Act Amendments, America experienced major demographic changes emanating from an immigrant tidal wave. During the past 35 years, between 35 and 40 million people have entered the United States. According to Keller (2001a), immigration since 1965 is ethnically very different from previous immigration, with 9 of 10 immigrants coming from Latin American, the Caribbean, Asia, and Africa. Prior to 1965, 9 of 10 immigrants came from European countries and Canada.

Since 1965, there have been other significant demographic shifts in the college population with regard to race and ethnicity, particularly with regard to significant increases in the number of African Americans, Latinos, and Asian Americans. The increase in the college-going rate of African-American students in the past 20 years alone is fairly dramatic; in 1983 only about 38% of African Americans went on to some form of postsecondary education; in 1998 this rate had increased to 61% (Mortenson, 1999). Significant shifts in gender patterns are worth noting as well. In the 1970s and 1980s, 77% of new students attending college were women (Mortenson, 1998).

Not only have demographics and family lives changed dramatically since the 60s, higher education has changed as well. It abandoned its elitist orientation in favor of an egalitarianism that brought an access revolution fueled by a 6000% increase in financial aid (Merante, 1987). As a result, enrollments quadrupled, curricular offerings mushroomed, and a multitude of highly specialized programs and services were created to meet the needs of increasingly diverse student populations. Today's students are indeed diverse, not simply in terms of race and ethnicity, but in terms of age, part-time or full-time status, expectations, attitudes, beliefs, learning styles, and social patterns. The next section examines some of these characteristics more closely.

Characteristics of Contemporary College Students

In recent years, the news media have constructed a national image of contemporary college students as an aimless, apathetic, and spoiled generation of slackers who detest hard work, snub political responsibility, and whine about their lot in life (Hayworth, 1997; Sacks, 1996). Faculty, staff, and others who accept these stereotypes may come to believe that this generation of students has a poor work ethic, is more comfortable shopping or loafing than working or studying, and is essentially apolitical, apathetic, and overly materialistic. Fortunately, a great deal of evidence suggests that the media have mis-portrayed many of today's students.

A major source of information on contemporary students is generated annually by the Higher Education Research Institute (HERI) at UCLA. For more than 30 years, the HERI staff, through their Cooperative Institutional Research Program (CIRP), have administered a national survey to numerous first-year students at two-year and four-year institutions. In 2001, for example, 411,970 students from 704 institutions participated in the survey. The results of these and

"As institutions have become more diverse, the campus political climate has undergone a basic shift."

other public surveys show that there is indeed a new breed of student on campus and that the behavior and attitudes of today's students are quite different from those of previous generations. The following general themes drawn from CIRP data and the literature (Astin, 1997; Hayworth, 1997; King, 1999; Kuh, 2001; Levine, 1998; Levine & Cureton, 1998; Lowery, 2001; Newton, 1998, 2000, 2001; Schroeder, 2000) are particularly worth noting.

High Stress Levels and Psychopathology

Students today are experiencing higher levels of stress than students of any previous generation. The stress appears to be twice as high for women, because they are concerned about financing college and developing successful career paths in highly competitive fields while maintaining many traditional female values. Regardless of gender, students' stress is attributed to the challenges of financing the escalating costs of a college education and to being "overwhelmed by all I have to do." Entering students are also in a more psychologically precarious position than those of previous generations, and increasing numbers seek personal counseling. Counseling center directors across the country report that eating disorders, suicide attempts, drug and alcohol abuse, sexual abuse and violence, as well as dysfunctional family experiences, are all on the rise (Newton, 1998). Staff psychologists also report more incidents of such stress-related disorders as depression, headaches, digestive problems, and hypertension.

Working More and Longer Hours

Unlike students of the 60s, national data indicates that 75% of contemporary college students (students enrolled in all types of postsecondary institutions) have an outside job that requires them to work an average of 37 hours per week. On many residential campuses that enroll traditional-aged students (17 to 22 years of age), students who work are trying to combine a traditional collegiate experience with an average of 25 hours of work per week (King, 1999). Although many students work to pay college expenses, a significant portion work to maintain a particular lifestyle that includes fashionable clothing, a new car, CD players, televisions, and other amenities. Many students are also overloaded with record debt levels, not only from college loans, but more alarming, from credit cards (Stanford, 1999; Kidwell & Turrisi, 2000). Data from *Student Monitor* show 59% of students who had a credit card expected to have a debt at graduation, and the debt level was expected to top $17,000 (Schroeder, 2000). Balancing work responsibilities with academic obligations has become a major challenge primarily because students who work long hours have less time and energy to devote to their studies and other educationally purposeful activities.

New Patterns of Socializing

The social life of contemporary college students is also quite different from that of previous generations. Because students feel overwhelmed in balancing work, academic obligations, and involvement in other activities, they often complain about their inability to have a "traditional social life." Furthermore, social connections and intimacy are taking on different patterns. Students are less likely to be paired off in couples and more likely to join group activities (Levine & Cureton, 1998; Newton, 2000). Indeed, group dating, which provides protection from deeper involvement and intimacy, has replaced traditional dating in many places.

At most institutions, the vast majority of social life occurs off campus—often in local bars that encourage drinking through discounts and promotions. Clearly, social life for college students is lubricated by alcohol. According to longitudinal research conducted by Wechsler (1996) at the Harvard School of Public Health, almost half of all college students binge-drink (defined as five or more drinks at one sitting for men and four or more for women). Students who binge-drink are more likely to damage property, have trouble with authority, miss class, experience hangovers, engage in unplanned sexual activities, and incur injuries. As recently reported by a federally appointed task force, abusive drinking by college students often results in tragic consequences: 14,000 college students are killed each year in alcohol-related accidents and abusive drinking by college students contributes to 500,000 injuries and 70,000 cases of sexual assaults or rape annually. Also, 400,000 students between the ages of 18 and 24 reported having unprotected sex as a result of drinking (Schroeder, 2000).

Dangerous drinking is particularly prevalent in fraternities because of the "alcohol-centered culture" of many Greek houses. On average, Greek men report being more than three times as likely to engage in "risky drinking" than independent men, and Greeks report almost twice as many negative consequences from their drinking. Recent research also indicates that female high school students are now binge drinking at the same rate as their male counterparts and that female college students are rapidly reaching parity with men in regard to drinking on campus (Schroeder, 1999). In addition, binge drinking is becoming more of a problem in sororities (Ozegovic, Bikos, & Szymanski, 2001).

Increased Academic Disengagement

Data from recent CIRP and other national surveys increasingly demonstrate an escalation in academic disengagement and greater numbers of students requiring remedial or developmental education. CIRP data, for example, indicate that 40% of students reported being "bored in class"; 63% said they came to class late; and more than 40% indicated they studied fewer than three hours per week while in high school. Fully one third reported taking a basic-skills or remedial course in reading, mathematics, or writing. Although students studied significantly less in high school compared with previous cohorts, record numbers got B or better grades in high school (Sax, Astin, Korn, & Mahoney, 1997). In 1999, high school teachers awarded more A grades than ever (almost 35%), compared with 12.5% in 1969. Paradoxically, more than 40% of first-year college students say they need to improve their reading and study skills; about the same percentage say they expect to earn at least a B average. These and other data suggest that many students today are unrealistic about what it takes to do well in college.

These trends have not gone unnoticed by faculty. Faculty often view students as economically motivated, inadequately prepared, uncommitted to the inherent worth of liberal learning, and apathetic about many contemporary issues (Sax, Astin, Korn, & Mahoney, 1997). Unfortunately, these perceptions contribute to the widening gap between how students best learn and how faculty teach. This disconnect in teaching and learning is a result of many factors, but none more important than the fact that more students today have learning styles that differ from previous cohorts and from their teachers. Based on more than 20 years of research, as many as two thirds of today's students exhibit a "concrete active" (field-dependent) learning pattern (Schroeder, 1993). Students who exhibit this pattern perform best in learning situations characterized by direct, concrete experience, moderate-to-high degrees of structure, and a linear step-by-step approach to learning. They often have difficulty with complex concepts and ambiguity, are less independent in thought and judgment, and are more dependent on the wishes and ideas of those in authority. Compared with their more traditional predecessors, they are more passive, display less tolerance for diversity, are more dependent on immediate gratification, exhibit more difficulties with basic reading and writing skills, and value knowledge primarily for its practical utility.

Three quarters of the faculty, conversely, exhibit a teaching style that not only is opposite of, but antagonistic to, that of the concrete active learner. Their style is referred to as "abstract reflective" (field-independent), and they prefer the global to the particular; are stimulated by the realm of concepts, ideas, and abstractions; love learning for learning's sake; and assume that students, like themselves, need a high degree of autonomy in their work (Schroeder, 1993). These fundamental learning style differences make working with college students more challenging, because most faculty and staff members were not exposed to such pedagogical strategies as active and collaborative learning that respond directly to the needs of concrete active students (Kuh, 2001).

When characteristics such as academic disengagement, inadequate preparation, and different learning patterns are coupled with outside employment patterns, it is not surprising that students are taking longer to graduate. At my institution, only 28% of the students graduate in four years, though 61% graduate in six. On many campuses, course loads now average 13 to 14 hours per semester, or slightly less for many entering students. In addition, students today are prone to drop courses more readily, particularly if they are not receiving the grades they desire (Levine & Cureton, 1998). Students often find they are closed out of courses they need, while at the same time external mandates from various professional accrediting agencies have increased credit requirements for fields such as business and engineering.

National data also indicate that academic dishonesty is on the rise (Cole & Kiss, 2000). In one survey of college-bound seniors, four of five said they had cheated, and the majority indicated they did not consider this a serious ethical violation. Reports from various campuses confirm that cheating has reached epidemic proportions, and that cheating on tests, downloading term papers off the Internet, and plagiarizing are common (Newton, 2000).

Changing Civic and Social Attitudes

According to the most recent CIRP data, three of four students perform some kind of volunteer work during their senior year in high school; however, once they enroll in college, these students are much less likely to continue performing community service work. Prior to the tragedy of September 11, students tended to be cynical about national politics and were often unfamiliar with national and world leaders and their views. There is increasing evidence, however, of a stirring of a civic renaissance which not only reflects a response to the September 11 tragedy, but also an increasingly tight job market. A recent study by the National Association of Colleges and Employers (2002) found that employers expect to hire 36% fewer

graduates this year compared with last year. Service organizations, such as Teach for America, the Peace Corps, and Ameri-Corps, are expanding and students are responding in record numbers. This emerging pattern is congruent with the emphasis on "think globally and act locally"—that is, volunteering in local schools, soup kitchens, and homeless shelters where students feel they can make an immediate impact (Levine & Cureton, 1998; Lowery, 2001).

National surveys also underscored the tremendous amount of campus tension and anxiety associated with multiculturalism and race relations. Levine (1998), in interviews conducted for his book *When Hope and Fear Collide*, found that students were much more willing to share the intimate details of their sex lives than to discuss multiculturalism and the status of race relations on their campuses. These concerns are particularly acute at large research and doctoral institutions, where increased evidence of racism, incivility, intolerance, and hostility toward different minority and international students makes these students feel marginalized and isolated.

As institutions have become more diverse, the campus political climate has undergone a basic shift. Traditional political groups have declined and been replaced by racial, ethnic, and gender support and advocacy groups (Chang, 2002). This new political climate has spawned increased student activism on such issues as high college costs, race-based scholarship, gay rights, and multiculturalism (Schroeder, 2000). Although contemporary students often take diversity for granted, primarily because of their diverse backgrounds and having more diverse friends, they often dislike others' self-grouping based on race, sexual orientation, or other characteristics. Caucasian students, in particular, sometimes view self-grouping of African Americans and other minority students as a desire on the part of these students to segregate and isolate themselves from the mainstream. Student organizations differentiated along racial and ethnic lines continue to proliferate, and some observers fear that "As the student body becomes more racially diverse, the campus necessarily becomes more racially divided and balkanized" (Chang, 2002, p. 5). These, among other attitudes, have created a relatively "chilly climate" for race relations on many campuses.

Advanced Technological Proficiency

Students born after 1979 have been exposed to computers in their school rooms, sophisticated electronic games, and the Internet as a search tool. Many, if not most, carry cell phones, pagers, and personal data assistants. Contemporary students have developed learning habits primarily in front of a computer screen; hence, they are much less used to reading books than prior generations. They are also accustomed to rapid-fire information from multiple sources and hence, quite impatient with long tasks. As a result, many students have difficulty focusing on one topic for a long time. Paradoxically, although students are often connected instantly to one another through electronic technology, it is much more difficult for them to form meaningful relationships with one another.

Campus-wide applications of technology are also expanding at a rapid rate—from basic, limited uses (such as e-mail, course web pages, and class chat rooms) to classroom enhancements (i.e., PowerPoint, one-way and two-way audio visual techniques, computer simulations) and co-curricular applications (residence hall rooms with ethernet connectivity, premium cable TV channels and asynchronous/CD ROM hybrids) (Upcraft & Terenzini, 1999). In addition, students today can take online courses, not only at their own institutions, but simultaneously at other institutions as well. Distance learning, particularly for non-traditional-aged college students, is becoming commonplace throughout the country and around the world.

In this section, I have attempted to highlight major trends and patterns in students' academic needs, social patterns, expectations, attitudes, and values. As previously stated, attempting to understand the collective dynamics of a generation of students is incredibly difficult and extremely challenging. Educators committed to designing effective first-year experiences, therefore, must engage in systematic assessment of entering students to achieve a thorough under-

standing of their unique needs and characteristics. By combining the results of national studies with institution-specific assessment data, educators are better equipped to design responsive, intentional, and effective first-year experiences. The following section demonstrates how to respond effectively to changing student characteristics and the needs summarized previously.

Responding Effectively to Students' Changing Needs

In recent reports on the status of higher education (Wingspread Group on Higher Education, 1993; Boyer Commission on Educating Undergraduates in the Research University, 1998; and Kellogg Commission on the Future of State and Land Grant Universities, 1997), researchers have stressed the need to connect all undergraduate experiences with student learning and development. Recommendations from these reports, plus the findings from empirical research on the impact of out-of-class experiences on student learning, have also led student affairs educators to view fostering learning as their mission and primary purpose. Three recent documents in particular—*The Student Learning Imperative (SLI): Implications for Student Affairs* (American College Personnel Association, 1994); *Principles of Good Practice for Student Affairs* (American College Personnel Association and National Association of Student Personnel Administrators, 1997); and *Powerful Partnerships: A Shared Responsibility for Learning* (American Association of Higher Education, American College Personnel Association, and National Association of Student Personnel Administrators, 1998)—all draw attention to the centrality of student

> "Educators committed to designing effective first-year experiences, therefore, must engage in systematic assessment of entering students to achieve a thorough understanding of their unique needs and characteristics."

learning and the need to provide students with a more cohesive, less fragmented, and more effective educational experience. These reports, documents, and perspectives have one common theme—putting student learning first (Whitt, 1999).

Putting student learning first requires fundamental changes in the way student activities are conceptualized, designed, and delivered. The phrase "student activities" itself conjures up images of big name entertainment, feature-length movies, comedy acts, tee shirt give-aways, and other "fun and games" events. Faculty and student affairs educators rarely view student activities as connected to the academic mission of the institution; in fact, faculty, at best, view student activities as a healthy diversion from the rigors of intense, academic work.

To become learning-centered, staff in student activities units must shift their current perspectives by (a) viewing themselves as educators; (b) intentionally designing activities and experiences that support and complement the academic mission of their institution; (c) formulating clear and measurable learning outcomes; and (d) forging educational partnerships with academic administrators, faculty, and other student affairs educators to promote student learning and success not only *within* their organizational boundaries, but *between* these boundaries and other divisions within the institution. To fully embrace this mandate, student activities educators committed to first-year students must reflect on two central questions: *What* should students learn and *how* should they learn it?

A review of current students' expectations, academic needs, attitudes, and values suggests that first-year programs and activities should focus significant attention on fostering academic engagement, humanitarian values, interpersonal and intrapersonal competencies, and character development. The content of this learning should not be separate and distinct from traditional "academic learning" that occurs in the classroom. To the contrary, academic and student affairs educators committed to high-quality experiences for first-year students must focus their efforts on creating seamless learning environments—environments that connect in a mutually supportive and coherent fashion, and that merge formal curricular experiences with informal co-curricular experiences (Kuh, 2001). Facilitating such powerful connections requires focusing on the second question—how can this learning be facilitated? By capitalizing on the educational potential of technology, using active and collaborative pedagogies, and innovative assessment tools, educators can design activities and experiences that respond effectively to the changing needs of today's students. Through active learning processes, students not only learn content, but also improve their critical thinking; learn to manage their time; practice interpersonal, listening, and speaking skills; become better writers; and gain sensitivity to cultural differences (Warren, 1997). The following sections examine some innovative programs, practices, and pedagogies that illustrate ways of making these kinds of connections. They also explore how student activities educators can adapt these practices and pedagogies in order to enhance the experience for first-year students on their campuses.

Fostering Academic Engagement

In the publication *Seven Principles of Good Practice in Undergraduate Education*, Chickering and Gamson (1987) argue convincingly that the following seven conditions are especially important for fostering academic engagement: (a) student-faculty contact, (b) cooperation among students, (c) active learning, (d) prompt feedback, (e) time on task, (f) high expectations, and (g) respect for diverse ways of learning. In recent years, many institutions have used these principles to foster academic engagement through the design and implementation of learning communities for first-year students. One highly successful model is residentially based Freshman Interest Groups (FIGs), which are organized around general education academic themes, enroll between 15 and 22 new students in three common general education courses, and assign these students to live together on the same floor of a residence hall. Each FIG also has a peer advisor who lives with the students and co-facilitates a credited first-year experience course with a faculty or staff member. The peer advisor organizes various activities directly linked to the academic theme of the FIG including service-learning activities, field trips, and guest speakers on topics related to the FIG (Schroeder, Minor, & Tarkow, 1999).

Although learning communities can take forms other than freshman interest groups, the literature (Love, 1999; MacGregor, 1991; Schroeder, 2002; Tinto, 1997; Tinto & Goodsell, 1993) clearly suggests they make major contributions to meeting the changing needs of new students by providing opportunities to integrate courses in an interdisciplinary manner; helping students form social networks among their peers; increasing student involvement and engagement; enhancing academic achievement, retention, and educational attainment; making the campus "psychologically small" by creating peer reference groups for new students; and purposefully integrating curricular and co-curricular experiences through the development of seamless learning environments. In addition to these benefits, recent research (Schroeder, 2002) indicates that residentially based learning communities for first-year students have a significant impact on reducing binge-drinking. As Kuh and his colleagues note in Chapter 1, learning communities have also been shown to improve cognitive complexity and knowledge acquisition and application.

Student activities educators can make significant contributions to the vitality of learning communities by serving as co-facilitators with faculty in pro-seminar and University 101 courses; designing co-curricular experiences (i.e., field trips, simulations, case studies) that support and reinforce classroom learning; and creating activities and experiences that promote interpersonal, intrapersonal, and practical competencies (i.e., self-awareness, confidence, time and stress management, credit card and debt management, and sound decision-making). Opportunities also exist for student activities educators to create their own learning communities—communities composed of student organization members and leaders who develop a common vision and meet regularly in "learning circles" to explore ways to improve the effectiveness of their organizations. An excellent example of a student organization learning community is illustrated by Motley and Corts (1996). At Samford University, the Student Government Association used a variety of Total Quality Management (TQM) and Continuous Quality Improvement (CQI) principles and methods to improve their organization. The student government president fashioned a 22-member "core learning team" that met every week to study organizational change strategies, practice systematic thinking, form cross-functional teams, and engage in strategic planning as team members envisioned the preferred future of student government at Samford.

In addition to participating in learning communities, student activities educators can foster academic engagement by collaborating with orientation staff to make orientation for first-year students a more academic and intellectually engaging experience. As previously stated, contemporary students are often unaware of the purpose of a college education and many have unrealistic expectations about what is required for success. To address these issues, student activities educators and first-year experience staff can introduce students to the two versions of the *Principles of Good Practice in Undergraduate Education*—the original version centers on expectations that students should have of their faculty members, and the second on student responsibilities. In addition, student activities educators can make clear and explicit the skills and competencies that students will acquire, not only from their general education courses, but from their involvement in co-curricular activities as well. Sharing the learning outcomes highlighted by Kuh and his colleagues in Chapter 1 with students will help demystify the college experience; additionally, making expectations and outcomes explicit will directly address the learning styles of concrete active students. These expectations and outcomes can further be reinforced by having alumni from various corporate and other settings describe during orientation the qualities they seek in recent graduates and how these qualities reflect the learning outcomes of general education (i.e., communication skills, reasoning abilities, writing and speaking skills). Distinguished alumni can also underscore the importance of co-curricular involvement in promoting student learning and success.

Finally, most institutions do a very poor job of establishing and communicating appropriate expectations for student performance in and outside the classroom. As a result, academic engagement suffers because for students, it is like "being on the job without a job description" (Schilling & Schilling, 1999, p. 9). To address this concern, student activities educators, in collaboration with faculty and orientation staff, can develop and implement a "new student job description" that clearly articulates expectations for student performance in and outside the classroom.

Capitalizing on the Educational Potential of Technology

In an attempt to address the consumer-oriented needs of contemporary college students, many campuses have installed premium movie channels in their residence halls. Although this amenity is highly prized by students, it can significantly detract from student engagement and academic pursuits. Instead of being a deterrent to learning, faculty and staff at Indiana University used this form of technology to improve performance in a high-risk math course (M118-Finite Math). Historically, 40% of students who enrolled annually in this gateway mathematics course received a D- or F grade or withdrew from the class. In addition to creating a reduced-pace equivalent to M118, a cross-functional team developed an extremely innovative, interactive TV supplement, the Finite Show, which was produced to appeal to media-oriented undergraduates, many of whom have nocturnal study habits. The show, which airs Monday through Thursday evenings over the campus cable system, is hosted by an accomplished M118 instructor and guest lecturers, uses a combination of problem solving and live calls from students, and is available in all residence hall rooms. This innovative intervention substantially enhanced

first-year student performance (Hossler, Kuh, & Olsen, 2001).

Technology can also be used to engage first-year students in the process of reflecting on and integrating their learning experiences and outcomes through the use of electronic portfolios (Pack, 1998). At Winona State University, for example, students include materials from courses, extra-curricular or co-curricular activities, and work experiences that document their achievement and learning. A similar initiative, developed at Kalamazoo College, was aimed at helping new students articulate the benefits of and connections among their coursework and educational experiences, learn to use cutting-edge technology, and effectively present themselves to prospective employers (LaPlante & Springfield, 1997). In both examples, students often reported that they are more aware of the knowledge and skills gained from their education than they were before creating and using their portfolios.

Student activities educators are in an excellent position to collaborate with faculty in the design of electronic portfolios and co-curricular transcripts. Such technological innovations not only chronicle achievements, they also provide a "road map" of expectations for directing student effort toward engagement in a variety of educationally purposeful activities both in and outside the classroom. The campus cable system can also be used by student activities educators to provide a range of timely and relevant educational programs on such topics as academic success strategies, registering for classes, developing leadership skills, managing time and money, and healthy lifestyles, among others, at times and in places that are accessible to students on and off campus.

Reaping the Benefits of Diversity

A number of national studies have demonstrated that all college students learn better in settings where they are confronted with others who are different from themselves (Clements, 1999; Pascarella, Palmer, Moye, & Pierson, 2001; Smith & Schonfeld, 2000). University of Michigan psychologist Patricia Gurin (1999), for example, found that students who experience the most racial and ethnic diversity in classrooms and during interactions on campus score higher on tests used to measure complex thinking, are more motivated to achieve, have greater intellectual self-confidence and engagement, and display the highest levels of interest in earning graduate degrees. Furthermore, these students are more likely to develop the ability to understand the ideas and feelings of others, which in later life make them more likely to live in racially diverse communities, maintain friendships with people of different races, and be able to function more effectively in diverse workplaces. Other researchers (Smith & Schonfeld, 2000) have found important links between experiences with diversity and increased commitment to civic engagement, democratic outcomes, and community participation.

Although the benefits of diversity are absolutely clear, engaging students in meaningful experiences and dialogues, particularly about race, has been extremely difficult and often disappointing. Baxter Magolda (1997) has created an active learning model that helps elicit understanding of ethnocentric views, invites students to talk about their backgrounds and experiences with diversity in a non-defensive fashion, and creates opportunities to move students in the direction of a mutually constructed meaning of race. This active, collaborative, and experiential approach helps students make intellectual and emotional connections essential for fostering humanitarian values—understanding, accepting, and respecting human differences.

Another challenge facing most institutions is how to foster greater interactivity among diverse campus groups. Student activities staff, in collaboration with first-year experience educators, can use experientially based adventure education to promote racial understanding. For example, heterogeneous groups of African-American and Caucasian students on an Alpine tower (a 40-feet climbing apparatus with multiple stations and activities) can become immersed in team challenge courses and novel problems that can only be solved through cooperative and collaborative efforts. Student activi-

ties educators can design similar learning opportunities with students in historically segregated clubs, organizations, and fraternities and sororities. Small heterogeneous groups of African-American and Caucasian students can adopt different elementary school classrooms and, by providing continuous and sustained service to those classrooms, can increase their racial understanding; model cooperation and collaboration; and deepen their understanding, acceptance, and respect for one another.

Another effective active learning pedagogy for fostering humanitarian values is videotaped simulations and case studies. Students at Miami University use an interactive video that they access via their computer to engage various scenarios in which race is a factor (Baxter Magolda, 1999). Student activities educators could use programs like this to stimulate meaningful conversations about race with students in various clubs, organizations, and learning communities. To enhance their effectiveness as discussion facilitators, student activities educators would need to be trained in Baxter Magolda's (1999) active learning model that includes the following four components: experience (immersion), reflection, integration, and application. When student activities educators incorporate these components into the learning process, students are helped to access, consider, and respect views different from their own and to determine for themselves what to believe about these views.

Promote Coherent Values and Character Development

Many campuses continue to experience random acts of incivility, intolerance, bigotry, cheating, alcohol abuse, sexual harassment, and violence. With the demise of *in loco parentis* and the rise of increasingly diverse student populations, we need a new approach to defining campus community and the duties and obligations new students must assume when they join our communities (Willimon, 1997; Willimon & Willimon, 1998). As documented by Keller (2001a, 2001b), Levine and Cureton (1998), and Newton (1998, 2000, 2001), students are coming to us from family and community situations in which the old boundaries are gone. Our society now offers a multitude of lifestyles. Students are examining these lifestyles and choosing those they believe to be most appropriate for themselves. Increasingly, they hunger to be guided through what Harvard University psychologist Bill Perry calls the "sea of relativism" (Schroeder, 2000).

Unlike students of the 60s, students today "do not seem possessed by the search for freedom. They seem much more interested in the search for roots, stability, order, and identity" (Willimon, 1997, p. 9). Such a search quite naturally impels educators to help students develop coherent values and ethical standards. The need for such an approach was recently highlighted by the Kellogg Commission report "Returning to Our Roots: The Student Experience" which argued

> The biggest educational challenge we face revolves around developing character, conscience, citizenship, tolerance, civility, and individual and social responsibility in our students. We dare not ignore this obligation in a society that sometimes gives the impression that values such as these are discretionary. These should be part of the standard equipment of our graduates, not options. (1997, p. v)

Institution-wide character education initiatives are usually effective if they involve the following five critical elements: (a) teaching about character (e.g., morality, ethics), (b) displaying character, (c) demanding character, (d) practicing character (e.g., apprenticeships), and (e) reflecting on character (Berkowitz & Fekula, 1999). The University of South Carolina incorporated many of these elements into the development of the Carolinian Creed—a document that captures and articulates the institution's standards, expectations, ideals, and aspirations. Fundamentally, the statement expresses the values to which the university expects its students to adhere in their peer relationships, and it helps students understand, appreciate and live the values of civility, compassion, empathy, and openness (Pruitt, 1996).

The student affairs staff at South Carolina, along with student leaders, were primarily responsible for developing the creed. Numerous student organizations were involved in planning activities to unveil the creed. South Carolina still sponsors an annual "Creed Week" each fall, and student organizations plan events and forums to underscore the tenets of the creed. It is also an integral part of the curriculum in each University 101 section; each student signs the creed in her U101 course early in the fall semester.

Promoting coherent values and character education can also be enhanced for first-year students through creating floor standards in residence halls (Piper, 1997), developing community constitutions (St. Onge & Crawford, 1999), creating campus-wide values programs (Kirby, 1998), and engaging students in various service-learning activities (Engstrom & Tinto, 1997). With regard to service-learning, in particular, there are a number of benefits to student participants including developing a habit of critical reflection; increasing their understanding of the complex issues underlying social problems; strengthening their sense of social responsibility; enhancing their cognitive, personal, and spiritual development; heightening their understanding of human difference and commonality; and sharpening their abilities to solve problems creatively and to work collaboratively (Jacoby, 1996).

Student activities educators can also promote coherent values and character development within student clubs and organizations by helping students create a "community covenant statement"—a statement that articulates mutual expectations and obligations. Drawing on the principles and processes derived from USC's Carolinian Creed, floor standards model, NASPA's Reasonable Expectations document (National Association of Student Personnel Administrators, 1995) and Baxter Magolda's (1999) active learning principles, student activities educators can help students explore ways to develop vibrant, value-centered organizations—ones characterized by high levels of student involvement, investment, commitment, and personal responsibility. Consider, for a moment, a student government creating norms for their work and a system for maintaining them to avoid the apathy that generally sets in early in the semester. Or, imagine fraternity men engaging in a genuine dialogue and exploring multiple perspectives about enculturation into their organization, particularly with regard to issues around pledging and new member education. Consider as well, immersing first-year students in powerful service-learning experiences, such as working in soup kitchens and homeless shelters, and then asking them to reflect on questions such as What does it mean to be human? To be a member of a community? To be moral, ethical, or just? (Perry, 1999). By becoming partners with students in initiatives such as these, student activities educators can create seamless learning experiences—ones that help students realize the full educational potential of their first-year of college.

Conclusions and Recommendations

Students activities educators committed to strengthening the first-year experience must not only understand changing student characteristics, but how these changes influence students' college experience and the learning outcomes prized by their institutions. As noted in this chapter, higher education has experienced profound changes during the past four decades; however, even more dramatic change is on the way. Undergraduates at the nation's colleges will increase by 2.6 million by 2015 and of this increase, 2 million, or roughly 77%, will be students of color. When dramatic demographic shifts such as these are combined with other major societal changes—such as shifts in family values, an increasingly interdependent global economy, an aging population, and the complexities associated with an on-going technological revolution, it is clear that institutions will be challenged, as never before, to provide high quality undergraduate experiences under very difficult circumstances. Addressing these challenges requires new forms of educational and administrative leadership because

Our challenges are no longer technical issues of how to allocate rising revenues, but difficult adaptive problems

of how to lead when conditions are constantly changing, resources are tight, expectations are high, and options are limited. We live in an age of transformational, not technical, change. Our leadership, like our institutions, must become transformational as well. (Kellogg Commission, 1997, p. v)

What must student activities educators do to become transformational leaders? What new perspectives, roles, and responsibilities are required to meet the needs of increasingly diverse students and to address major challenges associated with reforming undergraduate education? Here are a few recommendations worth considering:

1. *Putting student learning first must become a priority for student activities educators.* This will require a fundamental "mental model" shift in thinking—from a narrow focus on the traditional "programming" role to a broad, all encompassing focus on the role of "educator." Similarly, putting student learning first requires embracing the perspectives, principles, and behaviors associated with the student learning community of practice (student affairs professionals are active partners with faculty in the learning mission and students seen as learners) while simultaneously de-emphasizing characteristics of the student administration and student services communities of practice (students seen as customers or participants) (Blimling, 2001).

2. *Learning-centered student activities educators must monitor, understand, and respond effectively to the changing needs of students.* They must know and understand the latest theory and research about college students and how to use theory and process models, such as Baxter Magolda's active learning model, to enhance their professional practice. They must also know how to engage in unit-specific assessments that

"Putting student learning first must become a priority for student activities educators."

generate timely and relevant information, not only related to understanding the changing needs of students, but also for solving problems of consequence to their units, divisions, and institutions.

3. *Student activities educators must be willing to leave the comfort, security, and stability of their organizational boundaries and forge strategic partnerships with academic administrators, faculty, and other student affairs staff to create seamless learning environments that connect curricular and co-curricular experiences in a complimentary, mutually supporting, and coherent fashion.* By fostering collaboration and cross-functional dialogue, student activities educators, as transformational leaders, can begin to respond to the following challenge posed by Terenzini and Pascarella (1994):

> Organizationally and operationally we have lost sight of the forest. If undergraduate education is to be enhanced, faculty members, joined by academic and student affairs administrators, must devise ways to deliver undergraduate education that are as comprehensive and integrated as the ways that students actually learn. A whole new mindset is needed to capitalize on the inter-relatedness of the in- and out-of-class influences on student learning and the functional interconnectedness of academic and student affairs divisions. (p. 32)

Facilitating this kind of "integrative learning" (Newell, 1999) must also become a priority for student activities educators. By incorporating active learning pedagogies such as simulations, experiential, and collaborative learning, journaling and group discussions, student activities educators can substantially increase the level of student engagement in the first-year experience. They can also design activities and experiences that foster the development of humanitarian values, interpersonal and intrapersonal competencies, and civic responsibility.

Student activities educators committed to students and their learning are needed today more than ever. They can, and must, play a leading role in enhancing the first-year experience for undergraduates. Such an effort is surely worth their time and attention, so … *Carpe diem!*

References

American Association of Higher Education, American College Personnel Association, & National Association of Student Personnel Administrators. (1998). *Powerful partnerships: A shared responsibility for learning.* Washington, DC: Authors.

American College Personnel Association. (1994). *The student learning imperative: Implications for student affairs.* Alexandria, VA: Author.

American College Personnel Association & National Association of Student Personnel Administrators. (1997). *Principles of good practice for student affairs.* Washington, DC: Authors.

Astin, A. (1997). The changing American college student: Thirty year trends, 1966-1996. *The Review of Higher Education, 21*(2), 115-135.

Astin, A. W., Parrott, S. A., Korn, W. S., & Sax, L. J. (1997). *The American freshman: Thirty year trends.* Los Angeles: University of California, Higher Educational Research Institute.

Baxter Magolda, M. (1997). Facilitating meaningful dialogues about race. *About Campus, 2*(5), 14-18.

Baxter Magolda, M. (1999). Defining and redefining student learning. In E. J. Whitt (Ed.), *Student learning as student affairs work: Responding to our imperative.* Washington, DC: National Association of Student Personnel Administrators.

Berkowitz, M. W., & Fekula, M. J. (1999). Educating for character. *About Campus, 4*(5), 17-22.

Blimling, G. S. (2001). Uniting scholarship and communities of practice in student affairs. *Journal of College Student Development, 42*(4), 381-396.

Boyer Commission on Educating Undergraduates in the Research University (1998). *Reinventing undergraduate education: A blueprint for America's research universities.* New York: The Carnegie Foundation for the Advancement of Teaching.

Chang, M. J. (2002). Racial dynamics on campus: What student organizations can tell us. *About Campus, 7*(1), 2-8.

Chickering, A. W., & Gamson, Z. F. (1987). *Principles of good practice for undergraduate education*. Racine, WI.: Johnson Foundation.

Clements, E. (1999). Creating a campus climate that truly values diversity. *About Campus* 4(5), 23-25.

Cole, S., & Kiss, E. (2000). What can we do about student cheating. *About Campus, 5*(2), 4-12.

Engstrom, C., & Tinto, V. (1997). Working together for service learning. *About Campus, 2*(4), 10-15.

Gurin, P. (1999). Expert report of Patricia Gurin [on-line] Retrieved June 15, 2002. from http://www.umich.edu/~url/admissions/legal/expert/studies.html.

Hayworth, J. (1997). The misrepresentation of Generation X. *About Campus, 2*(4), 10-15.

Hossler, D., Kuh, G., & Olsen, D. (2001). Finding (more) fruit on the vines: Using higher education research and institutional research to guide institutional policies and strategies (Part II). *Research in Higher Education, 42*(2), 223-235.

Jacoby, B. (1996). Service-learning in today's higher education. In B. Jacoby & Associates, *Service-learning in higher education: Concepts and practices* (pp. 3-25). San Francisco: Jossey-Bass.

Keller, G. (2001a). The new demographics of higher education. *The Review of Higher Education, 24*(3), 219-236.

Keller, G. (2001b). The new demographics of higher education—Shifts in family values. *About Campus 6*(3), 2-5.

Kellogg Commission on the Future of State and Land-Grant Universities. (1997). *Returning to our roots: The student experience*. Washington, DC: National Association of State Universities and Land-Grant Colleges.

Kidwell, B., & Turrisi, R. (2000). A cognitive analysis of credit card acquisition and college student financial development. *Journal of College Student Development, 41*(6), 589-598.

King, J. (1999). Helping students balance work, borrowing and college. *About Campus, 4*(4), 17-22.

Kirby, D. J. (1998). The values program at LeMoyne College. *About Campus, 2*(6), 15-21.

Kuh, G. (2001). College students today: Why we can't leave serendipity to chance. In P. Altbach, P. Gumport, & B. Johnstone (Eds.), *In defense of the American university* (pp. 158-182).

Baltimore: The Johns Hopkins University Press, 158-182.

LaPlante, M., & Springfield, E. (1997). The Kalamazoo electronic student portfolio. *About Campus, 2*(5), 26-27.

Levine, A. (1998). *When hope and fear collide*. San Francisco: Jossey-Bass.

Levine, A., & Cureton, J. (1998). What we know about today's college students. *About Campus, 3*(1), 4-9.

Love, A. (1999). What are learning communities? In J. H. Levine (Ed.) *Learning communities: New structures, new partnerships for learning* (Monograph no. 26) (pp. 1-8). Columbia, SC: University of South Carolina, National Resource Center for The First-Year Experience and Students in Transition.

Lowery, J. (2001). The millennials come to campus [Interview with William Strauss]. *About Campus, 6*(3), 6-12.

MacGregor, J. (1991). What difference do learning communities make? *Washington Center News, 6*(1), 4-9. Olympia, WA: Washington Center for Improving the Quality of Undergraduate Education.

Merante, J. (1987). Organizing to manage enrollment. *College Board Review, 14*(5), 14-17 and 31-33.

Mortenson, T. (1998, October). Men behaving badly . . . Where are the guys? *Post Secondary Education Opportunity, 76*, 1-8.

Mortenson, T. (1999, June). College continuation rates for 1998 high school graduates. *Post Secondary Education Opportunity, 84*, 1-8.

Motley, E., & Corts, T. (1996). Student government: Friend or foe? *About Campus, 1*(4), 28-30.

National Association of Colleges and Employers (2002). *Grads salaries rise, jobs harder to find*. Washington, DC: Author.

National Association of Student Personnel Administrators (1995). *Reasonable expectations: Renewing the educational compact between institutions and students*. Washington, DC: Author.

Newell, W. (1999). The promise of integrative learning. *About Campus, 4*(2), 17-23.

Newton, F. 1998. The stressed student: How can we help? *About Campus, 3*(2), 4-10.

Newton, F. (2000). The new student. *About Campus, 5*(5), 8-15.

Newton, F. (2001). Students of the third millennium: Who are they? What are their needs? How do we respond? Unpublished Presentation, Northwestern University.

Ozegovic, J., Bikos, L., & Szymanski, D. (2001). Trends and predictors of alcohol use among undergraduate female students. *Journal of College Student Development, 42*(5), 447-455.

Pack, D. (1998). WINGS: The Winona State University electronic portfolio project. *About Campus, 3*(2), 24-26.

Pascarella, E., Palmer, B., Moye, M., & Pierson, C. T. (2001). Do diversity experiences influence the development of critical thinking? *Journal of College Student Development, 42*(3), 257-271.

Perry, M. (1999). The College of New Jersey first year experience: A learning partnership. *About Campus, 4*(3), 25-27.

Piper, T. (1997). Empowering students to create community standards. *About Campus, 2*(4), 22-24.

Pruitt, D. (1996). The Carolinian's Creed. *About Campus, 1*(4), 27-30.

Sacks, P. (1996). *Generation X goes to college: An eye-opening account of teaching in post modern America.* Chicago: Open Court.

Sax, L., Astin, A., Korn, W., & Mahoney, K. (1997). *The American college freshman.* Los Angeles: University of California, Los Angeles, Higher Education Research Institute.

Schilling, K. M., & Schilling, K. L. (1999). Increasing expectations for student effort. *About Campus, 4*(2), 4-10.

Schroeder, C. (1993). New students: New learning styles. *Change, 25*(4), 21-26.

Schroeder, C. (1999). Battling the alcohol culture on campus. *About Campus, 4*(3), 12-18.

Schroeder, C. (2000). Understanding today's students in a changed world. *Priorities, 15,* 1-5.

Schroeder, C. (2002). Do learning communities discourage binge drinking? *About Campus, 7*(2), 4-13.

Schroeder, C., Minor, F., & Tarkow, T. (1999). Learning communities: Partnerships between academic and student affairs. In J. H. Levine (Ed.), *Learning communities: New structures, new partnerships for learning* (Monograph No. 26) (pp. 56-69). Columbia, SC: University of South Carolina, National Resource Center for The First-Year Experience and Students in Transition.

Smith, D., & Schonfeld, N. (2000). The benefits of diversity—What the research tells us. *About Campus, 5*(5), 16-23.

Stanford, W. (1999). Dealing with student credit card debt. *About Campus, 4*(1) 12-17.

St. Onge, S., & Crawford, M. (1999). Developing community constitutions at the University of Wisconsin-Oshkosh. *About Campus, 4*(4), 23-25.

Terenzini, P., & Pascarella, E. (1994). Living with myths: Undergraduate education in America. *Change, 26*(1), 28-32.

Tinto, V. (1997). Classrooms as communities: Exploring the educational character of student persistence. *The Journal of Higher Education, 68*(6), 599-623.

Tinto, V., & Goodsell, A. (1993). Freshmen interest groups and the first-year experience: Constructing student communities in a large university. *Journal of the Freshman Year Experience, 6*(1), 7-28.

Upcraft, M. L., & Terenzini, P. T. (1999). Technology. In *Higher education trends for the next century: A research agenda for student success* (pp. 29-34). Washington, DC: American College Personnel Association.

Warren, R. (1997). Engaging students in active learning. *About Campus, 2*(1), 16-20.

Wechsler, H. (1996). Alcohol and the American college campus: A report from the Harvard School of Public Health. *Change, 28*(4), 20-25.

Whitt, E. J. (Ed). (1999). *Student learning as student affairs work: Responding to our imperative.* Washington, DC: National Association of Student Personnel Administrators.

Willimon, W. (1997). Has higher education abandoned its students? *About Campus, 2*(4), 4-9.

Willimon, W., & Willimon, W. (1998). On college and friendship. *About Campus, 3*(2), 16-21.

Wingspread Group on Higher Education (1993). *An American imperative: Higher expectations for higher education.* Racine, WI: Johnson Foundation.

The Impact of Involvement on Students at Various Points in Their College Careers

Jan Arminio
Shippensburg University
Stephen E. Loflin
National Society of Collegiate Scholars

Since Astin (1984) published his theory of involvement, defined as the amount of time plus physical and psychological energy students invest in learning, educators in higher education have been concerned with making it the cornerstone of student learning. Kuh, Schuh, Whitt, and Associates' (1991) research on institutions that encourage involvement demonstrated that institutional practice and campus environment can encourage student involvement. Currently, the task of educators in higher education is to apply the more complex findings that have been discovered subsequent to the early research. For example, it has become clear that not all involvement is equally beneficial to student learning (Anaya, 1996; Kuh, Douglas, Lund, & Ramin-Gyurnek, 1994). Also, involvement may not result in long-term learning gains (Berkowitz, 1994; Lenihan, Rawlings, Eberly, Buckley, & Masters, 1992). Finally, feelings of marginalization may make some students reluctant to get involved (Borrego & Guido-DiBrito, 2002; Fleming, 1984; Sutton & Kimbrough, 2001).

In considering the development of students along cognitive, psycho-social, identity formation, and other paths, it is intuitive that students would outgrow some aspects of involvement ("been there, done that") and seek other means that would provide increased challenges to en-hanced learning. This chapter seeks to explore this nuance of involvement. In particular, we seek to describe more clearly the impact of involvement along the college career continuum. What are the outcomes and what are the barriers? We accomplish this by discussing themes from the literature, by revealing our own involvement experiences, and by discussing results of our own study.

What is Involvement?

Astin (1985) defined involvement as a dynamic process in which the amount of learning gained as a result of being involved is directly related to the quantity and quality of participation. Moreover, institutional effectiveness is assessed according to its ability to marshal student involvement. Involvement in peer and faculty groups tends to have the greatest impact on student learning (Astin, 1996a). Yet, a "chicken and egg" dilemma tends to exist here. Student GPA is often a predictor of student involvement and student learning (Pascarella & Terenzini, 1991). Thus, do those students who are already academically successful seek out interactions with faculty, or might students seek out faculty to increase learning and academic competence?

The Goal of Involvement: Learning

The literature on involvement includes discussions of both in-class and out-of-class experiences. Learning indeed occurs in both. Regardless of where it occurs, the immediate goal of involvement is increased student learning. Boyer believed that learning in higher education should strike a balance between "individual interests and shared concerns" (1990, p. 64). Learning outside the classroom offers substantial opportunities for both but a preponderance for the latter. However, as classroom and out-of-class learning continue to merge through the creation of learning communities (Cross, 1998), freshmen interest groups (Schroeder, Minor, & Tarkow, 1999; Westfall, 1999), experiential learning opportunities (which includes both internships and service-learning) (Jacoby, 1996; Jones & Hill, 2001), and the continuation and creation of rituals and traditions (Kuh et al., 1991; Schlossberg, 1989), the distinction between in-class and out-of-class learning blurs. Pritchard (2001) noted that "educators have to consider goals of student involvement in project design, service experiences, curricular content, learning assignments, and assessments (p. 22).

Who is Involved and Who is Not Involved?

Before we explore the impact of involvement over the course of a student's college career, it is first necessary to explore which students are more likely to become involved and how involvement is influenced by institutional practice.

Race, Class, Gender, Residential, and Transfer Status

Fleming's seminal work *Blacks in College* (1984) addressed the disparities of Black student involvement at predominately White institutions (PWIs), Historically Black Colleges and Universities (HBCUs), and predominately Black institutions. Fleming found that patterns of intellectual development for Black students from 15 institutions in four states were consistently more positive at HBCUs or predominately Black institutions. In contrast to Fleming's findings, Mackay (1993), conducting research at 12 colleges, found involvement was related to educational gains for both White students and African-American students. Plus, there were no significant differences in the level of involvement. Yet, Mackay found that educational gains did differ depending on the type of involvement.

In a study conducted at the University of Maryland, Latino and Latina students were involved in campus activities at a substantially lower level than all other racial groups. For example, all of the African Americans who participated in the study stated they were involved (Grande, Guenzler-Stevens, Arminio, & Osteen, 1997). Consistent with Fleming's findings, however, African-American students were more dissatisfied with the quality of their experiences than White students.

Sutton and Kimbrough (2001) found in a multi-institutional study in seven states that of the 334 Black students surveyed, 85% described themselves as leaders. Black students at PWIs were significantly more likely to be involved in multicultural groups, whereas students at HBCUs were significantly more likely to be involved in student government and as orientation leaders or ambassadors.

Research has found that African-American women are significantly more involved than African-American men; Latinas are less likely to be involved than Latinos; and White women are more likely to be involved than White men (Grande et al., 1997; Sutton & Kimbrough, 2001). With all races combined, however, men are more likely to attend a film or see a comedian, attend social events at the student union, and participate in intramurals than are women (Grande et al., 1997). In Grande et al.'s study, the majority of Asian-American women were dissatisfied with their involvement activities, though a small portion were highly satisfied.

Social class may also impact involvement. In a study of three different types of institutions (public urban, private small liberal arts, and public regional), Borrego & Guido-DiBrito (2002) noted that "working class individuals in higher education often expressed the theme of being 'an outsider' or being invisible" (p. 23). Such feelings of marginalization may lead to less involvement on campus, but this is not always the case. Traditionally marginalized students (such as women, students of color, and transfer students) tend to use campus facilities, especially the student union, more than White students at PWIs (Grande et al., 1997; Watson & Kuh, 1996).

Other factors affecting involvement are transfer status and place of residence. The quantity and quality of involvement for transfer students has been found to be significantly less than their non-transfer counterparts (Grande et al. 1997; Young, 2002). For example, Grande et al.'s (1997) research suggests transfer students are less likely to be campus leaders. Despite lower levels of involvement, they used campus facilities more and were more satisfied with interactions with faculty (Grande et al. 1997). Much has been written about the impact of living on campus on involvement. Resident students tend to be more involved in the institution than commuter students (Astin 1977, 1993; Grande et al., 1997) and demonstrate more learning outcomes associated with involvement (Kuh et al., 1994).

Involvement Trends over the Course of a Student's Career

As Astin's (1984) definition indicates, involvement demands student and institutional effort. Kuh et al. (1994) suggest that involvement of college students is cumulative, mutually shaping, and requires "sustained effort" (p. 42). What does the literature and recent research indicate about this sustained effort? Does involvement change over the course of a student's college career?

The literature is inconsistent regarding the class year when students are most likely to be involved. The National Study of Student Engagement (NSSE) research (2001), however, found that first-year students were most involved and that subsequent involvement declines over the course of the student's college career. According to Grande et al. (1997) and Sutton and Kimbrough (2001), however, students in their junior year tended to be the most involved regardless of race, gender, or transfer status. In Grande et al.'s study, the largest percentage of non-involved students were those in their fifth year, followed by first-year students.

Eighty-six percent of the participants in this study were very involved in formal academic experiences, 50% in interpersonal relationships with fellow students, 48% in paid or volunteer experiences, 34% in student organization experiences, 32% as spectators, and 22% in interpersonal relationships with faculty. Though leaders were the most involved in terms of quantity and quality, interestingly, they were not the most satisfied with their overall student experience. The inconsistencies in which class year a student is most involved and why deserves further study.

Developmental Effects of Involvement

The essence of student development is the increasing complexity of a student's ability to make meaning of and interact effectively with the world. Development is usually considered along psycho-social, cognitive, and identity formation paths. Do students remain involved in the same activities over the course of their college career? First-year students have a high need for acceptance, to feel they belong, and that they matter (Astin, 1985; Pascarella & Terenzini, 1991; Schlossberg, 1989). Kuh et al. (1994) identified "fitting in" as one of the core student concerns of undergraduates. Many students fulfill these needs through becoming engaged in the institution or with people at the institution. Once these needs are met, do students seek other types of involvement that perhaps require more risk taking? Do belonging needs go unmet for students who wait to become involved or for those who never become involved? If indeed development occurs during college, it would seem logical that students become involved in either more activities or increasingly move from spectator to member to leader, increasing involvement qualitatively. The concept of spectator indicates involvement as an attendee at an event, activity, or meeting with little to no engagement

"The essence of student development is the increasing complexity of a student's ability to make meaning of and interact effectively with the world."

or sense of responsibility for the day-to-day functioning of the sponsoring organization. The member level of involvement suggests consistent attendance as well as accepting some minimal responsibility with the sponsoring organization that might include any of the following: paying dues, voting, participating in discussion regarding group functions, or identifying with the organization. Leaders are those who accept and engage in consistent and deliberate operation of the organization. They expend considerable psychological and behavioral energy on behalf of the organization.

Consistent with this line of thinking, over the course of a student's college career students would become more involved in organizations of which they are already members, or become involved in more complex roles in other organizations that offered increased learning opportunities. For example, a current college president articulated that he joined a fraternity as a first-year undergraduate student to become a member, but later realized that the behaviors reflected what he did not want to be, so he left the organization and became more involved in his academic work (Ceddia, 2002). A variety of studies have indicated that indeed students do develop as a result of involvement over the course of their college career. This literature is described below.

Membership and Leadership

In a study using the Student Development Task Life Inventory, the development of first-year students who would later become members of organizations were compared with those who would not become members. Those first-year students who would later become members scored significantly higher on the Life Management and Developing Purpose scales (Cooper, Healy, & Simpson, 1994). Scores as juniors indicated that organization members showed more growth than non-members in Educational Involvement, Career Planning, Lifestyle Planning, Life Management, Cultural Participation, and Academic Autonomy. When controlling for the entering measures, member juniors still showed more growth in Developing Purpose, Educational Involvement, Career Planning, and

Academic Autonomy. As first-year students, those who would later become leaders showed the following significant growth above their non-leader classmates: Developing Purpose, Educational Involvement, Career Planning, Lifestyle Planning, and Life Management. Junior scores demonstrated the same differences just mentioned and included Cultural Participation. Student organization leaders showed the highest growth over non-leaders.

Service

According to the National Survey of Student Engagement, 63% of seniors were involved in community service and 41% of seniors were involved in service that was directly connected to a course (Reisberg, 2000). There is now considerable literature advocating the educational potential of service (Astin, 1996b; Loeb, 1994; Jacoby, 1996; Jones & Hill, 2001). This potential includes learning about culture (one's own and other cultures) (Jones & Hill, 2001), coming to see people as individuals rather than stereotypes (Jones & Hill, 2001; Neururer & Rhoads, 1998), the ability to build relationships with others different from oneself (Astin & Sax, 1998; Jones & Hill, 2001), applying knowledge to new situations (Eyler & Giles, 1999); critical thinking (Eyler & Giles, 1999); and academic development (Astin & Sax, 1998). Astin notes that there is a clear link between service-learning activities and responsible citizenship (Astin, 1996b).

Astin and Sax (1998) found that those first-year students who later participated in service scored higher on civic responsibility measures than future non-service participants. Service participants demonstrated increased self-rated leadership abilities whereas non-participants' self-rated leadership abilities decreased slightly. The longer students participated the more likely they were to make gains in many measures of civic responsibility, academic development, and on several life skills measures. In general, the longer the duration of the involvement in service, the greater the learning outcomes. Jones and Hill (2001) discovered similar findings. They found that in order to gain multicultural competence sustained involvement in service was necessary and more easily achieved when service was performed with the same community partners.

Cognitive Development

In her five-year longitudinal study of 70 students at Miami University, Baxter Magolda (1992) explored the development of knowing and reasoning in participants over the course of their college careers and one year after graduation. She noted that student outcomes differed depending on the type of "knowers" they were. For example, absolute knowers (those who depended on authorities for truth) are primarily first-year students and sophomores. From their student organization involvement, they gain greater responsibility in their acclimation to college. Transitional knowers, those experiencing the "bridge" (p. 320) between reliance on parents and reliance on self, gain leadership skills and practical experience from their involvement. They also learn to appreciate diversity, to be more independent, and gain self-knowledge through their living arrangements. These students tend to be sophomores and juniors.

Independent knowing, knowing that is no longer reliant on authority figures, is characterized as thinking for oneself, sharing views openly, and creating a process for knowing. This type of knowing was not evident in Baxter Magolda's participants until the year after they graduated from Miami University. However, students note that their college involvement encouraged them to find their own voice. Participants explained that their voice was validated and individual effectiveness was increased through involvement in student organizations. This occurred by "getting out of situations themselves" (p. 346). Through their relationships with peers during college, they began to realize that others' views are valid and to balance their needs with the needs of others.

Personal Narratives

Creswell (1998) notes the renewed interest in the use of biographical and autobiographical writing in recent years, suggesting that it has roots in literary, historical, anthropological, and sociological views. Stories have the potential to bring epipha-

nies, "Theory meets story when we think with a story rather than about it" (Bochner, 1997, p. 436, emphasis added). In a discussion of students' involvement experiences over the course of their college careers, it is appropriate that we offer our own experiences of the search for self through college involvement. Our own experiences exemplify aspects noted in the literature above.

Jan's Story

A first-generation college student, I attended a small, rural, private liberal arts college. My parents insisted that I attend the same institution as a neighbor, the only institution with which they had any relationship. As a first-year student I immediately became involved in a sorority, as I appreciated the affiliation needs the sorority satisfied. It offered immediate friendships, plus later it also provided leadership opportunities that most likely I would not have sought out otherwise. Over the next few years, I became very involved in a number of activities, including Panhellenic Council, cheerleading, the residence hall association, and as a junior I performed in a foreign language theater production. During my senior year, however, I decided not to try out for cheerleading and instead I tried out for the volleyball team, though my skills were quite poor. I was selected as a manager only but decided to join the team anyway. It was here that I met new peers with interests far different from my sorority sisters.

Simultaneously, I had a profound experience in a sociology class. One day our professor told us that there was to be a "pop" quiz and to take out a sheet of paper. Instead of writing our names at the top of the page, we were instructed to indicate our gender without using the terms "male" or "female." Then he asked us 10 quiz questions and collected the papers. During the following class the instructor noted that almost all of the males in the class had indicated on their quizzes that they were "men," while almost all of the females in the class indicated that they were "girls." He asked why the discrepancy. I do not recall the subsequent discussion, but I do remember that I was very shocked that I had indicated I was a "girl." I looked across the aisle at a male peer and saw he had written "man." Why did he perceive himself to be more mature than I? My sorority sisters seemed uninterested in what to me was a profound insight. The women athletes, however, seemed more interested in being seen as strong women rather than sorority girls. Also, these athletes discussed politics, religion, sexual orientation, and topics other than dating and beer. I found myself withdrawing from the sorority (even though I was president) and engaged in more social activities with women athletes. Yet, because of my poor team athletic skills I lacked important commonalities with them as well. Out of necessity, I became more comfortable being on my own.

It was in this transition that I sought out the dean of women as a mentor. It was through her encouragement that I applied to graduate school. In fact, she drove me to my interview with the chair of the department, for which I am eternally grateful. Since receiving my master's degree in college student personnel in 1978, I have worked in student affairs in a variety of areas including campus programs. Currently, I teach in a graduate student affairs program.

Steve's Story

I spent my afternoons during high school working, and like many of my friends, not involved in extra-curricular activities. I looked forward to college as an opportunity to reinvent myself as a leader and person who would be engaged and make a difference. I had only considered one school since early childhood. As a result, I only visited and applied to this one, large state institution. I never considered that it might be challenging for me to find my place at such a big school with so many students also hoping to reinvent themselves. My orientation program clearly inspired and confirmed that my college experience was wide open for me to create. I decided that I would definitely be a joiner. I signed up for a University 101 orientation course, which had a requirement that I join an organization. My hope was that I could get extra credit for joining several. My first stop was the place with which I was most familiar, a religious student organization. I found it easy to be involved there because I was surrounded by people who had similar beliefs and interests. It was a good, comfortable

place to get started. Knowing that I needed to move beyond my comfort zone, I also joined a committee within the student government association. I was an eager volunteer, and they were happy to give me responsibilities. Between adjusting to the academic responsibilities, meeting people, and the organizational responsibilities, I felt confident about my first-year experience.

During my second year, I started taking on leadership roles within the religious organization and student government. I also started realizing that I liked to create clubs that are not already on campus. I worked to start a spirit organization and a new committee to address some clear needs in student government. I decided that being involved truly made me feel connected to the university. I was not just a student; I was contributing and making a difference there.

In my junior and senior years, I continued to be very involved. I was elected to an office in student government, elected to president and state president of the religious organization, served as an orientation leader and the president of two clubs, and at the last minute, agreed to fill a vacant RA position. I truly found myself engaged in a variety of amazing student life opportunities.

My major was marketing, and I had every intention of working to promote products at a large company. As a senior approaching graduation, that all changed when the vice president of student affairs, and my mentor, called me into his office for a career conversation. He asked me to summarize my undergraduate experience. After a long list of reasons why I had truly enjoyed being a student there, he asked me to consider student affairs as a career. Many of the people who had been a major part of my experience were in student affairs, but I had not thought about it as a career option. The conversation led me to make a decision to pursue a master's in college student personnel. I have now worked in several student affairs positions. I continue to create leadership opportunities just like I did in college, including a national honor society that engages students in making a difference.

Our stories demonstrate that we became involved to fulfill affiliation needs as new students and that we moved from spectator to member, to leader levels of involvement indicative of personal development. The feeling that we were important to others in the college environment provided the support necessary to risk new learning. Our stories also exemplify that, because we were White students at predominately White institutions, finding support was achievable. Both stories demonstrate how classroom learning was integrated with outside-of-class organizations to spawn even greater learning. Of note for us are the career implications of this integrated "meaning making" through the care of mentors. What are the involvement stories and experiences of current students and recent graduates?

A Study of Involvement Across the College Years

For this chapter, we employed a multi-method study to explore involvement patterns across the college careers of students with whom we interact. Specifically, we sought to address the following:

- ◆ Do students become more qualitatively and quantitatively involved, seeking increased involvement and increasingly complex involvement over the course of their college careers?
- ◆ What are the learning outcomes of being involved?
- ◆ What are the barriers to becoming involved?

Positivistic empiricism was used to determine if and how students' involvement changes during the college career. Using the database from the National Society of Collegiate Scholars (NSCS), a random sample of 150 students from a variety of institutions were invited to complete a survey indicating the types of organizations in which they were involved, their level of involvement (i.e., spectator, member, leader), the class year of their involvement, and lessons learned. This is similar to the survey distributed in the Grande et al. (1997) study. Open-ended questions were included on the survey to determine what students learned from their involvement and to ascertain what barriers to involvement existed for them. A copy of the survey is located in the chapter appendix. Seventy-six surveys were completed for a 51% return rate. Similar surveys were distributed to three classes in a graduate student affairs program. One class was a beginning introduction course, another, a mid-level course, and a third a capstone course. Students were asked to reflect on their involvement experiences over the course of their undergraduate careers. Twenty-five surveys were completed.

Both samples are exceedingly small and are samples of convenience. Caution should be taken in generalizing these results to other populations. Also, both populations consist of students who have proven to be academically successful. The samples are representative of their populations, however, as membership in this graduate student affairs program is predominately White women and the membership in the NSCS is predominately White women. The results are presented here, nonetheless, as samples of involvement assessments that could be accomplished by the reader. Nineteen percent of the combined samples are male, 77.8% women, 5.8% African American/Black, 3.8% Asian American/Asian/Pacific Islander, 81.7% White or non-Hispanic, 1.9% Latino and Latina, and 3.8% multi-racial.

Students participating in the NSCS random sample were invited to participate in a focus group. Also, members of one graduate student affairs class were invited to participate in a separate focus group. These focus groups were conducted to gain insight into how involvement changed over the course of a student's college career.

"The feeling that we were important to others in the college environment provided the support necessary to risk new learning."

Empirical Data

Interestingly, the only statistically significant difference noted between the two samples using a chi square analysis was that the undergraduate sample had been more involved in the performing arts. Otherwise, involvement experiences of the two samples were similar.

Consistent with the NSSE research, but inconsistent with the Grande et al. (1997) and Sutton and Kimbrough (2001) studies referred to above, students in our samples were involved in the most activities listed on our survey during their first year. Students were more likely to be involved with a faculty member than any other involvement activity. Yet, most were involved with faculty as a student, rather than as an advisee or mentee. Only 24% of the participants indicated they had a faculty member as a mentor, and only 43% of those who had reached their senior year had a faculty member as a mentor.

The second most likely involvement activity was having a paid job, followed by being involved in service-learning. Eighty-three percent of the participants had paid jobs as first-year students. Seniors in this study were the least likely to have a full-time paid job. Forty-seven percent of the seniors indicated that they had a paid job.

Over the course of the college career, involvement decreased in all of the opportunities listed: service-learning, Greek organizations, multicultural clubs and organizations, religious clubs, "other" clubs, print media, academic cohorts, student government, residence life, performing arts, involvement with faculty, recreational sports, intercollegiate athletics, and having a paid job. Involvement in multicultural clubs and print media increased in the sophomore year but then later declined below the first-year levels.

Regarding the model of increased quality of involvement (i.e., spectator, member, and leader), more participants followed such a model through residence life than any other involvement activity listed. Other students indicated that they became a leader in an organization soon after joining (often in clubs), but most students were leaders in organizations in which they were members early in their college careers. Throughout their college careers, students were far more likely to be involved as a member rather than a spectator or leader. Service-learning, clubs, residence life, and paid jobs provided participants with the most leadership opportunities. Using the Pearson Correlation, it was found that students who were involved in recreational activities were more likely to be involved in service, student government, residence life, and religious organizations than the other activities listed on the survey.

A substantial number of students in our study (67%) were satisfied with their involvement activities and felt they learned from their involvement. Yet, 62% wished that they had been more involved outside the classroom. Fifty-nine percent felt that their involvement contributed to their career choice.

Open-Ended Questions

Learning gained. For the graduate students, the most frequent response regarding what was learned from being involved was related to career aspirations. Graduate students indicated that through their involvement they learned more about their own skills and talents, were able to explore goals, network with people in various career fields, establish relationships with future career clients or colleagues, and learn valuable skills specific to career interests (such as teaching techniques). Some in the undergraduate sample mentioned that involvement was helpful in deciphering career aspirations, but did so less frequently than the graduate students. This is most likely due to the chosen field of the graduate student sample. The undergraduate sample listed gaining leadership skills as the most important benefit of involvement and management skills as the most important learning outcome of involvement. Specifically, they mentioned gaining organizational, time management, project management, and financial management skills.

Next, both samples mentioned learning associated with establishing relationships as the subsequent most important learning outcome associated with involvement. In particular they mentioned learning social skills, establishing relationships with peers and faculty, and gaining experience in working with "all kinds of people." Learning about diversity was salient in establishing relationships.

Both samples also mentioned learning about responsibilities. Graduate students mentioned learning about work ethic, the amount of responsibilities one can handle competently, and self discipline. Undergraduate participants also mentioned responsibility frequently, including realizing one's responsibility to others.

The undergraduate sample also noted that they were happier the more they became involved. This was not noted by any of the graduate participants.

Barriers to involvement. Time was the biggest barrier to involvement for both samples. Working, academic commitments, commitments to relationships, time for commuting, and lack of time management skills were all seen as barriers. So too, but to a lesser degree, lack of motivation, lack of awareness of the opportunities, and being shy were also named as barriers. One undergraduate noted, "I would find out about a meeting of a group I wanted to join the day after they had met. I couldn't seem to find out about them in advance." Another undergraduate stated that he thought he did not have the skills to be involved in an organization in which he was interested.

Several non-traditional students noted that involvement is still too geared toward traditional students. This was a frustration for several working and commuting students as well as those with families.

Focus Group Results

The focus groups were asked to discuss their needs and feelings as incoming college students and whether those needs and feelings were addressed, and if so, how. Similarly, they were asked what concerns and feelings they experienced later in their college lives and whether those were addressed. Additionally, students discussed what learning was salient during their undergraduate tenure and by what means this was achieved.

The two focus groups revealed that fear was a consistent feeling during the first year of college. Students were fearful of failing to fit in, be academically successful, or find things—friends, classrooms, books, and activities to join. Students negotiated these fears by making "convenient friendships." These were quickly made friendships based more on geographic proximity (roommates and classmates) than on mutual af-

fection. Closer, deeper, and lasting friendships were formed later. Convenient friendships were important because these relationships simultaneously validated and calmed fears. Students learned from and grew from the deeper relationships formed later. Involvement activities helped provide a forum for meeting convenient friends and also others who would become close friends. One student noted her institution's "call out session" where students became acquainted with involvement opportunities. Greek organizations, residence life, and learning communities were mentioned as opportunities where fears were reduced. However, one student commented that leaders of organizations were at times condescending to first-year students. Another noted, that though encouraged to speak with faculty outside of class, "You need something relevant to talk about. I didn't feel I had anything relevant to say to a faculty member."

Later in their college careers, students' concerns were future-oriented. Through confidence gained over the college years, these concerns could be addressed with less intimidation than might have been felt in the first year. Students noted how they had changed over their college careers, in particular becoming more concerned about others, especially those who were from different cultures from themselves. They also spoke about becoming less selfish and more responsible over the course of their college lives. Graduate students were more reflective of the overall undergraduate experience, whereas seniors noted concrete experiences that helped "shape the future." For both groups, however, the journey was life-altering.

Recommendations

We make the following recommendations based on the literature review offered above and our own study of student involvement.

Embracing Learning Centeredness

As higher education seeks to move toward enacting learning-centered education rather than teaching-centered education, it is imperative that student affairs also make this transition. Student affairs professionals and graduate students complain of faculty who teach only through lecture. But student affairs professionals may be guilty of this as well. For example, career development workshops on interviewing skills conducted through lecture alone offer little real learning to students. Residence life staff training and floor meetings that rely on lecture alone diminish possible learning outcomes. Many orientation programs are still lecture-driven. At the other extreme, Kuh (1996) notes that some orientation programs are often hard to differentiate from cheerleading camps. Neither atmosphere is likely to produce the gains we seek. Student affairs must intentionally create learning-centered environments, programs, and services. Since involvement contributes to learning, and increased learning occurs through making meaning of experiences, it is imperative that as many students as possible become involved in processing their learning. The literature discussed above, our own stories, and our survey indicated that sustained effort was most likely to lead to heightened quality involvement. To allow for this sustained effort (involvement over a considerable span of time), those responsible for first-year experience programs and campus programs must work diligently to involve first-year students and keep them involved.

Since students feel as if they "have nothing relevant to say" to faculty, student affairs professionals could serve as consultants in creating interventions that offer a structure to make engaging with faculty and staff easier. This would help students find their voice with faculty and others. For example, many institutions sponsor a first-year and faculty dinner during some portion of the transition process. Faculty could be given a discussion guide to create a structure for the interaction and be offered specific ice breakers or other means to engage students in meaningful conversation.

Finding Voice

Baxter Magolda (1992) stated that a critical component to one's cognitive development is finding one's voice. How can those of us involved in first-year experience programs and campus programs better ensure that students achieve this developmental goal? First, student affairs needs to increase the numbers of students who are involved. Remember that 62% of the participants in our study indicated that they wish they had been more involved. This can be achieved by broadening the means for inviting students to engage with others as in the dinner example given above. Those responsible for campus programs and student transitions must be intentional about inviting all students to participate and designing opportunities that are welcoming to all students (not just traditional students). Our data corroborated Baxter Magolda's (1992) findings that many students often fail to perceive themselves as leaders or see their work as worthy of leadership or faculty interest. Baxter Magolda suggests that student leaders should be taught to share their power with other students. This sharing could lead to increased involvement from students who previously never considered it. Too often student affairs educators rely on the rhetoric of "my door is always open." The reality is that many students will not walk through those doors due to family and job constraints, commuting issues, or because they have not typically felt welcome by "people like us." We must actively and passionately recruit and invite students to join us.

Baxter Magolda (1992) recommended that learning from involvement occurs through "confirmation and contradiction" (p. 347) and noted the importance of providing "creative tension" (p. 360). A similar notion is often referred to as support and challenge (Sanford, 1966). Baxter Magolda urges student affairs professionals who are trying to place students in residence life or mentoring positions or on judicial boards or campus committees to be less concerned about hiring or appointing students to "avoid uncomfortable situations" and more concerned about creating educational opportunities for them (p. 348). We are sure that the reader can think of students who failed to reach expectations in their involvement experiences. Yet, too, we are certain that the reader has encountered students whose potential exceeded expected boundaries. As representatives of educational institutions, appointing students with potential rather than students already skilled is the risk educators must take. This is especially true in the continuing era of doing more with less when institutions could use more students as peer educators.

Involving students is only the beginning of accomplishing the student affairs ideal of educating the whole student (American Council on Education, 1989). Student affairs must also concentrate on creating intentional learning environments, programs, and services. As indicated in our study and the recent NSSE research, students were most involved during their first year. Additional work must explore why the quantity of student involvement decreased. Was it because students became qualitatively more involved in fewer activities? Or did early involvement opportunities fail to keep students interested? Student affairs must be committed to ensuring that involvement is worthy of students' time. This can occur when student affairs professionals join students as equals in assessing their involvement experiences (Baxter Magolda, 1992; Gardner & Van der Veer, 1998).

We believe student affairs professionals must be better about noting student leadership and its subsequent learning in unfamiliar places. For example, might work-study students be unrecognized or potential leaders? We wonder how many educators discuss with their work-study students what those students have learned from their work. Might these students become more involved if invited? As the federal government increasingly encourages institutions to use work study wages toward community service, are campuses providing intentional opportunities for work-study students to reflect on and make meaning of their campus work responsibilities as well as their community service? We also wonder about groups of students not often considered for appointments, because they are shy, non-traditional, have transferred to the institution, or are marginalized in other ways.

To assure students' growth of voice, Baxter Magolda (1992) maintained that student affairs must be more intentional about processing involvement experiences. The service-learning community has recognized the potential of reflection for increasing learning (Jacoby, 1996). Campus program staff must recognize and use its powerful benefits as well. Gardner and Van der Veer suggest that those "who have opportunity to reflect on their learning are better learners" (p. 8). How often do those who advise student organizations ask students, "What have you learned from being an orientation leader? What did you experience in this organization that reminded you of something you learned in a class? What did you learn from planning this event? What insight did you gain about society from this fund raiser?" Baxter Magolda (1999) suggests that students be asked, "Who were you? Who are you? Who do you wish to become?"

Likewise, Baxter Magolda suggests that student affairs professionals spend more time making meaning than making rules. How better to enhance students' voice than in a shared process of problem solving? Baxter Magolda maintained that older students learn more from living arrangements off campus, since they have to negotiate rules with housemates, rather than being told the rules by housing and residence life staff.

Confronting Barriers to Involvement

Campus activities and first-year program professionals must become involvement specialists and intentionally confront barriers to involvement. Our study found that time was the biggest barrier to becoming more involved. Might further study reveal the hours students spend watching television, instant messaging, and playing computer games? If campus involvement opportunities cannot compete with these distractions, how might these distractions be used as involvement opportunities that encourage learning? For example, how might students be engaged in learning through instant messaging?

The important role of student affairs educators as mentors is increased when considering the percentage of seniors in our sample who had no faculty mentor. This is especially disconcerting considering that these students were all academically successful. Are students who are less academically successful even less likely to have faculty mentors? How can this void be filled? Student affairs professionals must be prepared to accept the role of educational mentor if necessary. The role of mentors in Steve and Jan's stories emphasizes this point.

Finally, each institution must assess involvement particular to that institution. For example, how must graduate student affairs programs respond to the fact that graduate students need to be prepared to engage commuter and nontraditional students? Student affairs can no longer rely on flyers in the residence halls to engage today's students. How do our own involvement experiences create a bias in our expectations of current and future student involvement? Should student affairs respond to the fact that their nationwide student populations are predominately White women? How does higher education engage students of color, increasing their numbers and their satisfaction? Responding to these trends and important assessment feedback is critical.

Summary

In summary, the following can be stated regarding college students' involvement over the course of their college career:

- Important learning and development occur outside the classroom. What students gain from involvement depends on their development. First-year students need, want, and gain different outcomes from involvement than students further along in their college careers. In general, first-year students want and need to matter and then need responsibility. Sophomores and juniors want and need some autonomy while they transition from relying on parents to relying on themselves. Juniors and seniors need and want encouragement in finding their own voice to negotiate their futures. This occurs through involvement in organizations but also through living arrangements where students negotiate guidelines with those with whom they live.
- When (in which class year) students are most involved is not clear. At least at some institutions, students appear to

drop out of involvement activities over the course of their college careers.

- Paradoxically, sustained effort (involvement over the course of several years) offers the greatest potential for learning. This is most effective when the environment, program, or service is planned to enhance learning intentionally.
- Students are most involved as members of organizations. Through membership, some later become leaders. However, many students never become leaders in college, remaining perpetual members.
- Frequent involvement occurs with faculty, but only as students, not as advisees or mentees.
- Large percentages of students continue to have paid jobs, especially first-year students.

References

American Council on Education (1989). The student personnel point of view. In *Points of View* (pp. 5-19). Washington, DC: National Association of Student Personnel Administrators.

Anaya, G. (1996). College experiences and student learning: The influence of active learning, college environments and cocurricular activities. *Journal of College Student Development, 37,* 611-622.

Astin, A. W. (1977). *Four critical years.* San Francisco: Jossey-Bass.

Astin, A. W. (1984). Student involvement: A developmental theory for higher education. *Journal of College Student Development, 25,* 297-308.

Astin, A. W. (1985). *Achieving educational excellence.* San Francisco: Jossey-Bass.

Astin, A. W. (1993). *What matters in college: Four critical years revisited.* San Francisco: Jossey-Bass.

Astin, A. W. (1996a). Involvement in learning revisited: Lessons we have learned. *Journal of College Student Development, 37,* 123-134.

Astin, A. W. (1996b). The role of service in higher education. *About Campus, 1*(1) 14-19.

Astin, A. W., & Sax, L. J. (1998). How undergraduates are affected by service participation. *Journal of College Student Development, 39,* 251-263.

Baxter Magolda, M. (1999). Constructing adult identities. *Journal of College Student Development, 40,* 629-644.

Baxter Magolda, M. (1992). *Knowing and reasoning in college.* San Francisco: Jossey-Bass.

Berkowitz, A. D. (1994). A model acquaintance rape prevention program for men. In A. D. Berkowitz (Ed.), *Men and rape: Theory, research, and prevention in higher education* (pp. 35-42). San Francisco: Jossey-Bass.

Bochner, A. P. (1997). It's about time: Narrative and the divided self. *Qualitative Inquiry, 3,* 418-436.

Borrego, S. E., & Guido-DiBrito, F. (2002). *A critical qualitative exploration of class culture at three institutions of higher education: Implications for student and academic affairs collaboration.* Unpublished paper.

Boyer, E. (1990). Foreword. In Carnegie Foundation for the Advancement of Teaching (Ed.), *Campus life: In search of community* (pp. xi-xiii). Princeton; NJ: Princeton University Press.

Ceddia, A. (2002). Personal communication with J. Arminio.

Cooper, D. L., Healy, M. A., & Simpson, J. (1994). Student development through involvement: Specific changes over time. *Journal of College Student Development, 35,* 98-102.

Creswell, J. W. (1998). *Qualitative inquiry and research design: Choosing among five traditions.* Thousand Oaks: Sage.

Cross, P. (1998, July/August). Why learning communities? Why now? *About Campus,* 3-10.

Eyler, J., & Giles, D. E. (1999). *Where's the learning in service learning?* San Francisco: Jossey-Bass.

Fleming, J. (1984). *Blacks in college.* San Francisco: Jossey-Bass.

Gardner, J. N., & Van der Veer, G. (1998). *The senior year experience.* San Francisco: Jossey-Bass.

Grande, S., Guenzler-Stevens, M., Arminio, J., & Osteen, J. M. (1997). *The senior involvement study: Examining the relationship between involvement in and satisfaction with the college experience.* Unpublished manuscript, University of Maryland.

Jacoby, B. (1996). Service-learning in today's higher education. In B. Jacoby and Associates (Eds.), *Service-learning in higher education* (pp. 3-25). San Francisco: Jossey-Bass.

Jones, S., & Hill, K. (2001). Crossing High Street: Understanding diversity through community service-learning. *Journal of College Student Development, 42,* 204-216.

Kuh, G. (1996). Guiding principles for creating seamless learning environments for undergraduates. *Journal of College Student Development, 37,* 135-148.

Kuh, G. D., Douglas, K. B., Lund, J. P., & Ramin-Gyurmek, J. (1994). *Student learning outside the classroom: Transcending artificial boundaries.* ASHE-ERIC Higher Education Report No. 8. Washington, DC: The George Washington University, Graduate School of Education and Human Development.

Kuh, G. D., Schuh, J. H., Whitt, E. J., & Associates (1991). *Involving colleges.* San Francisco: Jossey-Bass.

Lenihan, G. O., Rawlings, M. E., Eberly, C. G., Buckley, B., & Masters, B. (1992). Gender differences in rape supportive attitudes before and after a date rape education intervention. *Journal of College Student Development, 33,* 331-338.

Loeb, P. R. (1994). *Generation at the crossroads: Apathy and action on the American campus.* New Jersey: Rutgers University Press.

MacKay, K. A. (1993). A comparison of White and African American college student involvement and educational gains. *Dissertation Abstracts International, 53*(09), 3121A. (University Microfilms No. AAC 92-31563).

National Study of Student Engagement. (2001). *National Findings.* Bloomington, IN: Author.

Neururer, J., & Rhoads, R. A. (1998). Community service: Panacea, paradox, or potentiation? *Journal of College Student Development, 39,* 321-329.

Pascarella, E. T., & Terenzini, P. T. (1991). *How college effects students.* San Francisco: Jossey-Bass.

Pritchard, I. A. (2001). Raising standards in community service learning. *About Campus, 6*(4), 18-24.

Reisberg, L. (2000, November 17). Are student actually learning? *The Chronicle of Higher Education,* p. A67.

Sanford, N. (1966). *Self & society.* New York: Atherton.

Schlossberg, N. K. (1989). Marginality and mattering: Key issues in building community. In D. Roberts (Ed.), *Designing campus activities to foster a sense of community* (pp. 5-16). San Francisco: Jossey-Bass.

Schroeder, C. C., Minor, F. D., & Tarkow, T. A. (1999). Freshmen interest groups: Partnerships for promoting student success. In J. H. Schuh & E. J. Whitt (Eds.), *Creating successful partnerships between academic and student affairs.* San Francisco: Jossey-Bass.

Sutton, M. E., & Kimbrough, W. M. (2001). Trends in Black student involvement. *NASPA Journal, 39,* 30-40.

Watson, L. E., & Kuh, G. D. (1996). The influences of dominant race environments on student involvement, perceptions, and educational gains: A look at historically Black and predominately White liberal arts institutions. *Journal of College Student Development, 37,* 415-424.

Westfall, S. B. (1999). Partnerships to connect in-and-out of class experiences. In J. H. Schuh & E. J. Whitt (Eds.), *Creating successful partnerships between academic and student affairs.* San Francisco: Jossey-Bass.

Young, J. R. (2002, November 22). Transfer students feel disengaged from college life, survey shows. *The Chronicle of Higher Education,* p. A55.

Appendix

Campus Involvement Survey

Please indicate if you were involved in any of the listed events and then to the right, indicate how you were involved and when:

Type of Involvement	College Year(s) When Involved		Level of Involvement	
_____ service/volunteer	1 2 3 4 5	spectator	member	leader
_____ Greek organization	1 2 3 4 5	spectator	member	leader
_____ honor society	1 2 3 4 5	spectator	member	leader
_____ multicultural organization	1 2 3 4 5	spectator	member	leader
_____ student government	1 2 3 4 5	spectator	member	leader
_____ residence life	1 2 3 4 5	spectator	member	leader
		(resident)	(attended programs)	(RA, hall, gov't, etc.)
_____ intramurals/recreation	1 2 3 4 5	spectator	member	leader
_____ intercollegiate athletics	1 2 3 4 5	spectator	member	leader
_____ religious organizations	1 2 3 4 5	spectator	member	leader
_____ literary/newspaper/yearbook	1 2 3 4 5	spectator	member	leader
_____ on-line chats	1 2 3 4 5	spectator	member	leader
_____ theater/dance/performing	1 2 3 4 5	spectator	member	leader
_____ club or organization (any group that is not recognized in a category above)	1 2 3 4 5	spectator	member	leader
_____ peer academic cohort	1 2 3 4 5	spectator	member	leader
_____ paid job	1 2 3 4 5	employee	supervisor	leader
_____ relationship with faculty or staff	1 2 3 4 5	student	advisee	mentor

Please list any ways that you have developed or what you have learned that is a direct result of involvement in the above?

Was your involvement outside the classroom an important part of your undergraduate success?
_____ Yes _____ No

Did your involvement noted above contribute to your career choice? _____ Yes _____ No

Do you wish you would have been more involved in activities outside the classroom?
_____ Yes _____ No
If Yes, what prevented you from getting involved?

Personal Demographics
Race

_____   African American/Black

_____   American Indian

_____   Asian Pacific/Islander

_____   White/Caucasian/non-Hispanic

_____   Hispanic/Latino/Latina

_____   Multiracial/Bi-racial

Gender

____ M   _____ F

Undergraduate GPA

_____

Class Year _____

Thank you!

Building Community on a Commuter Campus

Nancy S. King
Brian M. Wooten
Kennesaw State University

In recent years higher education administrators have become increasingly concerned with retaining students. There are several reasons for this heightened interest in retention. First, educators focus quite naturally on student success, and an important measure of student success is retention and graduation rates. Because of the large numbers of students who leave college before graduating, college and university administrators are concerned with growing demands for accountability and the financial impact of student departure. Increasingly, state legislators are tying retention and graduation rates to institutional effectiveness and funding levels. Furthermore, it requires more money to recruit students than it does to retain students already enrolled (Moller-Wong, Shelley, & Ebbers, 1999). Thus, strong financial incentives to keep students enrolled exist for most colleges and universities.

Importance of Student Involvement

Authorities in the field of retention offer many explanations for the attrition problem. Some students are underprepared for college work and fail to achieve the academic success necessary to stay in school. For others, however, the fundamental problem is lack of connection with the institution. A basic principle of retention relates to a student's involvement with the campus culture. Kuh and Schuh (1991) acknowledge that the role of the student affairs professional in providing students with experiences outside the classroom is pivotal in helping them become involved with the campus community. According to Astin (1985), "the greater the student's involvement in college, the greater the learning and development" (p. 157). Tinto (1993) posits,

> There appears to be an important link between learning and persistence that arises from the interplay of involvement and the quality of student effort. Involvement with one's peers and with the faculty, both inside and outside the classroom, is itself positively related to the quality of student effort and in turn to both learning and persistence. (p. 71)

A student's success, then, is clearly related to her level of involvement with the institution.

Thus, Astin's theory of student involvement and Tinto's model have important implications for student activities professionals. As Tinto observes, "An institution's capacity to retain students is directly related to its ability to reach and make contact with students and integrate them into the social and intellectual fabric of institutional life" (p. 204). Through their integration into the campus community, students enhance their chances for success. Unfortunately, what occurs outside the classroom is often dismissed as being of little importance. Richard Light (2001), Harvard professor and author of *Making the Most of College: Students Speak Their Minds*, admits that his initial assumption was that most academic learning occurs inside the classroom, "while outside activities provide a useful but modest supplement" (p. 8). Based on 10 years of interviews with Harvard seniors, however, Light concludes that "the opposite is true: learning outside of classes, especially in residential settings and extracurricular activities such as the arts, is vital." When the students Light interviewed were asked about what incidents had changed them most, "four-fifths of them chose a situation or event outside the classroom" (p. 8). Certainly this finding validates the importance of out-of-class experiences.

Participation in events outside the classroom not only fosters intellectual engagement, but also creates a sense of community on the complex campuses of the 21st century, which is clearly critical in improving retention and fostering student success. Student life professionals can play a major role in facilitating a sense of community among students. Perhaps more than anyone else, staff involved in student activities are in an enviable position to build a campus culture that revolves around out-of-class interaction, events, and traditions essential to the development of community. Practitioners must evaluate the needs of the students and offer activities that meet those needs. To be effective in community development, student activities professionals must re-examine the definition of student activities and the events that make up programming calendars, and provide students with experiences that are engaging and interactive. Community development does not happen with one event, but with programs that build on each other and, as a result, provide frequent interaction with the participants. *Campus Life: In Search of Community* (Carnegie Foundation, 1990) suggests that students have significant blocks of time not spent in class or studying. If campus personnel wisely facilitate activities during these time blocks, the result will be greater student involvement that leads to a spirit of community on the campus.

Challenges to Building Community

It must be acknowledged, however, that building a sense of community on today's campuses presents a number of challenges. The first challenge many practitioners face is combining the theory of community development that centers on student involvement with a comprehensive plan that takes into account the diverse needs and interests of the students enrolled in higher education institutions. Community development is a slow, methodical process that must honor the individuality of each student yet connect them as a group in a bond that allows for open communication and trust. Rarely will students come together naturally or through disconnected program initiatives—rather, it requires comprehensive planning to create an effective system of programs that stimulate the development of community.

Today's college students struggle with multiple responsibilities, and more often than not college is not their primary focus. In addition, the profile of who is coming to college has changed dramatically in the past two decades. College campuses in the 21st century are seeing an increase in older adults who are balancing the demands of school with families and jobs. According to the U.S. Department of Education (DOE), "fewer than one in six of all current undergraduates fits the traditional stereotype of the American college student attending full-time, being eighteen to twenty-two years of age and living on campus" (cited in Levine, 1998, p. 49). Rather, this DOE report notes that by 1994 more than 40% of all college students were more than 25 years old, approximately half were working, more than half were female, and a significant portion were attending part-time (cited in Levine, 1998). The number of students working is increasing. By 1998, the National Center for Education Statistics reported that 79% of all undergraduates worked while taking classes during the 1995-96 academic year—up from 54% in the DOE report.

Another characteristic of today's student population that offers a challenge to building community is increasing diversity. According to Carnevale and Fry (2000), by 2015, African-American, Hispanic, and Asian/Pacific Islander students will account for 80% of the increase in undergraduate enrollment. Despite the enrollment gains, however, the playing field for these students is still not level because "a wide disparity persists between minority and white college students in the number and percentage of who actually graduates from college" (p. 31). It is essential that minority students at risk for dropping out become involved within the campus community if they are to succeed. Of particular concern to student affairs professionals is the trend toward minorities forming small groups, causing a fragmentation of the larger community. Levine (1998) gives a portrait of the current generation of college students in *When Hope and Fear Collide*: "As undergraduates search on campus for a place to call home, their clubs are dividing into smaller and smaller groups based on race, ethnicity, gender and sexual orientation" (p. xiv). Such fragmentation does not contribute to the development of community that fosters a greater appreciation of diversity. Moreover, Tinto (1993) suggests that while membership in multiple communities is important in meeting a wide range of needs, such membership is not a guarantee of persistence, especially if the communities with which students align themselves are not connected to the central values and mission of the institution.

Most educators view appreciating diversity and learning to work well with those unlike oneself as a critical goal of higher education. As Light observes, "If campus norms encourage students to develop groups built primarily on race or ethnicity, interaction across groups becomes harder" (p. 190). In order to break this cycle and create a community that reflects the institution's diversity, campus leaders must intentionally design and coordinate activities that strongly encourage inclusiveness. In *Diversity on Campus: Reports from the field*, Pike (2000) states that "the greatest gains in diversity education are achieved when institutions intentionally structure college experiences to promote high levels of in-class and out-of-class interaction and involvement" (p. 39). Student activities personnel can play a critical role in making certain that intentional experiences, leading to higher levels of involvement, are created. Without this deliberate interaction, students miss an opportunity to become part of a community whose diversity reflects the larger society beyond the campus.

Another obstacle to creating a sense of community is the large number of transfer students on many campuses. Because transfer students are at risk for leaving, special attention needs to be given to their needs. Tinto (1993) believes that providing programs tailored to the specific needs of transfer students "will enhance the likelihood that they will finish their degrees in the institutions to which they transfer" (p. 190). Transfer students frequently feel no attachment to the institution, and therefore it is often difficult to assimilate them into the campus community. Providing an orientation program especially for transfers can be a good first step in smoothing their transition. Commuter students, sometimes labeled "PCP students" (parking lot-classroom-parking lot), are also difficult to bring into the community. Once a problem primarily of metropolitan commuter institutions, more and more campuses are faced with engaging an increasing number of commuter students in the life of the campus community. Residential life presents a ready-made opportunity for creating a sense of community because students are living together; however, with both transfers and commuters, the challenge is helping students connect with the institution and develop a sense of belonging to the community.

Yet another challenge to building a sense of community on the college campus is

> "Another obstacle to creating a sense of community is the large number of transfer students on many campuses."

53

the increasing dependency on technology that can lead to isolation and a heightened sense of individualism. The current generation of college students grew up during the technological revolution—a time of enormous change and communication at stunning speeds. The fall 2000 survey of incoming first-year students conducted by the Higher Education Research Institute at UCLA's Graduate School of Education and Information Studies in association with the American Council on Education finds a record-breaking 78.5% of the new students used computers regularly during the year before attending college (Sax, Astin, Korn, & Mahoney, 2000). Although technological proficiency is critical in today's world and some campuses are making efforts to use technology to foster community, Anderson (2001) concludes that

> no matter how much information was efficiently transferred to the students, faculty, and staff, it was not until we physically came together that I truly felt as if I were part of a community... I realized that, no matter how much we try to build 'high touch' into 'high tech' services, we will never be able to replicate the human need for physical interaction. (p. 23)

Two other obstacles stand in the way of creating a community among current college students. First, most students are focused on preparing for a career and believe they lack the time to involve themselves in campus activities or may not see the relevance of activities to future career aspirations. Student affairs professionals can help students see the connection between out-of-class involvement and preparation for the world of work. Developing interpersonal skills and leadership ability, problem-solving skills, and working in teams are all important to employers, and participation in campus life affords opportunities for students to develop these critical skills. There may even be a connection between active participation in the campus community and future earnings. Pascarella and Terenzini (1991) point out that "with some exceptions the weight of the evidence suggests that

there may be a small positive and statistically significant correlation between involvement in extracurricular activities, particularly in a leadership role, and subsequent earnings" (p. 520). If students understood fully that participation in the campus community may enhance their career opportunities, they would perhaps take a more active role in the life of the community.

Finally, the most imposing obstacle that confronts community building on many campuses is student apathy. Fewer students are voting in campus elections, and while the variety of student activities has grown, those activities are attracting fewer students. According to Levine (1998), in 1979, on-campus activities topped the list of students' social outlets. Increasingly, today's students are going off campus for their social life, most often to clubs or bars, and this makes it very difficult to create a bond with the institution and a sense of campus community that are so critical to retention.

Opportunities for Building Community

Despite these challenges, student affairs professionals must not abandon hope of building a campus community. There are some very important times to provide opportunities for students to become a part of the campus culture. For example, orientation is an excellent way to begin establishing a sense of connection with the campus. Many orientation programs across the country do an excellent job in beginning the process of community development. Texas A&M (a four-year, public, residential institution with 44,000 students) sponsors a program called "Fish Camp." The Fish Camp works under the premise that "...every member of the organization through their actions, shoulders the responsibility to aid the freshmen's transition from high school to college in an unconditionally accepting environment." The program focuses on "build[ing] relationships with others, shar[ing] the Aggie spirit and welcom[ing the new students] to the Aggie Family" (http://stuact.tamu.edu/stuorgs/fishcamp). The weeklong program strives to connect students through team-building exercises and events such as square dancing, role-playing, and participating in camp games. All events are done in a camp located near campus. The student staff creates an environment that seeks to develop trust and engage students in the Aggie family.

Texas Christian University (a four-year, church-affiliated, residential institution with 7,800 students) also offers an orientation camp. Named after the school's mascot, a horned frog, "Frog Camp" includes a wilderness adventure and a Habitat for Humanity service project, with the goal of not only helping new students make the transition between high school and college but also creating a sense of community and identification with the university. The approach certainly has a positive effect on retention. "Only 15% of first-year students who participated in the 1995 Frog Camps did not return for their sophomore year in 1996. Among non-Frog Camps, the dropout rate was 27%" (Noel & Levitz, 1997, p. 7).

With the increase of non-traditional students whose schedules are not suited to events like Fish Camp, other ways have to be found to build a connection for them to the university. At Kennesaw State University, (a four-year, public, primarily commuter institution with 15,600 students) the one-day orientation program struggles to provide the necessary information for academic success while allowing time for students to develop relationships with each other. Kennesaw State University's orientation program is designed with a strong academic focus that educates students on the registration process and includes one-on-one advisement focused on identifying a challenging but not overwhelming schedule of classes. The second part of the orientation program focuses on the social aspect of college, introducing new students to university life and providing them with a current student leader to help them through the process of transition.

To ensure student interaction, a student leadership group was created at Kennesaw State University called LINK (Leaders Involving Newcomers @ Kennesaw). LINK leaders are assigned a group of 15 new students, and they work with that group throughout the entire orientation process. LINK leaders remain with the group during the official orientation day—es-

corting students to academic advising, discussing the "nuts and bolts" of student life, and celebrating their entrance into the university community at an event called BASH, which showcases student activities on the campus. Most importantly, LINK leaders remain in contact with the new students during the first weeks of school and encourage them to attend campus events that provide information about offices and services at KSU that help foster success. LINK members not only serve as mentors to the new students, but they also serve as active agents, recruiting students to campus life at KSU.

Some schools provide a more in-depth orientation program that includes outdoor activities. At Furman University (a four-year, private, residential institution with 2,800 students), new students report to campus a week prior to the beginning of classes. During the first day of activities, parents attend an orientation while their students move into the residence halls. Parents leave at the end of the day with a better understanding of campus life and some knowledge about the services available. During the remainder of the week, students are tested to determine class needs and meet with academic advisors. Simultaneously, they are encouraged to get to know residence hallmates as well as other new students by participating in various activities including a square dance, a meeting with the university president and staff, and a rafting trip. Each of these activities is part of Furman's tradition. Students gain a better sense of the community because of these events and become more connected to the institution because of the rituals. Upper class students serve as guides during the week and seek to involve new students in campus life while giving them a thorough introduction to the university.

Orientation is not the only important time to focus on building a community, however. According to Moller-Wong, Shelley, and Ebbers (1999), the majority of students who drop out during the first year do so during the first six weeks—a critical time for many students. By the fifth week, the newness of college seems to wane. Students appear to be less excited about college as they begin to face the realities of tests, papers, and projects. This is also the time when professors start to return graded material. Frequently students receive grades that fail to meet their expectations, and they begin to think they might not be capable of succeeding in college. Many students question whether college is the right choice for them and many consider dropping out.

At Kennesaw State University a comprehensive week of activities entitled "Bust Your Rut" is planned to combat this fifth-week slump. Services, workshops, and activities are held in an attempt to encourage students to identify their current patterns and break out of "ruts" that might prevent them from being successful. The week includes workshops on developing effective study habits, dealing with stress, and maintaining balance. Support offices are also highlighted for students. KSU 1101 (first-year seminar) professors distribute a list of support offices to their classes and encourage their students to visit these offices if they need help. In addition, support offices are invited to participate in a student services fair held at the student center during lunch in an attempt to reach as many students as possible. Tables contain information and representatives are there to raise students' awareness about support services. Kennesaw State University's 2002 Bust Your Rut Week also includes a "learning styles" workshop. Student participants take a test to determine their individual learning style. Each style is explained, and students develop an understanding of the different methods by which information is learned. Students then determine the teaching style of the professors for each of their classes and learn specific tactics to help them succeed in the classes taught in a style that is not their preference. Tutors are available and learning labs are open to raise awareness of those services. Finally, a campus-wide cookout for faculty, staff, and students celebrates the completion of the first five weeks of the semester.

There are other times during the year when the entire campus community should come together. Convocations, campus-wide celebrations, and commencements are just a few examples. Offering cultural events such as concerts, lectures, and debates is an excellent vehicle for developing a sense of community as well as extending the opportunity for student learning outside the classroom. Most student programming boards include lecture series and cultural events. The importance of these events for student learning and community development should not be understated. Hearing a lecture by a well-known figure, attending a political debate, or seeing an artistic performance adds richness to what students are learning in the classroom and needs to be an important part of programming activities.

Events coordinators should keep in mind that there are three types of events within student activities programs that contribute to community development. First, there are events that enrich the environment and make the community attractive and enjoyable, such as concerts; speakers; and the distribution of novelty items such as video buttons, inflatable games, and goofy IDs. Novelty give-aways can be stand-alone events, but using them to emphasize a particular theme or to lead up to a bigger event generates increased community recognition. All of these events make the environment enticing by offering activity and leisure programs that extend learning and create an enjoyable environment. Clearly students are more likely to persist if the environment is interesting and engaging. The second type of event develops skills and offers support focused on individual empowerment. Examples of these events include diversity workshops, one-on-one mentoring activities, and support service fairs. These events are usually topic-driven, single-focused initiatives that seek to provide special training and information in a given area. Increasing students' skills also makes a positive impact on retention. The third category includes events that deepen participants' understanding of themselves and the larger community while challenging them to be leaders in that community. These events usually take place in a cohort model, bringing the same students together on a consistent basis and providing activities focused on the group experience. This type of ongoing participation with a group is a most effective community builder because it offers opportunities for building relationships, a powerful retention tool. Leadership groups that meet on a regular basis or learning communities are good examples of this category. Effective programming calendars combine all three types of activities and work to challenge students to increase their commitment to the institution by prioritizing student activities.

Planning activities throughout the year makes the environment attractive to students and contributes to ongoing community engagement. However, identifying events that are of interest to students and keeping the campus "alive" with activity are ongoing challenges for programming boards and student activities professionals. Students enjoy a certain amount of pride when they are part of a campus that offers high-profile speakers, comedians, concerts, and other performers. But "walk-up" events, those events that students do not have to make a conscious decision to attend, can be equally important in shaping students' perceptions of the campus culture. For example, the Kennesaw Activities Board (KAB) regularly sponsors ice cream give-aways, distributing ice cream across campus from the back of a golf cart. This event does not require a student to go to a special location—instead the event comes to the student. KAB's office has a tree where free pens, pencils, and highlighters are hung for students to pick up. All freebies are imprinted with upcoming event information and this works well to publicize future events. Students learn to identify KAB members, who wear brightly colored shirts and whose office is decorated in an eye-catching manner, as members of an important organization that provides entertainment and opportunities for involvement on campus. Novelty events, such as those during which students can have caricatures made, create wax models of their hands, or record their lip-synced performance to a popular song or video do not require large time commitments from the students and frequently have many participants. At the same time, these events help develop a community spirit because they involve students with one another and create an enjoyable and engaging atmosphere.

Inclusion of Faculty and Staff in Community Development

Community development professionals should establish opportunities for interaction among students and faculty and staff. Students often enter the university with a preconceived idea of a rigid divide between students and faculty and staff members. When this gap is collapsed and a collegial relationship is established, students learn more and become more closely connected with the institution. Failure to establish these relationships between faculty and students negatively impacts the development of a meaningful campus community. William Willimon, (1997) Dean of the Chapel at Duke University, feels that faculty do students a disservice when they do not interact with them: "We have structured the modern university in such a way that the chances of faculty befriending students are slim" (p. 6). He argues that "the time has come to recover the classical ideals of higher education, to reclaim a sense of the campus as an environment meant to foster friendship between the generations, and to recognize the specific educational needs of this particular generation of students" (p. 9). In the early days of the academy, these interactions occurred quite naturally. In today's colleges and universities, opportunities for faculty and students to interact outside the walls of the classroom must be intentionally created.

Many universities have designed programs that bring students and faculty and staff members together outside the classroom. At Furman University, a program entitled "Dialogue" was created to provide this service (http://www.student.furman.edu/dialogue/). At the end of orientation week, new students are divided into cohort groups of 12 and assigned a senior group leader as well as a faculty or staff co-facilitator. The Sunday prior to the start of classes, the groups meet at the faculty or staff person's house for dinner and plan events for the next five weeks. Each group has a budget of $150 to plan a service project, an outdoor event, and other activities at the discretion of the group. The focus of this initiative is to

"Community development professionals should establish opportunities for interaction among students and faculty and staff."

answer questions and discuss the atmosphere of the institution. Satisfaction for this program has been very high, and it offers students a unique opportunity to connect with older members of the community.

Kennesaw State University also gives faculty the opportunity to host classes in their home. A program called Faculty Firesides offers $50.00 to help faculty provide food for the event. Faculty and student participants have consistently stated that this was one of the best experiences they had during the course of the semester. Faculty Firesides create a strong relationship between the faculty and students by connecting them beyond the in-class faculty-student relationship. The program, coordinated through the Division of Student Success and Enrollment Services, works well to enhance the learning environment in the classroom. Communication between teacher and student is improved through this out-of-class interaction and students become more active contributors to the learning experience.

Assistance of Peer Mentors in Community Development

In addition to involvement with faculty and staff, an effective peer-mentoring program gives new students the comfort and knowledge that they are not alone at the university; there is someone who cares about their success. These relationships can ease new students' transitions by providing them with someone who has already gone through the process. Peer mentors understand what the new student is going through at a particular time, because they have already had the same type of experience. The mentoring program can also be used as an intervention tool. The peer mentor has an excellent vantage point and can determine how the new student is adjusting. If there is a situation the new student cannot handle, the peer mentor must be able to refer the student to the appropriate office to ensure that the situation does not escalate and jeopardize the student's success.

A strong peer-mentoring program is fundamental to ensure that commuter students make a successful transition into the college community. The Odyssey peer-mentoring program at Kennesaw State University connects students with similar backgrounds and interests. Primarily designed to provide mentoring for specific populations of minority students, adult learners, international students, and students with disabilities, the Odyssey peer mentoring program has contributed to the development of a sense of community. Students who wish to serve as mentors must enroll in an intensive training session to understand the mentoring role. Matching mentors to new students who have similar interests and talents is essential. After the initial meeting between mentor and student takes place, specific events are not planned; however, the new students are able to learn more about the university and ways to be a successful student with the help of their mentors. These relationships also help new students establish themselves within the university environment. For this reason mentoring programs can be invaluable for new students. In its annual "Colleges of the Year" edition, *Time* cites the mentoring program at William Jewell College (a four-year, private, church-affiliated institution with 1,500 students) as one of the primary reasons "it would be tough for a freshman to fall through the cracks" (Goldstein, 2001, p. 73). Mentors at William Jewell contact their 8 to 10 students well in advance of their arrival on campus. In addition, they leave gifts for the new students outside their doors their first day on campus. Clearly the feeling of being welcomed into the community begins early for these newcomers to the campus.

Importance of a Sense of Place

Students also need to have common areas where unstructured interactions can occur. A strong sense of place contributes to the establishment of community on campus. One way institutions attempt to address this need is through the creation of student centers with television areas; recreation areas; and places for specific populations such as adult learners, African-American students, and international students. These, too, are part of an active student activity program. While communal areas are not activities in the traditional sense, they do provide a place for students to congregate and develop relationships and strong peer networks—all of which contribute to community development. Kuh and Schuh (1991) cite the importance of the physical environment in involving students in the campus community. The student center is often a focal point for out-of-class activities and a place where students can interact with one another. Kuh offers the student union at Grinnell College (a four-year, private, liberal arts institution with 1,400 students), known as the Forum, as an example of how a student center can become the hub of student life. Like many student centers, it contains meeting rooms, a snack bar, student life offices, student government offices; and, as the name implies, it is intended to be a "forum" for students to discuss issues and concerns that affect the college community.

Academic and Student Affairs Collaborations for Community Development

Some other excellent ways to build community on campus exist primarily in academic affairs, but student life professionals can also play a significant role in these opportunities. For example, on many campuses, first-year seminar courses are taught by both faculty and student affairs personnel. These courses can have a profound effect on the development of community because they foster relationships among students. Common themes include not only study skills, time management, and an introduction to the resources of the institution, but also involvement in campus organizations and events. One of the most encouraging results of these first-year-experience courses is the fact that most students develop a support group of peers and a faculty or staff mentor that help connect them to the institution.

The establishment of the freshman interest group (FIG), or learning community, is another important collaboration between academic affairs and student affairs. Learning communities offer both an academic component, through enrollment in common courses, and a social component, through an emphasis on the out-of-class connection. The primary goal of most learning

communities is to establish a strong sense of community among the students and a connection to the intellectual and social life of the campus. The FIG at the University of Oregon (a four-year, public, residential institution with 18,000 students), established in 1982 by the Office of Academic Advising and Student Services, is a prototype of a learning community (Love & Tinto, 1995). The FIG program at the University of Washington (a four-year, public, residential institution with 36,000 students) is another example of such a program (Love & Tinto, 1995). Groups of about 20 students are enrolled during their first term in a cluster of three courses that are linked by a common theme. The FIG members also participate in meetings facilitated by a junior or senior peer advisor. These meetings are yet another opportunity for building a sense of community.

One of the major advantages of learning communities and FIGs is the social interaction they afford among peers both inside and outside the classroom. Such interaction may be "of special importance at large institutions [where] learning communities allow students to aid each other with one of the key points of transition—learning their way around campus and meeting people" (Love & Tinto, 1995, p. 85). Through participation in learning communities, students build relationships and enhance the likelihood that they will become involved in student organizations and extra-curricular activities. In addition, they are more likely to use the services of the institution such as advising and counseling. Most important, participation in a learning community appears to have a positive effect on retention rates and a students' satisfaction with the learning environment (Pascarella & Terenzini, 1991; Tinto, 1993). At Appalachian State University (a four-year, public, residential institution with 13,000 students), for example, there is a strong sense of a community where students feel "nurtured and challenged" (Rutherford, 2001, p. 68). This is especially true for those students who enroll in small first-year seminars and learning communities. These students return to Appalachian for their sophomore year at a higher rate than do their peers who do not participate in the program (90% versus 84%

for 1999's first-year class). Nearly 650 students at Seattle Central Community College, one of the nation's most diverse campuses, are involved in learning communities, and their retention rate is an amazing 97% (Goldstein, 2001, p. 77).

Another activity frequently connected to academic units is service. Indeed, service-learning has become an integral part of many college curriculums. Programming boards should not overlook the value of offering opportunities for students to work together on projects that will not only result in work that benefits the larger community but also create a stronger community spirit among participants. Many college and universities, for example, sponsor groups to build Habitat for Humanity houses; others are actively involved in local, national, and international service projects. In Boyer's (1987) view, "Service constitutes a vital part of an undergraduate education. It offers opportunities that cannot be obtained in any other way" (p. 214). Service also helps build community on a college campus.

Community Rituals and Traditions

Under Boyer's leadership, the Carnegie Foundation (1990) reminded the higher education community that "a college or university is a celebrative community, one in which the heritage of the institution is remembered and where rituals affirming both tradition and change are widely shared" (p. 55). Clearly the development of rituals and traditions are central to the creation of a sense of community. Traditions frequently develop around key periods in the students' college journey, particularly at the beginning and end of their academic odyssey. Western Washington University (a four-year, public, residential institution with 12,000 students) has an excellent example of a welcoming ceremony that involves the entire university community. The Welcoming Convocation at WWU includes words of welcome from campus leaders, a keynote address that sets forth the community's values and expectations, and a goal-setting exercise that the president challenges each new student to complete. As first-year students walk out of the auditorium into a candlelit corridor

of returning students and staff who are cheering them on, they deposit their written goals into a time capsule. Following the ceremony, a reception sponsored by the alumni association is an ideal way for former students to greet and welcome the newcomers to the community (Carey & Fabiano, 1999). Such an event communicates to the new students the core values and expectations of the community they are joining. The participation of returning students and faculty and staff contribute to a powerful tradition that helps to create a sense of belonging to an established community.

Traditions vary from campus to campus. Kuh and Schuh (1991) describe a variety of traditions that communicate institutional values and "affirm the importance of student learning and development through out-of-class experiences" (p. 19). Traditions frequently connect to a college's history. For example, at Berry College (a small private liberal arts college in Rome, GA), Mountain Days celebrates the college founder, Martha Berry, and her emphasis on the value of work and the college's proximity to the mountains. For some colleges and universities, traditions spring up around their athletic programs. These sports traditions persist beyond graduation; and alumni who return to the campus years later still feel a connection to the institution's community because of these rituals and traditions. It is important to note, however, that participating in sporting events contributes more to the development of community than being a spectator does. Relatively few students participate in organized athletics; however, intramural programs offer an excellent way to involve large numbers of students in a community building activity. Many schools have developed traditions associated with the beginning and ending of the college journey—for example, at Kennesaw State University the "WINGS" (When in Need Gives Support) ceremony has become a valued tradition for adult learners who are able to honor those individuals who have been "the wind beneath their wings" during their college careers.

The importance of traditions to a sense of community cannot be overstated. Although *Built to Last* (Collins & Porres, 1997) focuses on the business world and outlines the characteristics of those companies whose success persists, many of the characteristics may apply to colleges and universities as well. For example, one of the characteristics relates to what the authors refer to (in a positive sense) as "cult-like cultures." The authors define this as an intense sense of identity with the community that exists within the organization. They stress the importance of community building activities that one may easily translate to a college or university setting including

- Orientation and programs that teach values, norms, history, and traditions
- Socialization by peers and immediate supervisors (for higher education substitute students, faculty, and staff)
- Corporate songs, cheers, or affirmation
- Celebrations that reinforce successes, belonging, and specialness

In the same way that businesses prosper when employees buy in to the traditions and core values of a corporate culture, colleges and universities likewise benefit from a strong sense of community built on shared values and traditions.

In *What Matters in College*, Astin (1993) says that the lack of student community has stronger direct effects on student satisfaction with the overall college experience than any other environmental measure. On the positive side, however, the establishment of a strong sense of community that occurs when students are involved on campus can definitely improve retention and students' satisfaction with their college experience. There are clearly challenges facing complex institutions that desire to build community; however, the rewards are certainly worth the effort. As an important component of our higher education institutions, student affairs practitioners have a major role to play in creating a campus community where students are able to reach their full intellectual and social potential as they become involved in the life of the institution.

References

Anderson, C. (2001). Community in cyberspace. *NASPA Forum, 23*(2), 23.

Astin, A. W. (1985). *Achieving educational excellence: A critical assessment of priorities and practices in higher education.* San Francisco: Jossey-Bass.

Astin, A. W. (1993). *What matters in college?* San Francisco: Jossey-Bass.

Boyer, E. L. (1987). *College: The undergraduate experience in America.* New York: Harper & Row.

Carey, A., & Fabiano, P. M. (1999, January/February). Welcome to Western: A community's approach to convocation. *About Campus,* 23-25.

Carnegie Foundation for the Advancement of Teaching. (1990). *Campus life: In search of community.* Princeton, NJ: Author.

Carnevale, A. P., & Fry, R. A. (2000). *Crossing the great divide: Can we achieve equity when Generation X goes to college?* Washington, DC: Educational Testing Service.

Collins, J. C., & Porres, J. I. (1997) *Built to last.* New York: Harper-Collins.

Goldstein, A. (2001, September 10). Time's colleges of the year: Seattle Central. *Time,* 76-77.

Kuh, G. D., & Schuh, J. H. (1991). *The role and contribution of student affairs in involving colleges.* Washington, DC: National Association of Student Personnel Administrators.

Levine, A. (1998). *When hope and fear collide.* San Francisco: Jossey-Bass.

Light, R. J. (2001). *Making the most of college: Students speak their minds.* Cambridge, MA: Harvard University Press.

Love, A. G., & Tinto, V. (1995). Academic advising through learning communities: Bridging the academic social divide. In M. L. Upcraft & G. L. Kramer (Eds.), *First-year academic advising: Patterns in the present, pathways in the future* (Monograph No. 18) (pp. 83-90). Columbia, SC: University of South Carolina, National Resource Center for The Freshman Year Experience and Students in Transition.

Moller-Wong, S., Shelley, M. C., & Ebbers, L. H. (1999, Fall/Winter). Policy goals for educational administrators and undergraduate retention: Toward a cohort model for policy planning. *Policy Studies Review,* 243-277.

National Center for Education Statistics. (1998). *The condition of education 1998.* Washington, DC: Department of Education Publications Center.

Noel, L., & Levitz, R. (1997). Recruiting graduates-to-be. *Recruitment & Retention, 11*(12), 4-7.

Pascarella, E. T., & Terenzini, P. T. (1991). *How college affects students*. San Francisco: Jossey-Bass.

Pike, G. R. (2001). The effects of students' backgrounds and college experiences on their patterns of interaction and acceptance and appreciation of diversity. In *Diversity on Campus: Reports from the field*. Washington, DC: NASPA, Magnificent Publications, Inc.

Rutherford, M. (2001, September 10). Time's colleges of the year: Appalachian State. *Time*, 68-71.

Sax, L., Astin, A. W., Korn, W. S., & Mahoney, K. (2000). *The American freshmen: National norms for fall 2000.* Los Angeles: UCLA, Higher Education Research Institute.

Tinto, V. (1993). Leaving college: *Rethinking the causes and cures of student attrition* (2nd ed.). Chicago: University of Chicago.

Willimon, W. H. (1997, September/October). Has higher education abandoned its students? *About Campus*, 4-9.

Shifting Mindsets to Accommodate the Explosion in Distance Learners

Zav Dadabhoy
Metropolitan State College of Denver

Colleges across the country are rapidly developing online classes to address the higher education needs of a quickly increasing student population and using the Internet to expand classroom space. In some ways, we seem to be in a collective race in which the rules have not been established, and the finish line (the end product) not yet set:

> Everyone seems to want to "do it" but many are not sure what "it" is or how to do it. The new technologies hold promise to help lead higher education into a period of rapid change. Student affairs practitioners need to be prepared to deal effectively with the change, as they can be critical to a successful learning experience. (National Association of Student Personnel Administrators—Distance Learning Task Force, 2000, p. 1)

Despite this suggestion that student affairs professionals take a proactive stance toward technology, many campus-based educators adhere to notions that distance education will strictly revolve around the faculty and the curriculum. Resources, program planning, and institutional foci for distance education efforts seem to be concentrated on academic and course-specific interactions between the instructor and the student.

This is unfortunate, because as Pascarella and Terenzini (1991) remind us, Americans expect their colleges and universities to accomplish several lofty goals, many of which are met outside the classroom. These goals include

1. Transmitting the intellectual heritage of Western Civilization
2. Fostering a high level of verbal and mathematical skills
3. Developing an understanding of political, social, and cultural institutions
4. Facilitating reflective, analytical, critical, and evaluative thinking
5. Developing value structures and moral sensibilities
6. Facilitating personal growth and self-identity
7. Fostering a sense of career identity and vocational competence (p. 1)

A shift in the medium of instruction or the physical relationship of the student to campus should not change our concept of education as a rich, purposeful endeavor with countless learning stimuli. It should not change our commitment to the goals outlined above. The challenge educators face in distance learning is to find ways to provide the depth and breadth of quality education needed to stimulate student interests, to evoke critical thinking skills, and to weave this new mode of education delivery into a total learning environment. Assuming that online education is merely a teacher-to-student web-based interaction is too simplistic a view, and akin to a conceptual sell-out of all the noble values educators have cherished, nurtured, and practiced for so long.

Student affairs professionals have been instrumental in leading institutions forward in their efforts to help students achieve the holistic learning outcomes at the center of American higher education. But, they have been slow to apply this developmental focus to distance education. This chapter calls attention to the need for such a holistic approach to distance learners and provides recommendations for how campus activities professionals can enhance the entire educational experience of distance learners.

The Emphasis on Distance Education

Distance education can be defined as formal academic programs in which the student and the instructor are not working together in the same physical space or at the same time. Technically speaking, there is nothing new about distance education. Correspondence courses; off-site continuing education; and television, radio, and satellite-based education have been a routine and normal part of the higher education landscape for years. In fact, correspondence courses have been offered in Europe and in the United States for more than 100 years. During this time, formal education has depended primarily on print media. Whether on campus or at a distance, people read, wrote, and learned from the physical page. In today's education environment, however, the medium of choice is rapidly becoming the digital screen as we increasingly use the Internet, digital video, and other computerized forms of communication to share knowledge with students and each other.

New technologies, and in particular, the Internet, have transformed our society and our institutions. Indeed, the impact of these new technologies has been so prodigious that many have labeled the phenomenon as a revolution, the digital revolution. These technological advances have also influenced education, changing our concept of distance learning. Colleges and universities across the country are quickly designing and developing new modes of delivering education at a distance. In doing so, many observers have begun to contemplate whether the traditional values of education can be sustained in the new distance learning medium.

Some years ago, it would have been hard to imagine that distance learning could be such a dominant topic for educators. Today, the percentage of universities and colleges offering distance education courses has exploded, and it is imperative that campus activities professionals participate in determining the quality of the educational experiences being provided to distance learners. A survey by the National Center for Educational Statistics (NCES) found that more than 1.6 million students were enrolled in distance education courses in 1997-98. When compared to the total college enrollment of approximately 15 million college students, this is clearly a significant percentage—and a number that is certain to be far higher today (NCES, 2000). During the 1997-98 academic year, 44% of two- and four-year higher education institutions offered distance-learning courses, up from 33% in 1995.

Reflective of the relative importance of this phenomenon, much of this chapter discusses distance education through the lens of Internet-based service delivery. Yet, all of the suggestions, recommendations, and illustrations have implications for students accessing the campus through other media.

The Diversity of the Distance Learner

We may be tempted to view distance learners as a homogeneous group. Yet, in reality, wide diversity exists among distance students. This diversity is reflected in the variety of reasons students enroll as distance learners and suggests a wide range of programmatic and developmental needs to which campus activities professionals must respond. Oblinger and Kidwell (2000) offer the following profiles of distance learners.

- ♦ Life-fulfillment learners, who enjoy learning for its own sake, enroll in distance courses because of the ease and convenience with which they can achieve their personal fulfillment.
- ♦ Corporate learners seek education because of their need to further their careers. These learners usually enroll through their companies' career development programs.
- ♦ Professional development learners seek to advance their careers or change careers. They are more likely to be seeking job mobility through additional or new educational attainments.
- ♦ Degree-completion adult learners enroll as distance learners to complete degree requirements at a later stage in life.
- ♦ Traditional learners usually enroll in distance-learning classes for the experience, flexibility, and the convenience these programs offer.
- ♦ Pre-college learners take distance classes to experience baccalaureate-level work while completing high school.
- ♦ Remedial learners enroll to complete prerequisites for an examination or for enrollment in other academic or professional programs. (p. 34)

In addition to these multiple reasons for distance enrollment, we should recognize the variety of possible demographic differences within the distance-learner population such as age, income, family obligations, place of residence and other factors. The motivation for enrolling in distance education and the demographic diversity of this population needs to be considered as we design programs and services for distance learners.

Our Role as Student Development Educators

Student affairs educators provide much of the out-of-class learning at colleges and universities. In recent years, achievement of student development and holistic educational outcomes has been a focus of much scrutiny and discussion for our profession. Boyer (1987) urged educators to pay attention to the intellectual and social quality of the undergraduate experience. In 1990, he entreated educators to develop coherence between in-class and out-of-class activities. Similarly, the Wingspread Group on Higher Education (1993) took higher education to task for its lack of emphasis on student learning:

> It is also time to readdress the imbalance that has led to the decline of undergraduate education. To do so, the nation's colleges and universities must for the foreseeable future focus overwhelmingly on what their students learn and achieve. Too much of education at every level seems to be organized for the convenience of educators and the institution's interests, procedures and prestige, and too little focused on the needs of the students. (p. 6)

Professional organizations such as National Association for Campus Activities (NACA), National Association of Student Personnel Administrators (NASPA), and American College Personnel Association (ACPA) have joined this call to pay attention to student learning outcomes and have cooperatively developed discussion papers and projects promoting the emphasis of student learning in the profession. The Student Learning Imperative (American College Personnel Association, 1994) is an example of this initiative. Evans, Forney, and Guido-Dibrito (1998) theorize that student development is one of the main goals in student affairs practice and that "for the sake of our students we must help the academy recognize the value of the

"In recent years, achievement of student development and holistic educational outcomes has been a focus of much scrutiny and discussion for our profession."

whole person concept" (p. 14). Nuss (1996) suggests that two concepts define the profession: "the development of the whole person and the fact that student affairs was established to support the academic mission of institutions of higher education" (p. 39). She suggests that these two concepts are at the heart of the future evolution of the field.

In their report "Powerful Partnerships: A Shared Responsibility for Learning" (1998), the American Association for Higher Education (AAHE), NASPA, and ACPA urge us to work cooperatively across divisional boundaries to achieve common student learning outcomes: "We ask that administrative leaders rethink the conventional organization of colleges and universities to create more inventive structures and processes that integrate academic and student affairs; align institutional planning, hiring, rewards, and resource allocations with the learning mission..." (p. 15). In *Good Practice in Student Affairs*, Schroeder (1999) also proclaimed that the creation of seamless learning environments must be a priority for student affairs, arguing that "[a]ddressing this issue is not an option for student affairs, but an obligation" (p. 134). Boyer (1990) also urged colleges to be actively involved in building community on campuses, and Astin (1984) proposed that students' involvement in their academic environment has a direct impact on their success in college, championing the call to get students involved on campus.

Yet, other concepts that define the work of campus activities and student life professionals include concepts of civility and diversity: "A college education should include being aware of cultural and class differences and societal reward structures." (King, 1996, p. 2). Other outcomes are encapsulated by concepts of citizenship, leadership, and experiential learning. Terenzini and Pascarella (1994) summarized most of these views by claiming that both academic affairs and student affairs are central to the educational mission of colleges. They claim that the real quality of undergraduate education depends on factors such as the institution's educational climate, social involvement, peer interactions, and co-curricular experiences.

Two things seems clear from the literature:

An explicit set of theoretical expectations guides the profession, and the concepts of student learning and out-of-class experiences are inextricably tied to the heart of our professional practices.

The Challenge and Our Response

American higher education has traditionally claimed to provide enlightenment through high-quality learning opportunities designed to result in a holistic education. The concept of developing well-rounded students who will become community leaders with articulate and well-developed critical reasoning skills is central to its mission. Intrinsically, most scholars will insist that the goals of education outlined by Pascarella and Terenzini (1991) capture the fundamental essence of holistic education toward which most colleges and universities strive. In this schema, student development educators and campus activities professionals insist that the collegiate experience is more than merely passing courses and earning degrees.

The rapid rate of innovation in Internet and computer technology, the creation of new and growing cyber-networks, and the resulting knowledge revolution are transforming culture and society in quite dramatic ways. Higher education has not been immune to these changes, and it has responded to demands to include these new technologies in their daily business (Palloff & Pratt, 1999). Colleges and universities are beginning to determine what the implications of Internet-based education are as it forces a shift in educational paradigm from professor-centered to student-centered (Van Dusen, 1997).

Already, educators are engaged in an exploding trend in Internet education termed "distance education." Citing cost benefits and other concepts such as student-centered education, new courses and even universities are being rapidly created. It challenges our very assumptions about what a college education should be, with little provision for the rich out-of-class interaction that is so essential to our current concept of a well-rounded, holistic education.

Unfortunately, higher education, and in particular student affairs units, often react to technological advances rather than being proactive in our approach to and use of them. Even though we acknowledge the importance of technology, we are often not prepared to use it effectively. Student affairs professionals constantly scramble to keep up with the newest technology, and sometimes blame this lack of strategic management on constraints such as budget and training. Another reason for the slow adoption of technology can be ascribed to the traditional culture of student affairs. Student affairs practice is grounded in face-to-face and one-on-one interactions with students, and student affairs professionals have been trained in cognitive and interpersonal development theories that stress people and events, not technology.

But technology is not going away, and we must find ways to provide holistic education ideals through alternative media such as the Internet. To date, much of student affairs' online interests and presence have revolved around essential support services. Those responsible for administering distance education have examined distance education in relation to its impact on enrollment and institutional budget—the perennial bottom line. For example, registration, admissions, and financial aid processes are provided on the web at many colleges and universities. Little, if any, emphasis has been placed on implementing online mechanisms to develop community or provide out-of-class experiences. Student life, campus activities and other such services have yet to make the transition to providing actual experiences on the Internet rather than just using their web sites as one would a bulletin board outside the campus activities office or in the student union. Campus activities professionals can and must assume a leadership role in shifting the focus of these programs toward holistic educational outcomes.

Providing information about campus-based activities and services is important, but we must also begin to develop ways to provide intentional learning opportunities through distance media. Thus, the challenge for educators is how to strike an effective balance between using the Internet and other distance media for information and knowledge transmittal and using them as tools to deliver holistic and co-curricular learning experiences. Smallen (1993) proposes a test to determine the effectiveness of Internet use and information technology applications within the context of the higher education mission:

> Successful applications of technology to the learning process, at any institution, will be ones that address variances from the ideal learning environment. Technology applied in a manner oblivious to these variances will not improve teaching and learning, and will waste critical institutional resources. (p. 22)

Unfortunately, there is currently a lack of vision and imagination about how these new Internet technologies could be used to improve the quality of learning (Bates, 2000). Rather than a comprehensive strategy, various departmental units and individuals within each institution have adopted independent, entrepreneurial approaches to creating their own web presence. As a collective, what we have is a piecemeal approach to the digital revolution. Departments have gallantly taken the "Lone Ranger" approach and done the best job they could with the resources available to them. What we need is a collective vision, an approach to harness the digital age as a strategic asset. What we need is a vision to use technology to bring distance learners a taste of the richness and variety of a traditional on-campus learning experiences.

Transforming Our Approach for Distance Learners

In the long term, visionary strategic planning that overcomes academe's intrinsic preference for the status quo is imperative, because of the need to respond quickly to the changing face of academe with the advent of the digital revolution. At the same time, we must not allow the digital revolution to change who we are or our fundamental role as educators (Blimling, Whitt, & Associates, 1999). Higher education has long been a center of thought; a thriving community of scholars; and a bastion of culture, intellectualism, and innovation (Mitchell, 1999). The issue at hand is the need for leadership and vision to sustain the traditional characteristics of our institutions while adapting to and using technology as a strategic asset and a value rather than adopting it as an end in and of itself (Katz, 1999; Blustain, Goldstein, & Lozier, 1999; Blimling et al., 1999).

The Internet is merely an alternate medium for campus activities professionals to conduct their work. Technology itself is not the panacea that people believe it to be. Dyson (1999) points out that it will not solve existing organizational problems nor will technology, by itself, drive educational leadership to incorporate a holistic learning paradigm into distance education endeavors. "It is a fallacy to believe that the technology is automatically going to change culture.... Information age technology won't fly if it is hobbled by industrial age organizational cultures" (p. 144). Dyson's point is that we need to change the way we organize ourselves if we are to realize the full educational benefits of technology.

The question, therefore, is how can campus activities professionals use their traditional pedagogies in the profession's distance-based endeavors? Some of the policy considerations that campus activities departments must identify include

1. How does the use of the Internet achieve the overall learning mission of the college and the co-curricular goals of student affairs areas? How can campus activities areas begin to use the Internet to provide levels of service similar to those provided on the physical campus?
2. How do campus activities areas plan for distance learners to get involved with their institutions? What plans have been implemented to provide a sense of connection between the college and the student? Are distance students even invited to participate in campus-based activities? Are they provided with information about the variety of opportunities available?
3. Have strategies been explored and implemented to connect distance learners to each other, thereby building a sense of community among them?

4. What are the organizational and web-based barriers that need to be addressed? Internet users are less likely to understand campus-based organizational boundaries and may be more interested in functionality than in which department offers what service. As such, special attention should be paid to the navigation system that could lead such students to explore campus activities sites. Essentially, online students would be better served by a navigation system that was based on functional need clusters than some type of departmental directory system.
5. How can campus activities staff begin to conceptualize the Internet as another medium for the provision of services? And then, what must they do to provide this content using the Internet? Finally, if such content is made available, how is it advertised to distance learners?
6. How can the college, and in particular campus activities staff, assume responsibility for its students' technological preparedness? How can this become another goal in a campus activities' endeavor to graduate well-rounded citizens?

As educational administrators who can become obsessed with the technology and the mechanics and financial issues of online delivery, it is crucial to remind ourselves that the educational pedagogy is the same, and the developmental needs of distance learners (such as the need for co-curricular learning or student involvement) are the same as the requirements of other students—but perhaps even greater. And that the theoretical imperatives pertaining to student success for campus-based students apply to all students, even distance learners.

Models

Campus activities professionals on some campuses have provided leadership in developing meaningful co-curricular opportunities for distance learners. The success of these and similar ventures requires educators to do a paradigm shift, where they learn to use distance media, including the Web, as a strategic asset rather than as a bulletin board outside the office door. The trick is to conceive of distance services as an online presence in much the same way as we think of campus-based service.

For example, distance students require an orientation to university study that supports goal commitment; provides real and symbolic interaction between academic staff and students; provides informal as well as formal contact to promote social integration; acts as a living institution in which the student feels an integral part; and, most important, allows the student to become acquainted with and trained in the techniques of independent learning and distance study through the use of new forms of technological interaction. Most distance-learning programs do not provide any substantive or creative orientation programs. Targeted orientation programs for distance learners could form the foundation on which students connect with each other and the institution and learn about resources they may need for their program of study.

Increasingly, student service units are taking their "show" on the road. Community-based orientations, outreach by campus health professionals, and other similar programs are being offered away from the campus in community-based, remote locations. Of course, when considering Internet-based services, we are not only transcending the barriers of space (or location) but also of time.

Boyer (1990) urged colleges to be actively involved in building community on campuses, suggesting that the dynamics of support and collaboration that a community provides should be an outcome that we actively seek. Tinto (1993) emphasized the importance of interaction between individual students and the campus communities, suggesting that this will enhance student success and persistence. Student activities units are largely responsible for developing interventions that contribute to building this sense of community.

Yet, one of the most frequent criticisms heard about the push toward distance education is the lack of community among distance learners. It is almost as though people perceive

there is a barrier and subsequently define the concept of "college-community" to be outside of the purview of distance programs. This is not correct. While colleges and universities' virtual presence provides new challenges for creating community, educators cannot expect the strategies of yesterday to provide solutions for tomorrow. It requires some innovative, creative thinking, and perhaps even some trial and error.

In fact, Frankola (2001) emphasizes the need to find strategies through which distance learners are engaged with each other, and with their institution. She claims that strategies that accomplish these outcomes will lead to higher completion rates among distance learners and increased student success.

Virtual Student Services: Taking the Show on the Road

The examples highlighted in this section demonstrate how student affairs educators think outside the box through distance learning. They are grounded in the premise that we can use Internet technology to emulate a campus-based student outreach system based on frequent contact, resulting in student support and interaction with the campus community.

Western Kentucky University offers "The Virtual Residence Hall" for campus-based students. The system is designed to create an environment of user-friendly, computer-based services and seeks to achieve the following goals:

1. Provide increased computer-based personal outreach and contacts within the college community
2. Provide students with high-quality, useful information
3. Tailor information provided to students based on user-identified personal preferences
4. Increase the number and type of computer access opportunities so that students have sufficient access to computer use
5. Increase the amount of time students can access computer-based resources
6. Provide value-added computer-based services to students

7. Provide for a community-emulating electronic forum in which students collaborate and share information
8. Provide social interaction online
9. Provide a variety of computer-based help resources to students
10. Provide Internet-based opportunities for personal development, experimentation, and learning growth
11. Provide support, security, and privacy so students feel secure and comfortable living and operating in their Virtual Residence Hall.

While designed for a campus-based audience, this concept illustrates some of the structures that might be included in a system developed for distance learners. Such a service would address distance learners' developmental needs and provide significant co-curricular opportunities.

The University of Pennsylvania offers another example of virtual student services for their distance learners through their virtual learning center, The Learning Exchange. This initiative offers information and interactive opportunities for distance learners so that students can access the resources of traditional learning opportunities online. Students navigate through menu choices to access printer-friendly versions of materials and tips on a variety of topics. During weekly online office hours, they meet with a learning specialist in a virtual workshop on topics ranging from studying and test-taking to leadership information and service opportunities. The Learning Exchange encourages reflective thinking and offers exercises through which distance learners can explore their own habits, discover their strengths, and identify areas for improvement.

The Bulletin Board as a Tool for Community Building

An electronic bulletin board (often called a discussion board or forum) is another possible strategy for reaching distance students. If setup as a virtual student lounge, it can be an opportunity for students to engage in community building, networking, and information sharing

using the electronic medium as a tool. In practical terms this provides an opportunity for students to share ideas; voice concerns; make friends; and network with other students, faculty, and staff. The initiative seeks to create an online community of learners interacting with each other to discuss shared college experiences.

Discussion board topics could vary from the general (discussions about student interest, student life issues) to the specific (such as information sharing, off-campus housing, and peer advice). Note that this is not a "chat-room"; rather, it is a hierarchical discussion board archived for a period of time and open for use by any student. Imagine the potentially lively debate about campus issues, extensive campus questions, and other collaborative ventures.

An example of a viable bulletin board is offered through the Metropolitan State College of Denver's Discussion Board. As students' conversations have evolved, a community of learners has formed. Through "conversations" in five areas (Student Lounge, Study Hall, Classifieds, Tech Talk, and Soap Box), students encourage one another as they share ideas and concerns and provide mutual support.

Online Moderated Chats or Online Co-curricular Events

The online moderated chat provides a medium for real-time conversations and communication between students. However, the real value of moderated chats are programmed online events such as chat sessions with a featured personality, celebrity, or expert in the field. Much like a co-curricular lecture series, the moderated chat provides an online opportunity for opening statements and questions and answers between students and the featured guest. Students log onto the "chat-line" at a pre-determined time, and can read and follow the ongoing "conversation" and even participate by asking questions. The moderator feature allows online events programmers to monitor inappropriate questions or clarify issues.

"Online socials" and community-wide online events such as orientation and advising are other possible programs that can be enhanced using the online chat system. Clearly a deviation from the archetypal campus activities, these online events will not just require a paradigm shift, they will also require much trial and error on the part of activities professionals.

Online Games as Community Building Tools

When one thinks of computer games, we usually conger up images of gunfights, exploding targets, vivid neon lights, bedlam, loud music, and obnoxious sound effects. The thought of using such games as educational tools is usually far from the minds of traditional educators. However, the use of games and simulations in education is well-documented in history and recent literature. They have been used in preschool, K-12, the university, the military, business, and by older adults (Dempsey, Lucassen, Hayes, & Casey, 1997).

Many of today's most powerful educational possibilities push educators to move beyond traditional views of teaching and learning. We must consider and adapt these in our student development work. For example, we know that fantasy football and computer-based stock market games have long been of interest to many students. Passionate indulgence in a variety of similar stimuli has become a part of everyday life for many. Colleges and universities could harness this trend and provide comparable opportunities online for students as a tool to build community.

Online competitions offer community building and involvement tools and can be used to provide opportunities to develop leadership skills as well as an understanding of economics, finance, and management. As with many such experiential learning opportunities, building occasions for reflection is crucial to ensure successful co-curricular outcomes.

Simulations as Experiential Learning

A simulation, basically, is anything that models reality. According to Cruickshank (1980), simulations are reality games in which students are given a simulated environment in which to play. These games are intended to provide in-

sight into the process or event from the real world. Simulations offer opportunities to simplify complex systems, to develop empathy, and to solve problems from the inside out. They can also help students gain vivid and personal insight to even the most abstract concepts and models, such as physical systems; military, industrial, and economic systems; and social systems.

Computer simulations are increasingly being used in all areas of education. Mathematics and physics have particularly benefited from the computer revolution by being able to simulate and show complex equations in graphical form. The languages have become benefactors as well, especially with the ability of students to hear digital words and sounds in other languages from their computers. But it is in the social sciences that simulation gaming first came into its own, with such (non-computer) classics as Star Power™ (Shirts, 1993) and Bafá Bafá™ (Shirts, 1974). These games provide powerful learning moments for participants. In Bafá Bafá, the moment of consciousness comes when participants suddenly grasp the idea that good intentions can actually worsen cultural misunderstandings. In Star Power, the realization occurs when participants unexpectedly discover that the only way to keep power over others is not to use it. Both these games have been used in traditional campus settings for many years. The question is: How can campus activities provide parallel opportunities for distance learners?

The Global Leadership Simulation at the Metropolitan State College of Denver is an exercise in developing a safe, healthy, creative environment for students to practice leadership skills in a variety of real life situations, such as diplomacy, politics, and international finance. Used in a setting of international politics and economics, the simulations series has the power to give students a perspective far beyond traditional lecturing, research, and reading. Simulation-based learning can be used as an experiential learning tool, allowing opportunities for students to apply knowledge, skills, rhetoric, and the possibility of self-exploration in relation to contexts of decision making not ordinarily provided to them.

The Global Leadership Simulations (GLS)

is a diplomatic exercise. Campus activities professionals and student coordinators offer a world where the students are the leaders and must depend on their personal and group organization, strategy, and communication tools to resolve problems between people with different perspectives, resources, and power levels. The simulations involve conflicts within groups and between groups, personalities, and alliances. Links, research material, and advisors are provided for those players who wish to learn more about the simulation being developed.

The simulation is offered through the Web using e-mail, threaded discussion, and moderated chat programs. Students communicate with each other in numerous ways, and such communications will depend on the type of simulation run and how the students are grouped. For example, in a Middle-East conflict simulation, each group will represent a nation, state, or world entity such as the news media, World Bank, IMF, or War Crimes Court. Players will have specific responsibilities, such as playing the role of the country's CEO (e.g., king, president, prime minister). These responsibilities and roles may be altered depending on the type of entity or simulation.

The simulations emulate contemporary international conflict events (like discussions surrounding the proposed U.S. invasion Iraq in the fall of 2002) or ongoing social and financial issues. These simulations demonstrate how political events are often determined by international economic policies. The goal is to incorporate the technology of web-based programs with new and interesting pedagogical approaches to learning. By putting students in positions of power within cultures and political climates that are different from their own, we can encourage new thinking and understanding. The GLS also encourages players to feel free to make moves and decisions they would not normally make—essentially, to make mistakes.

Conclusion

Even as we observe the phenomenon of technology in higher education, we are beginning to witness the formative years of a new network, the Internet2. While the Internet2 will be between 100 and 1,000 times faster, this next generation is more than just a faster web service. It will enable completely new possibilities such as digital libraries, virtual laboratories, and tele-immersion, all of which can be transmitted in seconds, in real-time, and with little or no degradation of quality. Concepts such as real-time videoconferencing, virtual reality simulations, 3-D imaging, multicasting, gigaPoPs will become conversational terms of the future, just as dotcoms, portals, and the Web currently are. The Internet2 will provide a convergence of multimedia capacities, with services such as telephone, radio, television, and other multimedia technologies becoming standard practice on the net. And just as the current version of the Internet has done, the Internet2 will certainly impact society, and in turn, our system of education.

Thus, possibilities for reaching distance students seem to be endless, limited only by an educator's imagination and willingness to "think" in the new media. Examples of programs and opportunities that can be offered online include student organization accounting services, leadership education sessions, networking possibilities with alumni and prominent professionals in various academic fields, virtual reality narrations of campus-based traditions, and online databases offering information about service-learning opportunities and matching student interests with service opportunities. While it would be unrealistic to expect that all aspects of student life can be re-created for distance learners, certainly campus activities staff could go further than they have to offer an environment that is more nurturing, friendly, and supportive of distance learners.

References

American Association for Higher Education, American College Personnel Association, & National Association of Student Personnel Administrators. (1998). *Powerful partnerships: A shared responsibility for learning.* Washington, DC: Authors.

American College Personnel Association. (1994). *The student learning imperative: Implications for student affairs.* Washington, DC: Author.

Astin, A. W. (1984). Student involvement: A developmental theory for higher education. *Journal of College Student Development, 25,* 297-308.

Bates, A. W. T. (2000). *Managing technological change: Strategies for college and university leaders.* San Francisco: Jossey-Bass.

Blimling, G. S., Whitt, E. J., & Associates (1999). *Good practice in student affairs: Principles to foster student learning.* San Francisco: Jossey-Bass.

Blustain, H., Goldstein, P., & Lozier, G. (1999). Assessing the new competitive landscape. In R. N. Katz & others (Eds.), *Dancing with the devil: Information technology and the new competition in higher education* (pp. 51-72). San Francisco: Jossey-Bass.

Boyer, E. (1987). *College: The undergraduate experience in America.* New York: Harper Row.

Boyer, E. (1990). Foreword. In Carnegie Foundation for the Advancement of Teaching (Ed.), *Campus life: In search of community* (pp. xi-xiii). Princeton; NJ: Princeton University Press.

Cruickshank, D. R. (1980). Classroom games and simulations. *Theory Into Practice, 19*(1), 75-80.

Dempsey, J. V., Lucassen, B. A., Hayes, L. L, & Casey, M. S. (1997). *An exploratory study of forty computer games* (COE Technical Report No. 97-2). Mobile, AL: University of South Alabama.

Dyson, E. (1999). Aligning corporate culture to maximize high technology. In F. Hesselbein, & P. M. Cohen (Eds.), *Leader to leader: Enduring insights on leadership* (pp. 143-150). San Francisco: Jossey-Bass.

Evans, N. J., Forney, D. S., & Guido-DiBrito, F. (1998). *Student development in college: Theory, research and practice.* San Francisco: Jossey-Bass.

Frankola, K. (2001). The e-learning taboo: High dropout rates in online courses. *Syllabus, 14*(11).

Katz, R. N. (1999). *Dancing with the devil: Information technology and the new competition in higher education.* San Francisco: Jossey-Bass.

King, P. (1996, May/June). The obligations of privilege. *About Campus, 1*(2), 2-3.

Mitchell, T. (1999). From Plato to the Internet. *Change Magazine, 31*(2), 17.

National Association of Student Personnel Administrators-Distance Learning Task Force. (2000). *Distance learning and student affairs: Defining the issues.* Washington, DC: Author.

National Center for Education Statistics (NCES), *Distance Education at Postsecondary Education Institutions: 1997-98,* NCES 2000-013.

Nuss, E. M. (1996). The development of student affairs. In S. R. Komives, D. B. Woodard, & Associates (Eds.), *Student services: A handbook for the profession* (3rd ed.) (pp. 22-42). San Francisco: Jossey-Bass.

Oblinger, D., & Kidwell, J. (2000, May/June). Distance learning: Are we being realistic? *Educause Review, 30-34,* 36, 38-39.

Palloff, R. M., & Pratt, K. (1999). *Building learning communities in cyberspace: Effective strategies for the online classroom.* San Francisco: Jossey-Bass.

Pascarella, E., & Terenzini, P. (1991). *How college affects students: Findings and insights from twenty years of research.* San Francisco: Jossey-Bass.

Schroeder, C. (1999). Forging educational partnerships that advance student learning. In G. S. Blimling, & E. J. Whitt (Eds.), *Good practice in student affairs: Principles to foster student learning* (pp. 133-156). San Francisco: Jossey-Bass.

Shirts, G. (1974). Bafá Bafá™. Del Mar, CA: Simulation Training Systems.

Shirts, G. (1993). Star Power™. Del Mar, CA: Simulation Training Systems.

Smallen, D. (1993). Reengineering of student learning? A second opinion from camelot. In R. Heterick, Jr. (Ed.), *In reengineering teaching and learning in higher education Vol. 10* (pp. 15-20). Boulder, Co: CAUSE ED.

Terenzini, P., & Pascarella, E. (1994, January/February). Living with myths: Undergraduate education in America. *Change Magazine,* 28-32.

Tinto, V. (1993). *Leaving college: Rethinking the causes and cures of student attrition* (2nd ed.). Chicago: University of Chicago.

Van Dusen, G. C. (1997). *The virtual campus: Technology: Technology and reform in higher education* (1st ed. vol. 25, no. 5). Washington, DC: The George Washington University, Graduate School of Education and Human Development.

Wingspread Group on Higher Education (1993). *An American imperative: Higher expectations for higher education: An open letter to those concerned about the future.* Racine, WI: Johnson Foundation. Retrieved November 15, 1999 from http://www.johnsonfdn.org/library/foundpub/amerimp/index.html

Developing Curricular and Co-Curricular Leadership Programs

Jonathan C. Dooley
Marquette University
Kathy M. Shellogg
Nebraska Wesleyan University

Empowering students to learn and experience leadership on campus, become stakeholders in their institution, and understand the value of leadership and civic engagement is a component of institutional missions for many colleges and universities. It is also an issue of satisfaction and importance for today's students. We are past the era when undergraduate leadership experiences are luxuries for a few campuses or can be designed to reach only an elite portion of the student population. In its 1993 report on imperatives of American higher education, the Wingspread Group articulated society's needs from higher education, including "stronger more vital forms of community, ...an informed and involved citizenry, ...[and] graduates able to assume leadership roles in American life." However, it warned, *"higher education is not meeting these imperatives"* (Opening section, para. 9). Thus, all students must learn the new paradigms of citizenship that will be expected of them as they emerge from their institutions to assume leadership roles in their professions and communities.

In addition to the benefits to society, leadership education at the undergraduate level has tremendous positive impact on the individual student participant. The Council for the Advancement of Standards (CAS) recommends that institutions of higher education provide activities, both curricular and co-curricular, that include three elements: leadership training, education, and development (2001). This chapter explores the benefits of leadership programs for undergraduate students, particularly first-year students, and examines several models that effectively involve first-year students in the development of leadership. We also present a planning model that serves as a guide for campuses to assess current leadership education and identify the gaps in programs and experiences. The model provides a framework for engaging the campus community (academic and student affairs educators and students) in a five-step process that fosters institutional commitment to leadership development. Such commitment is crucial to the incorporation of leadership education into the institutional fabric. We recognize that organizational structure and culture, regardless of mission, may not allow even the best leadership planning and implementation process to take root. To assist campuses in their efforts to enhance leadership training, education, and development, the chapter also describes barriers and limitations in using the model and lessons learned from educators involved in undergraduate leadership programs and courses.

Importance and Benefit of Leadership Development Programs

Many of the issues facing American society are compounded by problems of leadership. In recent years, government, corporations, educational institutions, and religious organizations have suffered crises of leadership. In *Leadership Reconsidered*, Astin and Astin (2000) suggest that the "important 'leadership development' challenge for higher education is to empower students, by helping them develop those special talents and attitudes that will enable them to become effective social change agents" (p. 2). To help students meet the challenges of leadership, colleges and universities must marshal their resources to maximize opportunities for students to engage in the work critical to society and the community. Campuses must serve as models of effective leadership and creative problem solving early and throughout a college student's career.

Early research on the generation of students entering colleges and universities today suggests that these students are more confident, team-oriented, and focused on achievement than previous generations. After years of free agency, social splintering, and declines in civic participation, some speculate that the current generation of students is more likely to balance the needs of the community with the individual, collaborate effectively to develop creative solutions to social problems, and engage actively as citizens in their communities. They are challenging their adult mentors, who have been vocal supporters of community service but less frequently active participants in it. Today's teens, on average, spend more hours doing community service than members of the "Baby Boom" generation (Howe & Strauss, 2000).

The combination of a crisis in leadership and the emergence of a generation with tremendous potential to reverse recent negative trends means colleges and universities are poised to have a positive impact on leadership in American society. Research suggests that the development of leadership skills as an undergraduate is associated more with the college experience than with mere maturation or other factors (Astin, 1993). This is due, in large part, to the fact that higher education institutions provide unique opportunities for students to learn and experience leadership. Curricular and co-curricular experiences engage students in the collaborative process of leadership and encourage them to explore values and develop skills, which in turn foster an understanding of the opportunities they have to create positive change in the broader community. Institutions have developed a number of creative approaches to expose students to leadership development and to solicit their participation in a variety of activities serving the institution or broader community (Boatman, 1997; Zimmerman-Oster & Burkhardt, 1999). These approaches include leadership courses, workshops, and seminars; orientation and new student programs; participation in clubs and organizations; community service and service-learning; mentoring and tutoring programs; and student employment and volunteer work experiences.

In their survey of research on student learning outside the classroom, Whitt and Miller (1999) summarize the impact of student experiences on a variety of personal competencies. Involvement in clubs and organizations and participation in leadership roles are tied to gains in cognitive development, interpersonal competence, intrapersonal competence, and practical competence. Several of these competencies are also correlated with participation in volunteer service activities, attendance at racial or cultural awareness workshops, and interaction with faculty outside the classroom—important components of many leadership development programs.

In its research on the impact of two leadership development experiences for first-year students, the Office of Institutional Research and Planning (2002) at Central Michigan University found that students who participated in two of the university's leadership programs for first-year students earned higher first-term grade point averages and had higher average rates of retention than their peers who did not participate in one or both programs. Although these leadership development experiences tended to attract students with higher than average entering credentials and first-year performance, the positive relationships between first-term GPA and retention were associated with the programs even after the effects of ACT scores, gender, and ethnicity were addressed.

Broader research has confirmed that involvement in extra-curricular activities and interaction with peers and faculty have a positive influence on retention, attainment of a bachelor's degree, and graduate school attendance (Pascarella & Terenzini, 1991). Leadership development is also associated with activities such as tutoring other students, performing community service, and participating in campus demonstrations (Astin, 1993). Involvement in leadership development and extra-curricular activities also has the potential for future personal benefits for students—including improving self-confidence and interpersonal and leadership skills. Alumni report that the effects of this participation were also important to their job success, although not necessarily career mobility or earnings (Pascarella & Terenzini, 1991). Students who experience leadership development through mentoring initiatives report greater satisfaction with their undergraduate experience, and LaVant, Anderson, and Tiggs (1997) found this to be especially true for minority students— African-American males, in particular.

Tinto (1985) reports that students who are involved in student activities are more likely to continue their education than their less-involved peers. He suggests that successful retention plans must pay attention to both the academic and social aspects of the student experience. Bedford and Durkee's (1989) review of research on the impact of orientation courses and student leadership programs on retention concluded that orientation courses were an important means of assisting new students with their adjustment to college. In addition, leadership development programs such as retreats and workshops and involvement in leadership roles within student organizations were seen as important factors in the retention of students and their social orientation to college and peers. Simply put, "encouraging participation and leadership in extracurricular activities helps students feel a part of the institution, develop friendships, and find their place on campus" (Bedford & Durkee, 1989, pp. 170-171). To the degree that students' participation in leadership training, education, and development helps them forge a connection with the campus and local communities, institutions benefit from including these activities as important core experiences for first-year students.

Models of Curricular and Co-Curricular Programs for First-Year Students

A number of colleges and universities provide excellent leadership development experiences targeted specifically to the unique needs of first-year students. Each of the programs described below represents a creative response to the desire to help students develop their leadership potential from the start of their college experience. The examples provided certainly are not an exhaustive list of programs but represent a diverse array of approaches to leadership development.

Leadership Camp and Leadership Safari, Central Michigan University

Even before students take their first class at Central Michigan University, they have an opportunity to involve themselves in leadership experiences that develop their skills and encourage growth. Leadership Camp takes place in mid-May, and two three-day sessions are conducted for approximately 80 incoming students who have accepted admission to the university but are still completing their high school careers. The itinerary for the program guides students through a series of experiences that reinforce the seven values of *The Social Change Model for Leadership Development* (Higher Education Research Institute, 1996): (a) consciousness of self, (b) commitment, (c) congruence, (d) common purpose, (e) collaboration,

"A number of colleges and universities provide excellent leadership development experiences targeted specifically to the unique needs of first-year students."

(f) controversy with civility, and (g) citizenship. During the Leadership Camp, students explore these individual, group, and community values, and they are challenged to put their definition of citizenship into practice through a service-learning experience.

Leadership Safari, another program under the umbrella of the Central Michigan Leadership Institute, has grown from 65 participants in its inaugural year in 1997 to 950 participants in 2001. The program takes place just prior to the start of classes and targets first-year and transfer students, encouraging them to learn more about leadership and leadership opportunities at Central Michigan. Using a character development model, conference participants are assigned to small groups led by upperclass student leaders. These facilitators help students reflect on the experiences of the two main conference components: speakers and team activities. Topics covered in the program include ethical decision making, respect for diversity, caring for team members, and active involvement as a community member.

Students Taking Active Roles, Marquette University (WI)

Created in 1986, the Students Taking Active Roles (S.T.A.R.) program at Marquette University offers character development activities to new student leaders at the institution. Students apply to the program during their first two weeks on campus, and many are recommended for participation by upperclass orientation leaders and resident assistants, or by faculty and administrators. The program is intentionally small, involving only 80 students, in order to foster strong relationships that encourage a climate of growth and trust.

The experience begins with a weekend retreat, led by a team of diverse upperclass student leaders. The retreat introduces participants to the program and each other and orients them to the learning cycle of action and reflection used throughout the remainder of the semester. A series of bi-weekly seminars are led by upperclass student leaders and are sequenced to foster the development of character and leadership in par-

ticipants. Seminar topics include empathy, diversity, leadership expressed in service to others, leadership styles, gender roles, and facilitating change efforts. The program challenges students to consider how the discussions they have with their peers will help them become more empathic student leaders when interacting with others. At the conclusion of the program, students reflect on how they might use what they have discovered about themselves to contribute to student organizations or campus leadership roles in offices such as residence life or new student orientation. Participants indicate that they feel more equipped to recognize social injustice or gaps in leadership within the Marquette or Milwaukee communities and communicate with peers, administrators, and faculty to initiate change. In the semester following the program, many S.T.A.R. participants continue the experience on their own by organizing a group service project and facilitating the sessions they have experienced for their peers on residence hall floors or in student groups.

Leadership, Excellence, and Community, Miami University (OH)

The Leadership, Excellence, and Community program was created in 1996 as a cooperative effort of the offices of Residence Life; New Student Programs; and Student Leadership, Campus and Community Life at Miami University. Developed to address a need for leadership education, the program is one of several theme learning communities offered at Miami for first-year students. The goal of the program is to help students develop their philosophy of leadership and understand how they can have an impact on the practice of leadership at any level of an organization. Participants enroll in a two-credit seminar on leadership and are involved in a variety of activities, including an opening convocation for the community, a campus-wide leadership conference, and service projects. The partnership used in the design of the program not only brings faculty and instructors into the residence halls, but also reinforces the concept that learning is everywhere and leadership is gained in a variety of settings and through diverse experiences.

In addition to an intentional integration of curricular and co-curricular experiences, the course is heavily dependent on technology, using online course materials, quizzes, discussion boards, and journals to supplement traditional classroom activities. With multiple sections of the course taught throughout the theme community, the technology also facilitates consistency of content across sections while allowing for instructor flexibility in the group process. Course content emphasizes historical approaches to leadership, student analysis of these approaches, and conceptualization of how both historical and emergent leadership perspectives are related to students' personal understandings of leadership. In an evaluation of the program conducted with student participants in 2000, students reported that although their ideas about leadership had not drastically changed, they had reinforced concepts such as "collaboration in leadership is paramount; leadership is not positionally defined; diverse perspectives must be encouraged; and the leader is an agent of change" (Roberts & Ahren, 2001, p. 42).

Residential Leadership Program, Nebraska Wesleyan University

Leadership development opportunities in most residential facilities are focused on resident assistants, hall council members, and residence hall association leadership. Beginning in 2000, Nebraska Wesleyan University modified a traditional community standards model, based on a developmental perspective of learning (King & Baxter Magolda, 1999), to provide all students in residence with the opportunity to learn individual and group skills of transformational leadership. The changes were made in response to the challenge facing many residence life professionals to develop programs for all students living in residential units, not just those serving on the staff or involved with the hall council. Nebraska Wesleyan also bases its model on the work of Astin and Astin (2000), who encourage the formation of "communities of reciprocal care and shared responsibility where every person matters and each person's welfare and dignity is respected and supported" (p. 11).

All residents receive "initial standards" during the first week of the academic year. These standards focus on basic tenants of safety and security for the floor. Within the first four weeks, floors use the initial standards and, as a community, establish a first set of their own standards. They must collaborate as a group to reach consensus in developing the community's standards (no voting is allowed). At the same time, individual living units establish roommate standards, which focus on self-knowledge, authenticity, empathy, and commitment to the created standards. All individual standards are given to peer assistants to review so that they are assured that each resident has a commitment to upholding the standards. If the peer assistant believes that the effort made on the roommate standards does not show commitment, then he or she works with each resident to explore his or her skill readiness for creating the agreement. During a conflict, peer assistants always use roommate standards as the basis for resolving the issue. Thus, the process models continuous learning. Because both floor standards and roommate standards are based on a process model of leadership, they change throughout the year. As issues arise on a floor, midterm exams approach, or standards are broken, residents revisit standards and make changes to accommodate new concerns. One student can call a meeting if he or she would like to revisit or propose modifications to standards.

An essential component of the program's success is the training of peer assistants. Experiential learning techniques are used with peer assistants; the process of developing individual and community standards for the hall is modeled in the creation of standards for the training experience. They also learn a set of skills called FLASH tools (Schultz, 2002) that encourage individuals and groups to approach disagreements with respect and empathy. The tools were initially established to teach confrontation skills relating to alcohol misuse and abuse and include five main concepts: (a) say what you see, (b) say how you feel, (c) say what you know, (d) set your boundaries, and (e) offer hope. The tools are modeled by the peer assistant staff and taught to residents through the development and revision of the standards.

Evaluation of the residential climate has shown that the standards approach fosters responsible communities and helps residents and peer assistants learn more about the process of leadership and the skills needed for the development of transformational leadership.

Leadership Development Studies, Phi Theta Kappa International Honor Society

Community colleges often enroll a broader student population than their traditional four-year counterparts, serving everyone from traditional-aged students studying full-time and preparing to transfer to four-year institutions to older students attending classes part-time for workforce retraining or career change. Traditional-aged students attending two-year colleges full-time often have greater opportunity than their peers at four-year institutions to become involved in significant leadership roles earlier in their educational careers. Shorter tenures for community college students, however, can create problems of continuity as organizations and programs transition between leadership teams. These factors combine to present a unique challenge for leadership training, education, and development programs for students in their first year at a two-year college. Many community colleges take advantage of the curriculum offered by the Phi Theta Kappa International Honor Society of the Two-Year College to offer a course in leadership studies that encourages students to explore the concept of leadership, consider their own philosophy of leadership, and develop and improve their leadership skills. Eleven units with titles such as "Articulating a Vision," "Leading with Goals," "Empowering and Delegating," "Initiating Change," "Applying Ethics to Leadership," and "Leading by Serving" are designed to integrate contemporary and classic readings, films, and experiential learning to foster knowledge acquisition and skill development. To remain accessible to the broad audience that community colleges serve, the curriculum is interdisciplinary and centers on readings from the humanities.

In addition to the course curriculum, Phi Theta Kappa provides faculty certification seminars, a certificate of applied leadership program, newsletters, and other resources to support participating institutions. The resources are designed to disseminate lessons learned from implementation of the program at individual campuses. Strengths of the program include the well-developed curriculum and teaching documents and the administrative support provided by Phi Theta Kappa, including faculty and administrator professional development activities. Students are also happy with the program: "The majority of students have rated the course as useful and the transfer of concepts as substantial" (Zimmerman-Oster & Burkhardt, 1999, p. 50). More than 450 institutions nationwide have access to the Leadership Studies program of Phi Theta Kappa through the certification process.

Leadership, Ethics, Achievement and Development (LEAD), Sigma Nu Fraternity, Inc.

Greek organizations historically have provided opportunities for first-year students to connect to each other and their institution and to gain leadership experience. Many national fraternities have instituted leadership education programs for new members. One exemplary program is offered by the Sigma Nu Educational Foundation, which provides a means for individual chapters to engage members in a four-phase leadership program that "fosters ethical leadership and a high sense of achievement... encouraging [members] to exemplify leadership in government, business, academia, and the community" (Sigma Nu Fraternity High Council, 2000, p. 3). As part of a broader movement by fraternities nationwide to improve operations and renew a commitment to founding values, individual Sigma Nu chapters have been encouraged to change the culture in their chapters since 1988. Beginning with new members, chapters can become more productive and members more confident and able to provide leadership in their chapters, campuses, and their future careers. New candidates participate in Phase I of the program, which is composed of 10 sessions devoted to traditional orientation education as well as communication and teamwork, project management, values, ethics, and an understanding of the differences between leadership and leading. Phase II and III continue members' individual and group leadership development after they have become fully initiated members of the fraternity. During Phase IV of the program, upperclass members become facilitators of the program and are supported by an alumni consultant and the national headquarters. The program is funded through a campaign launched in 1988 by the national organization, and thus chapters require only time and dedication to implement a well-developed leadership education program that spans a collegian's four years.

A Process Model to Enhance Leadership Education and Development

Most post-secondary institutions offer opportunities for leadership training, education, and development for their students. In this respect, campuses can be viewed as "leadership laboratories" (Boatman, 1997), but not all students, particularly first-year students, have opportunities to participate. All campuses should provide a comprehensive approach to leadership development or education that takes root during the critical first year of a student's college career. An intentional approach to leadership education that fosters retention requires planning and analysis so that gaps in leadership education and development opportunities can be evaluated. We provide a model planning process that can be used in a community or higher education setting to encourage a more coordinated and collaborative approach to leadership education between student affairs and faculty educators. It evolved from an economic and community development approach to coordinating planning and development efforts in communities. The process model can help campuses enhance, redirect, or connect co-curricular and curricular efforts, creating a more seamless leadership education experience for all students. One of the authors has used the model in a variety of settings, including a comprehensive public university and two private liberal arts institutions.

Creating the Work Group

Selecting a diverse ensemble of stakeholders will ensure effective planning and implementation. This group should be committed to leadership, the planning process, and gaining institutional commitment to pursue opportunities that are uncovered. A typical work group would involve key faculty, administrators, and students who are engaged in the study or practice of leadership or in the education of leaders on campus. Faculty in social sciences, business, education, and communication often study and teach courses about leaders and leadership. These faculty, along with staff from campus activities, leadership programs, Greek life, orientation, and other student affairs educators, can form a team. A work group committed to reviewing leadership education for first-year students might also include admissions or enrollment management staff and faculty who teach first-year courses. Key to the success of the work group is a phenomenon Bennis and Biederman (1997) call "dual administration." Two individuals support the effectiveness of the group: a visionary leader or facilitator, who leads the group and believes in the planning process and its intended outcomes, and a key administrator, who will support, protect, and embrace the group's work in the overall institutional structure. This dual leader structure allows the group to be creative with few constraints and protects it from outside interference and politics.

Phase I: Aligning the Work Group

Once the group has formed, a series of questions must be addressed in order to align the members and clarify goals. First, the compelling reasons for developing, enhancing, or coordinating leadership efforts in the campus community must be ascertained. The group members must then determine what values will guide their planning process. They must identify what leadership education and development means or should look like at their institution. Using the answers to these

"Most post-secondary institutions offer opportunities for leadership training, education, and development for their students."

questions, the alignment phase results in a statement of philosophy for the campus community about leadership development and education. Finally, the group must agree to a set of assumptions about leadership education that will drive the planning process and resulting program modifications. For example, some assumptions might be that leadership is a process; leadership opportunities are open to all students; a special emphasis should be placed on opportunities for first-year students; or the institution's mission will guide leadership training, education, and development.

Phase II: Assessment

The overall goal of Phase II of the planning process is for the group to discover their feelings about leadership, the current opportunities for leadership development and education, the climate for creating new initiatives, and the perceived need for an intentional leadership education emphasis on the campus. The activities in this phase focus on identifying the gap between the group's new philosophy and assumptions and the values, beliefs, and facts about leadership that exist in the campus climate and culture. Thus, bridging the gap becomes the work of the group and lays the foundation for what leadership development and educational opportunities might look like in the future. In this phase of planning, the work group must determine benchmarks or milestones that will guide the pace of the process. Group members must also explore both the facts and feelings about leadership in their current campus climate. Assessment strategies often include focus groups, surveys, faculty and staff discussions, as well as curricular and co-curricular audits. Once the assessment is complete, a gap analysis provides the group with an opportunity to stop the planning process or move forward. The outcome of this phase is the development of a mission, goals, and objectives that will guide the actual development of curricular and co-curricular programs. Siegel's chapter in this monograph provides a more in-depth treatment of assessment practice related to the first year of college.

Phase III: Development

The goal of the development phase is to close the gap between current leadership opportunities and the campus' desire to enhance existing programs or develop new initiatives. Setting long- and short-term goals that account for institutional budget cycles, external funding objectives, reorganization strategies, and curricular cycles helps to prioritize the opportunities that may emerge during the development phase. Modifications and new courses or programs are prioritized with funding and staffing needs in mind. Examples of short-term goals include the creation of a new co-curricular program, implementation of a change to an existing training activity, or revision of a course syllabus. Longer-term goals might include the development of new curricular programs, enhancement of leadership resources and libraries, reorganization of individual responsibilities or organizational systems, or solicitation of external funding sources for new initiatives. The outcome of the phase is to describe what current programs or courses can be enhanced and establish the priority for those goals.

Phase IV: Implementation

The results of the development phase are put into action during implementation. The focus of the work group's role now becomes monitoring the progress of the key stakeholders responsible for implementing the changes proposed by the group in the previous phase. Although the group does not disband, formal work is over until short- or long-term goals are completed and ready for evaluation. During this phase, the members of the work group may be involved in providing recommendations for components of pilot programs, reviewing a proposed curriculum, or assisting with training activities. The time required for implementation may vary from a semester to three years, but if the process has been well designed time is not wasted.

Phase V: Evaluation

The final formal stage of the planning process is evaluation. How and when evaluation occurs and the model used is determined by the strategies and solutions used by the work group in each of the previous phases. The following questions guide the evaluation work:

1. Have the short-term program goals been achieved?
2. Are the mission and objectives still relevant or do they require modification?
3. Have any changes in the institutional climate occurred that impact the program goals?
4. What has been the impact of new knowledge, actions, or attitudes about leadership on campus as a result of the implementation process?

Depending on the results of the first phase of evaluation and on the stability in the organization's climate, continued implementation would typically follow the results of a first evaluation. The length of time that has passed since the initial formation of the work group, the number and significance of changes in group membership, or shifting institutional priorities will all help determine the appropriate phase of the model that should follow evaluation. Major changes may require realignment and return to the first phase, while some evaluation results may call for further assessment or point to a need to simply re-tool the goals that were outlined in the development phase. If progress is positive, the group can seek institutional commitment to its ongoing work and continue its attention to leadership training, development, and education.

Barriers and Limitations of the Model

Although most institutions of higher education make it a goal to develop citizen leaders for the future, not all colleges and universities see it as a priority. During times of financial crisis, the landscape of higher education changes for many institutions. Some of the strongest institutions must refocus goals and plan for long-term fiscal health and stability, laying off staff and faculty, eliminating departments, or reorganizing to create leaner, more adaptive institutions. Unless leadership education is already woven into the fabric of an institution's culture, it may not be fiscally prudent to enhance and increase leadership training, education, and development activities on a campus that is trying to adapt to changing economic conditions and student demographics. In simple terms, timing is critical.

Other barriers can impede the success of even the best-developed and executed process model to enhance leadership education and development. One of the most devastating organizational barriers to the planning process is what is commonly referred to as the "silo mentality," either among colleges and departments who view their role as *the* leadership educators or between academic and student affairs divisions. An institution's "comfort factor" can also be a barrier to developing comprehensive leadership opportunities for all students. The fear of change in an uncertain climate can prevent the work group's recommendations from being instituted. Individuals must come to the process in an environment that embraces change, created by a community, not just *within* a community. Members of a planning group must feel free to redirect their energy and talent in order to realize a vision that is best for the community. Without an environment that supports collaborative change, the model will not be successful.

There is no substitute for good data on enrollment and retention when planning for leadership education and development. For example, if first-year students are not connecting to campus and retention numbers between the end of the first year and the beginning of the second indicate a pattern of poor retention, a strong justification can be made for a planning process that explores leadership education and development for first-year students. Without this data and other supporting evidence, assessment strategies critical to an effective gap analysis cannot be conducted.

Finally, because many higher education institutions are hierarchical, they operate in a manner that aligns leadership with positional power. Heifetz (1995) notes that we have always had a tendency to "equate leadership with authority," (p. 49) even though those in positions of authority may not be engaging in effective leadership. In organizations where the mode of operating is always "someone else is in charge of making those decisions," the process model described above has a formidable obstacle in creating a comprehensive model for leadership development and education.

If timing is right, assessment data is reliable and accessible, institutional leadership is effective, and a critical cadre of faculty, administrators, and students can be enlisted, then the planning model can serve as an important process for enhancing leadership training, education, and development.

Lessons Learned

All students, faculty, staff, and administrators in an educational community hold the responsibility of leadership education and development in their collective and individual hands. The imperative to grow a new generation of citizen leaders is everyone's responsibility. No group is more important than another, no individual more or less critical. If leadership education for students is not a community concern, then it will remain a single program or series of efforts that fail to encourage students to discover their capacity for leadership. Leadership programs, both curricular and co-curricular, are critical for first-year students. Many students entering higher education institutions today want to be involved in the campus community, but often require additional skills, education, or general knowledge to do so effectively. Leadership experiences during the first year will prepare students for deeper levels of involvement and provide a stronger connection to community, both of which will improve rates of student retention.

Research on the impact of involvement and leadership development on students and the example of model leadership development programs, as well as our own experience, suggest tremendous benefits to students, the institution, and the broader community when leadership training, education, and development programs are presented to students throughout their undergraduate career. Not only must the institutional community value and collectively engage students in leadership development, but it must also couple these values with a systems approach that explores retention and provides first-year opportunities for leadership development. Such an effort will yield the greatest results. Engaging the campus community in a process that explores both the current and potential impact of leadership training, education, and development programs and working collectively to address the gap between them will not only benefit individual students, but also potentially transform the institution and broader community.

References

Astin, A. W. (1993). *What matters in college: Four critical years revisited.* San Francisco: Jossey-Bass.

Astin, A. W., & Astin, H. S. (Eds.). (2000). *Leadership reconsidered: Engaging higher education in social change.* Battle Creek, MI: W. K. Kellogg Foundation.

Bedford, M. H., & Durkee, P. E. (1989). Retention: Some more ideas. *NASPA Journal, 27*(2), 168-171.

Bennis, W., & Biederman, P. W. (1997). *Organizing genius, The secrets of creative collaboration.* Cambridge, MA: Perseus Publishing.

Boatman, S. A. (1997). Student leadership development: Approaches, methods, and models. In N. Walborn, & M. Cuyjet (Eds.), *Management of Campus Activities Series* (No. 2). Columbia, SC: National Association for Campus Activities Educational Foundation.

Council for the Advancement of Standards (CAS). (2001). *The book of professional standards for higher education 2001.* Washington, DC: Author.

Heifetz, R. (1995). *Leadership without easy answers.* Cambridge, MA: Harvard University Press.

Higher Education Research Institute (1996). *A social change model of leadership development: Guidebook, Version III.* Los Angeles: Graduate School of Education and Information Studies, University of California.

Howe, N., & Strauss, W. (2000). *Millennials rising: The next great generation.* New York: Vintage Books.

King, P., & Baxter Magolda, M. B. (1999). A developmental perspective on learning. *Journal of College Student Development, 40,* 599-609.

LaVant, B. D., Anderson, J. L., & Tiggs, J. W. (1997). Retaining African American men through mentoring initiatives. In M. Cuyjet (Ed.), Helping African American men succeed in college. *New Directions for Student Services* (No. 80), San Francisco: Jossey-Bass.

Office of Institutional Research & Planning. (2002). *Analysis of Camp and Safari participants 1998-2001.* Unpublished manuscript, Central Michigan University.

Pascarella, E. T., & Terenzini, P. T. (1991). *How college affects students.* San Francisco: Jossey-Bass.

Roberts, D., & Ahren, C. (2001). *Technology enhanced leadership education: Miami University 1st-year leadership seminar.* Presented at the American College Personnel Association National Convention, Boston, MA.

Schultz, O. (2002). *Flashing your brights: Toolkit for participants.* Lincoln, NE: Starfish Enterprises, Ltd.

Sigma Nu Fraternity High Council (2000). *Sigma Nu ethical leadership manual: Phase I participant manual.* Lexington, VA: Sigma Nu Fraternity, Inc.

Tinto, V. (1985). Dropping out and other forms of withdrawal from college. In L. Noel, R. S. Levitz, D. Saluri, & Associates (Eds.), *Increasing student retention.* San Francisco, Jossey-Bass.

Whitt, E. J., & Miller, T. E. (1999). Student learning outside the classroom: What does the research tell us? In E. J. Whitt (Ed.), *Student learning as student affairs work.* NASPA Monograph Series (No. 23). Washington, DC: National Association of Student Personnel Administrators.

Wingspread Group on Higher Education (1993). *An American imperative: Higher expectations for higher education.* Retrieved December 1, 2002 from http://www.johnsonfdn.org/library/foundpub/amerimp/

Zimmerman-Oster, K., & Burkhardt, J. C. (1999). *Leadership in the making: Impact and insights from leadership development programs in U.S. colleges and universities.* Battle Creek, MI: W. K. Kellogg Foundation.

Authors' Note

Special thanks to Monika Byrd, Phi Theta Kappa International Honor Society; Lucy LePeau, Marquette University; Dennis Roberts, Miami University; and Kim Voisin, Central Michigan University, for providing information on their leadership program models. We are also grateful for Mark McCarthy, Marquette University, and Nancy Mathias, St. Norbert College, who provided review and commentary on earlier drafts of this chapter.

Providing Alternatives to Less Positive Activities: A Case Study of Changing Campus Culture

Kenneth D. Gray
Gerald E. Lang
Mary L. Collins
West Virginia University

Crisp, fall afternoons in a football stadium full of cheering fans, animated classroom debates, putting on the cap and gown after the last test is over and the final paper turned in—as administrators, we do our best to ensure our students enjoy a positive college experience in and out of the classroom.

But what about the less positive activities that are also often part of college life, all those things we don't mention in our view books or discuss on our campus tours? What about house parties and all-you-can-drink bar specials?

While it is not pleasant to consider the reality of this aspect of college life, especially the abuse of alcohol, ignoring it is not only foolish but also dangerous. By now the reality is, or should be, familiar to most college administrators. Several national studies confirm the problem of alcohol abuse at our schools, linking it to numerous negative outcomes including property damage, unprotected sex, assaults, injuries, and even death. (Abbey, 1991; Presley, Leichliter, & Meilman, 1999; Wechsler, Lee, Kuo, & Lee, 2000). Alcohol and drug abuse are linked to poor academic performance and are likely the reason that many students do not complete their education (Eigen, 1991). Moreover, campus alcohol abuse also often affects those who do not drink, as approximately 600,000 students are assaulted by a drinking student each year (Engs, Diebold, & Hansen, 1996).

As administrators at institutions of higher education, we must be concerned when the education we provide is compromised by students engaged in these less positive activities. Closing our eyes won't make these problems disappear and often makes them worse. In this chapter, we present a case study of West Virginia University, describing a campus culture that necessitated change and outlining a series of programs implemented on the campus over the last seven years to create that change and provide alternatives to less positive activities.

WVU's Approach: Creating Alternatives in Partnership with Students

WVU is a land-grant institution recognized by the Carnegie Foundation for the Advancement of Teaching as a Doctoral/Research University-Extensive. WVU is also the state's comprehensive institution of higher education, with a College of Law and the complete suite of health science disciplines—medicine, dentistry, pharmacy, nursing, and physical and occupational therapy. As an institution, it is also a top-100 research university.

These parameters define the academic environment of the campus. Faculty are hired to pursue an aggressive research agenda, students are involved in research, and rigorous academic programs change continually to meet challenges of an ever increasing knowledge base.

But if the staff at WVU had any inclination to keep their heads in the sand and push on with the traditional way of doing business, that notion was quickly changed in the mid-90s. Enrollment had been dropping, and the school was facing a decline in the state high school population through 2011—this in a state that already had one of the lowest college-going rates in the nation.

At the same time, student behavior was deteriorating, and a party image was prevalent. Each year a back-to-school student block party, where thousands of young people would take to the streets to celebrate the first day of classes, was attracting revelers from far and wide. Throughout the years, as the tradition grew in popularity and attendance, so did the unruly behavior. In 1994 the block party spiraled out of control when two students were shot by non-students.

Football season each year brought its own worries. An unsanctioned student tailgating area became a mire of mud, fights, and assaults before each game. Numerous injuries and arrests occurred in the area during the 1996 season, culminating in a night game during which more than 75 people were taken to local emergency rooms. In the stadium itself, spectators sustained injuries from cups and bottles thrown by students and other fans. Not surprisingly, WVU received very negative press around the state and country.

As a capstone marker, the *Princeton Review* in 1997 bestowed upon WVU the title of number one party school in the nation. This led to another flood of negative publicity and caused both potential students and employers to shy away from the university. Parents and alumni were rightly concerned about campus safety and our image, respectively.

In spite of this, WVU's underlying academic foundation was still strong enough to continue producing well-educated students, some recognized as Rhodes Scholars, Goldwater Scholars, and Truman Scholars. The majority of the students went on to successful careers. However, that foundation was being severely tested, and it was clear that fundamental changes would have to be made, and soon.

Change is Needed

In 1995, as David C. Hardesty, Jr. prepared to assume the presidency of WVU, he took the advice offered to former Harvard president Derek Bok to heart, that the most creative ideas about the future of Harvard would come to Bok before he took office and got involved in his official duties as president of the institution. (Bok, 1986). Seeing the wisdom in those words, Hardesty carefully reviewed the situation at WVU after he was appointed president but before taking office. He identified several problems in addition to the party scene and the dropping enrollment, including a general lack of respect both to students and by students.

By the time he arrived on campus, Hardesty was prepared to address these issues. On his first day as president, July 5, 1995, he held a press conference and announced that West Virginia University was going to become a student-centered institution. A new vision statement confirming that commitment was established:

> West Virginia University is a student-centered learning community meeting the changing needs of West Virginia and the nation through teaching, research, service, and technology.

Realizing the immediate and imperative need to make the student-centered and service aspects of WVU's new vision a reality, President Hardesty created a Student Affairs Task Force, comprised of 20 representatives from the campus and community. This group evaluated and suggested improvements for all aspects of student life at WVU and in the surrounding community, including technology, administrative organization, quality-of-life, student services, class attendance, early intervention strategies, facilities, advising, and career development.

Several recommendations were implemented, the first being a restructuring of student affairs leadership, from an associate provost position to a vice president, whose primary role would be as an advocate for students. A retired major general and assistant judge advocate general of the U.S. Army was hired as vice president. This was a non-traditional choice for a student affairs leader, but he brought strong administrative, leadership, and management skills.

Together, the president, provost, and the new vice president for student affairs, along with many others from across the University, led a slow but steady redirection of the focus of West Virginia University. To implement a student-centered environment, we turned away from bureaucracy and red tape and toward student service and friendliness, away from top-down administration and toward collaboration with students and their families, away from the party image and toward a focus on learning.

These changes were promoted through various marketing efforts. Through brochures, viewbooks, ads, and recruitment literature, programs were featured individually and also as part of a collective suite of offerings from WVU. Both potential and current students and their families were targeted in an effort to increase enrollment and retention. The first-year orientation course was also used to introduce the changes taking place on campus. Student government became vocal, proactive supporters for the new programs. Students and parents were included on committees, ensuring that the foundation of these new programs would be student-centered.

Creating the Ultimate First-Year Experience

To provide a foundation for future academic and personal success for our students, we created what we believe is the ultimate first-year experience. A diverse series of programs and initiatives under the umbrella Operation Jump-Start provide a solid start for students. The focal point of this program was and is to personalize the first-year experience. We hoped this firm foundation would result in improved retention and an improved student experience.

The goals established for Operation Jump-Start include

- ◆ Recruiting and retaining quality students and faculty
- ◆ Ensuring academic success
- ◆ Personalizing the first-year experience
- ◆ Changing the culture of residence halls and campus to a more student-centered, academic focus
- ◆ Providing opportunities for student-faculty involvement
- ◆ Encouraging healthy lifestyles
- ◆ Raising expectations
- ◆ Demonstrating that WVU is student-centered
- ◆ Developing residential learning communities

Residential learning is one of the cornerstones of the program. Developed in 1996, residential learning communities feature outstanding faculty mentors who live near each residence hall. Resident faculty leaders (RFLs) provide motivation and encouragement to students living in the residence halls, and help first-year students with the transition to college life, thereby creating a support system of Residential Education on WVU's campus.

Giving First-Year Students a Jump-Start

To further assist first-year students with the transition to college life, we developed a three-day orientation program called Jump-Start Academy that takes place the weekend before classes begin and in which the entire first-year class participates. Jump-Start Academy addresses many issues faced by students through a series of workshops and seminars. Students attend talks on campus safety; they learn about making safe choices regarding sex,

> "To provide a foundation for future academic and personal success for our students, we created what we believe is the ultimate first-year experience."

alcohol, drugs, and dating; and in small groups they meet with their individual RFL, resident hall coordinator, and resident assistants.

Jump-Start Academy is highly successful and not only gives students important information and advice, but also sets an important tone for the beginning of the semester. It culminates on Sunday afternoon with the New Student Convocation, during which the WVU administration, dressed in full academic regalia, join with local community leaders to welcome the students and provide encouragement for their academic careers.

Our efforts to support first-year students have continued to evolve through a partnership between student affairs and academic affairs.

Creating a Mandatory Orientation Course for All First-Year Students

The faculty senate approved a mandatory orientation course, University 101, as a one-credit, graded course, effective fall 2002 for all first-year students who are not enrolled in a major that already has an orientation course. To strengthen the sense of community, each class section is filled with students from the same residence hall, with the classes taught in the residence halls. Each residence hall hosts 9 to 10 sections of the orientation course.

An associate dean of student affairs and residential education and director of the RFLs re-wrote the syllabus and textbook for the course. Rather than using a generic textbook, he wrote a student workbook personalized to our campus that includes chapters on study skills, learning strategies, campus life, and resources at West Virginia University.

An important component of the University 101 course is the Jump-Start Programming Series, a faculty and staff lecture series that is implemented in each of our seven residence halls. This series includes five talks on health education topics and four academic and faculty topics. Students enrolled in University 101 are required to attend six of the talks offered in their own hall and to provide a brief written abstract.

Bringing Faculty and Education into the Residence Halls

Each year, faculty members are invited to the residence halls to give talks about their research or current events or social issues. They are also invited to have dinner with students before the program. Topics have included American society's fascination with the icon of the angel, censorship and the Internet, witchcraft trials in 17th century New England, triumphs and tribulations in African-American history, what killed the dinosaurs, terraforming Mars, and the possibility of life on Mars. In addition, professional staff members from University Health Services Center give talks on sexual assault prevention, alcohol awareness, stress and coping with college, and sexually transmitted diseases.

Students turn out in the hundreds to attend these talks. These programs break down the barriers that sometimes exist between first-year students and faculty and help the students become comfortable in approaching and talking to faculty.

Providing Academic Support in the Residence Halls

When the mid-term grades are released in the fall and spring semesters, RFLs meet with each student individually, discussing his or her academic performance and, if necessary, providing suggestions for getting focused and back on the right track. In these sessions, it sometimes emerges that the student is having a problem with a particular faculty member or course. In such cases, the RFL can speak to the professor on the student's behalf, serving as a true student advocate. These counseling sessions are highly successful. As an example, 75% of the students in Boreman Hall improved their grades to C or higher, and Boreman Hall went from the residence hall having the lowest GPA to having the highest GPA, second only to the honors hall.

Developing Study Skills

The Office of Residential Education has also developed a study skills course that is given in the spring semester to all first-year students with a GPA under 1.0. This provides added support and encouragement to these students and helps them enter their sophomore year in better academic standing.

Fostering Supportive Relationships Between Students and Faculty

RFLs not only provide academic support, they also befriend the students, inviting them to their homes for ice-cream socials, dinners, and meetings. These social events provide an opportunity to find out how the students are adjusting to college, if they are feeling homesick, if they are finding any classes difficult, or if they have problems with residence hall life.

Promoting Cultural and Entertainment Events

In addition to on-campus activities, students also enjoy a wide variety of trips throughout the year. Some trips focus on cultural events (e.g., outings to the opera, ballet, and symphony in Pittsburgh); others are geared toward recreation and outdoor sports (e.g., trips to a nearby theme park, midnight ice-skating, white-water rafting), while others take students to nearby points of historic or cultural interest (e.g., a trip to the Frank Lloyd Wright house, Falling Water). All of these are very successful and the student participation is high.

Listening to the Customers

With the establishment of our new vision and the goals of Operation Jump-Start, a different climate on the campus of West Virginia University began to emerge. The attitude toward our students became one of providing exceptional customer service. As we evaluated our programs, we also began to change our approach. Instead of keeping students at a distance, we pulled them into every committee on campus.

We also involved their families through the newly established Mountaineer Parents Club, based on the successful model at Texas A&M and supported by President Hardesty's wife Susan Brown Hardesty. Today the club has nearly 11,000 members and provides an exceptional venue for communication and support. Out of the Parents Club came the establishment of a Parents Hotline for families with problems, which each year receives thousands of calls and provides just as many solutions.

Throughout all of this, we listened, and we learned, especially as related to those less-positive activities. Several of our students told us that they knew the risks they were taking by indulging in high-risk drinking at bars and house parties, but some continued such behavior because, quite simply, few, if any, alternative social activities were available on the weekends.

They explained that they celebrated before football games in a dangerous, unsanctioned area because no other location was available for them. They attended the block party because they wanted to see their old friends after a long summer and share the excitement of starting another school year.

Our students' families told us that they heard repeated complaints from their students that there was nothing to do on the weekends. Concerned parents related stories of parties and a bar scene too easily accessible to students and shared with us their worries over the atmosphere on campus.

Providing Choice:
The Ultimate First-Year Experience Becomes the Ultimate Student Experience

We were determined to offer our students something they were obviously lacking: alternatives to less positive activities. It wasn't always easy, but students, faculty, administrators, and staff worked closely together to create a series of safe, enjoyable alternatives that were added under the umbrella of Operation Jump-Start. What began as the ultimate first-year experience has since grown into the ultimate student experience, and, we believe, has made WVU a national leader in successfully creating a culture of choice.

Back-to-school still brings a gathering of students, but instead of an unsanctioned block party, more than 15,000 students enjoy FallFest in our student union. This festival includes movie marathons, comedy performers, and musical bands on the student union plaza. The infamous Grant Avenue Block Party, and its inherent risks, has become nothing more than a memory.

Football Saturdays still find student fans tailgating and cheering on the Mountaineers before the game, but now it's in a safe, regulated area where they can enjoy free hotdogs and soft drinks and listen to a local band. Hundreds of gold shirts will be seen in the area, donned by members of the Mountaineer Maniacs, a sports booster club started by the students.

Weekends find our student union packed with thousands of students and guests, enjoying the free food and entertainment of the award-winning and internationally recognized weekend alternative program WVUp All Night. This program was one of the first major initiatives of the new vice president for student affairs. He established a committee chaired by his special assistant and within three months WVUp All Night was in full operation. Up All Night is held on Thursday, Friday, and Saturday nights and attracts 1,000 to 4,000 students to the student union. The wide variety of activities gives students a choice of going to the student union rather than staying in their rooms, going home, or going downtown to the bars.

The summer of 2001 brought the exciting opening of the student recreation center. Students have many choices at the recreation center, including swimming, climbing, jogging, lifting weights, playing basketball, and much more. Thousands of students take advantage of the center daily.

Operation Jump-Start isn't just for first-year students anymore—last year we implemented an enhanced senior year experience. A Senior Council, representing each of WVU's schools and colleges, guides decisions about senior fairs, celebrations, and assistance. This year, members of the senior council began making presentations to first-year students in University 101 courses on how to succeed in college.

Alcohol Abuse Education and Prevention

We have made a long-term commitment toward educating students about the use and abuse of alcohol and other drugs, adding to or strengthening our initiatives. Recognizing that the Greek system has a history of encouraging alcohol abuse, through our Parthenon 2000 program we are limiting the number of parties that fraternities may have and encouraging fraternities to move toward all-dry houses.

Education is an essential component in our efforts and is incorporated into the first-year orientation programs and courses, in residence hall programs, through information tables in the student union, and in more formal classroom settings. This education occurs among peers and with our on-staff alcohol educators.

Other initiatives focused on alcohol education and prevention are described below.

- The Department of Public Safety (DPS) routinely distributes and displays alcohol awareness brochures at various locations around campus and has a booth with an officer on hand to answer questions each semester at the Mountainlair (student union)
- DPS also speaks with students at orientation, advising them of the laws surrounding alcohol use. Students also learn that the crimes for which students are criminally prosecuted most often—date rape, battery, destruction of property—are crimes that typically involve alcohol use.
- The residence life staff receives training on alcohol issues and how to discuss this topic with students.
- University Health Services (UHS) cooperates with the Community Health Promotion (CHPR) program to offer special topics classes. One is "Drug and Alcohol Education for Student Athletes." A second UHS/CHPR class is a drug and alcohol course for student leaders that targets individuals in student organizations. UHS/CHPR also offers a Peer Education Program. Students receive education concerning drug and alcohol issues, particularly as they relate to issues of sexual assault, relationships, and STD and HIV prevention.
- All WVU local and national Greek chapters are required to hold programs edu-

cating members on alcohol and substance abuse.

♦ WVU's School of Medicine operates a web site developed to provide alcohol education for our students and the community.

♦ All fraternity and sorority pledges are required to take a pledge orientation class, which includes a mandatory alcohol education course. This is done in conjunction with University 101 and the Office of Residential Education.

WVU also provides alcohol/substance abuse treatment and interventions. Specific initiatives are described below.

♦ UHS has a Student Assistance Program (SAP) for assessment, treatment and referral of individuals with drug and alcohol problems.

♦ Students sent to Student Life who have on-campus alcohol violations are automatically referred to SAP. The SAP staff determines student treatment and education needs. Students involved in off-campus alcohol-related incidents are required to have a conference with the assistant dean of students. Referrals are made on an as-needed basis.

♦ The Carruth Center for Counseling and Psychological Services Center, part of student affairs, provides individual counseling—confidential, voluntary, and unlimited sessions with licensed psychologists. There is also a telephone hotline in service 24 hours a day, seven days a week, every day the University is in session.

♦ RAs, staff, or residence life administrators refer students to SAP and occasionally Alcoholics Anonymous. Also, our RFLs work closely with students to provide academic support and personal, alcohol, or drug-related help as needed.

♦ All WVU athletes sign a detailed "no-substance abuse" contract and are subject to random drug screening. They at-tend life skills courses and special classes on the dangers of substance abuse.

♦ DPS officers spot check ID cards at athletic or other events to deter underage consumption of alcohol.

♦ WVU sends a congratulatory letter to all students on their 21st birthday, offering them best wishes and tips for a safe celebration.

President Hardesty also reconstituted the WVU Advisory Council for Alcohol and Other Drugs. Chaired by the vice president for student affairs, the Council evaluates and supports efforts impacting the University community relative to alcohol and other drugs. The Council is made up mainly of representatives from the following units: student affairs, student government association, academic affairs, athletic department, communications, general counsel's office, office of social justice, parents club, human resources, and more.

In addition, we work with the state alcohol board and the local police concerning area bars and nightclubs, and were even successful in shutting one bar down for a period of time. Our commitment to student service and safety involves not only staff, faculty and administrators, but also parents through the Mountaineer Parents Club.

Results

If there is any doubt that President Hardesty meant what he said during the press conference on his first day as president about changing WVU's campus culture, the complete list of Operation Jump-Start programs listed in the appendix will put such doubts to rest.

> "These efforts demonstrate what is possible when leadership is provided and a philosophy of collaboration is fostered throughout the organization."

These efforts demonstrate what is possible when leadership is provided and a philosophy of collaboration is fostered throughout the organization. The response has been overwhelming, as demonstrated by higher residence hall occupancy, fewer incidents of vandalism, and increased retention.

West Virginia University's efforts were validated by the Kellogg Commission's (1997) recommendations that all public institutions focus on becoming more student-centered. This report confirmed we were headed in the right direction and gave us renewed commitment to providing excellent service to our students.

Positive indicators give us additional confirmation that we are on the right path, as numbers from 2000-03 illustrate:

Enrollment

♦ 2002-03 overall and first-year enrollment numbers are the highest in the history of WVU.
♦ WVU's overall enrollment for fall 2001 was 22,774, the second largest total in our history.
♦ Average test scores and high school grade point average for first-time admitted residents are higher for fall 2002. The average ACT is 23.4 (compared with 22.6 in fall 2000), average SAT is 1098 (1070 in fall 2000), and average GPA is 3.55 (3.40 in fall 2000).
♦ Average test scores and high school grade point average for first-time admitted non-residents are higher for fall 2002.

The average ACT is 21.6 (21.3 in fall 2000), average SAT is 1028 (1016 in fall 2000), and average GPA is 3.07 (2.96 in fall 2000).

Housing and Residential Education

♦ We were able to accommodate more than 500 students beyond housing capacity without a single complaint.
♦ Retention in the upper classes is the highest in recent history.
♦ Residence hall occupancy is the highest it has ever been.
♦ Vandalism expense is the lowest it has ever been.
♦ The number of incidents in the residence halls related to student conduct issues decreased by about 60%.
♦ Approximately 40% fewer first-year students were academically suspended.
♦ The number of students below a 2.0 GPA decreased by 4%.
♦ Student participation in programs and activities is quite amazing — each hall has an average attendance of 100 for each academic program, and students and RAs are reporting that the halls are much quieter and the students more focused.

Student Life Incidents

The number of incidents reported by Student Life has also dropped (Figure 1).

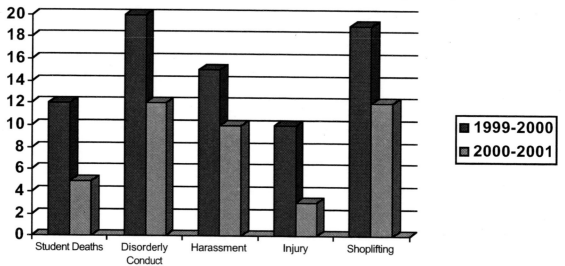

Figure 1. Incidents reported during the 1999-2000 and 2000-01 academic years.

94

Campus Incidents

Overall campus incidents declined markedly in the first fours years of Operation Jump-Start. Although the past two years show the total number of incident reports overall as slightly higher, the new numbers do indicate a reduction in the categories of larceny, simple assault, and arrests for drug law violation (See Table 1).

How Others Can Effect Change

West Virginia University is certainly not alone in providing alternatives to less positive activities. Colleges and universities nationwide have recognized that education is not enough. Students have told administrators that they understand how they can be harmed by abusing alcohol and drugs. However, they also tell us that when Saturday night rolls around, they want to be part of something. They want to belong. And if the only place to belong is at a house party or bar, then that is where they will go.

Recognizing the need to go beyond education, college and university administrators nationwide are providing viable entertainment alternatives for their students. In Ohio, for example, 79% of the colleges and universities in 1999-2000 were promoting non-alcoholic social,

recreational, and extra-curricular and public service alternatives. (Mitchell, 2001)

More than 100 schools across the nation have contacted WVU for information on how to establish late night alternatives, and WVU administrators have presented information on providing alternative activities at several national and international conferences. WVUp All Night has been featured in the national and international press, including segments on ABC's *Good Morning America* and on a British Broadcasting Company radio program. The *NCADI (National Clearinghouse for Alcohol and Drug Information) Reporter* and national honor society Golden Key's journal *Concepts,* along with many other magazines and newspapers, have also featured WVUp All Night.

WVUp All Night also received Innovative Program Awards from the National Association of Student Personnel Administrators (Region II) and the West Virginia Association of Student Personnel Administrators, and was included in the 2000-01 *Promising Practices Sourcebook* and in the 1999-2000 *Templeton Guide to College and Character.*

It took an entire University community—administrators, faculty, staff, students, families, and members of the surrounding community—to implement a program such as Up All Night and to affect the many other positive changes at

Table 1
1996-2001 Safety Statistics from West Virginia University Department of Public Safety

Year	1996	1997	1998	1999	2000	2001
Incidents of Larceny	306	273	232	212	244	211
Incidents of Simple Assault	44	37	32	14	29	22
Arrests for Drug Law Violations	62	43	38	46	48	38

Note. Provided by Lt. Randy Friend, WVU Department of Public Safety, April 2002

West Virginia University. It has been a daunting, difficult, and at times overwhelming task, but it has also been greatly satisfying. As other colleges and universities strive to change the cultures of their campuses by providing alternative activities, we offer them the advice of WVU's President David C. Hardesty, Jr. Hardesty speaks from his position as campus CEO, but his advice is applicable to faculty, staff, and administrators at all levels.

When change is really required, announce your intentions. Boldness is rewarded. Timidity is not.

Look outward, listen to, and involve those you serve in the change process. Ask for feedback and involvement from the people that you serve, inside and outside the organization. They will tell you where the problems are, and as they gain confidence in the institution's responsiveness, the institution will reap rewards.

Make and document the case for change. A leader has to build a case when change is needed. This is time-consuming, but very important. It requires facts, data, and personal involvement. The chapter on assessment in this monograph offers suggestions on how you might begin.

Build, mold, balance, and nurture a strong change leadership team. The strengths of WVU's leadership team have been critical elements to our success in the last several years, sharing special talents for leading change, focusing on goals, and producing results in record time.

Persevere. Winston Churchill said, "Never, never, never, never, never give up." When you know you are on the right track, stay the course despite pressures to give up and leave the status quo in place.

Allow change to occur. It is important to work together with students, listening to and supporting their suggestions.

Communicate and celebrate successes. Leading change requires storytelling. Stories make the abstract more real and personal. It was important for us to identify the right problems and have strong internal and external mechanisms in place to communicate both problems and solutions. And, we provided constructive means for input along the way, and took time to celebrate successes.

Get lucky. Expect some bad breaks. Many events are beyond our control, so we must react as best we can. The designation as the "Number One Party School" was no doubt bad, casting a lot of negative publicity on the institution. But, on the other hand, the ranking helped underscore the case for change with greater urgency. Within a year, we were not on the top 10 list of party schools. But more importantly, the culture had turned the corner. In short, when making change, expect curve balls, relapses, and resistance.

Allow time for change to occur. We are not done at WVU. We do believe in ourselves and know that change on campus is possible. There are countless individuals who have contributed their time, energy, and ideas. Change takes that kind of input and help, and it takes time. Change is never easy. The truth is that there is a constant need for change on campuses. We must identify the areas where change is most needed and then provide a vision for how it can come about. (Hardesty, 2000)

Conclusion

We have offered the alternatives to less positive activities developed for WVU. Some are academic, but most are related to student life or are some merger of the two. In higher education, the focus is often on academic quality. But to achieve quality, there is a need for the academic community to focus on the status of student life, a focus somewhat foreign to faculty. To be a student-centered institution means meeting the personal needs of today's students. It is about taking steps to change the culture of the campus. We hope this case study identifies ideas for change and provides sufficient, positive outcomes to make the risks worth taking. For additional information, please visit West Virginia University's web site at www.wvu.edu.

References

Abbey, A. (1991). Acquaintance rape and alcohol consumption on college campuses: How are they linked? *Journal of American College Health, 39,* 165-169.

Bok, D. (1986) *Higher learning*. Cambridge, MA: Harvard University Press.

Eigen, L. D. (1991). *Alcohol practices, policies, and potentials of American colleges and universities: An OSAP white paper*. Rockville, MD: Office for Substance Abuse Prevention, U.S. Department of Health and Human Services.

Engs, R. C., Diebold, B. A., & Hansen, D. J. (1996). The drinking patterns and problems of a national sample of college students, 1994. *Journal of Alcohol and Drug Education, 41*, 13-33.

Hardesty, D. C., Jr., (2000). Remarks made at the annual meeting of the National Association of State Universities and Land-Grant Colleges (NASULGC). Retrieved April 15, 2002 from http://www.nis.wvu.edu/wvu/Strategies.htm

Kellogg Commission. (1997, April). *Returning to our roots: The student experience.* Retrieved April 15, 2002 from http://www.nasulgc.org/publications/Kellogg/Exp.pdf

Mitchell, M. (2001). *Colleges promote late night activities as healthy alternatives to high risk alcohol consumption.* Higher Education Center for Alcohol and Other Drug Prevention (HEC). Retrieved April 15, 2002 from http://www.edc.org/hec/news/hecnews/0796.html

Presley, C. A., Leichliter, J. S., & Meilman, P. W. (1999). *Alcohol and drugs on American college campuses: Findings from 1995, 1996, and 1997.* A Report to College Presidents. Carbondale, IL: Southern Illinois University.

Wechsler, H., Lee, J., Kuo, M., & Lee, H. (2000). College binge drinking in the 1990s: A continuing problem-Results of the Harvard School of Public Health 1999 college alcohol study. *Journal of American College Health, 48*(10), 199-210.

Appendix

Below is a complete list of specific initiatives that modify student behavior and provide alternatives, all of them new programs created under Operation Jump-Start to ensure students are and remain WVU's number one priority:

1995 — FALLFEST
This successful replacement of an off-campus, unsanctioned back-to-school block party attracts an average of 15,000 students each August, on the first night of fall semester classes, for a major outdoor concert, free movies, comedy clubs, and more. It's free!

1995 — MOUNTAINEER PARENTS CLUB
Nearly 11,000 families have joined 68 clubs across the state and nation to "stay connected" to and involved in their students' university experiences. A toll-free parent helpline is set up to provide hard-to-find answers to difficult questions.

1995 — NEW STUDENT CONVOCATION
Creates an immediate connection to the University experience for our new first-year and transfer students and their families.

1996 — RESIDENT FACULTY LEADERS
These faculty couples who live next door to the residence halls serve as mentors and friends, providing motivation and encouragement, and helping first-year students with the transition to college life.

1996 — FESTIVAL OF IDEAS
This program brings renowned speakers to campus each spring semester, raising awareness and challenging our understanding of relevant and exciting issues. In 2002, speakers included Daniel Goleman, author of *Emotional Intelligence*; Fareed Zakaria, author of the Newsweek article Why They Hate Us: The Roots of Islamic Rage and What We Can Do About It"; and Monster.com CEO Jeffrey Taylor. Spring 2001 featured Maya Angelou, Cornell West, and Jerry Greenfield of Ben & Jerry's Ice Cream.

1996 — SOPHOMORE LAUNCH
Held at the end of the first year, the Sophomore Launch is a celebration that acknowledges students' successes in their first year of college and encourages them for the future.

1996 — PARTHENON 2000
Through this program, WVU fraternities are committing to healthier lifestyles, including "dry" houses. Parthenon 2000 is tied in closely with a national movement among Greek organizations to choose substance-free living.

1997 — THE NEW PIT

University leaders and students developed the "New Pit," a regulated tailgating area where students can tailgate on football game days in a safe, fun atmosphere. This replaced a potentially dangerous, unsupervised area.

1997 — CAREER SUCCESS ACADEMY

The Career Success Academy helps students establish successful, enjoyable careers by helping them choose a major, find summer jobs in their field, write resumes, and prepare for interviews and by providing guidance through the first two years of their jobs. It connects students to highly-successful University alumni.

1998 — ADVISORY COUNCIL ON ALCOHOL AND OTHER DRUGS

This council addresses substance abuse problems and has the authority to make the changes necessary to help students stay healthy and make positive choices.

1998 — SAFETY TASK FORCE

This group of students, faculty, staff and city representatives was established to review safety issues on campus. As a result, improvements continue to be made in lighting, emergency phones, and pedestrian safety.

1998 — WVUP ALL NIGHT

Recognized on ABC's *Good Morning America* and the BBC, among others, this late night weekend activity in the student union (the Mountainlair) features study rooms with snacks, free food (including a midnight breakfast bar), movies, astro bowling and billiards, and major events such as dances and comedy clubs. There is little or no charge to the students.

1999 — NITE RIDER AND 2002 - CAMPUS PM

WVU Nite Rider was an experimental Thursday, Friday, and Saturday night transportation system for WVU students, providing one round trip per evening, per student and guest. It eventually evolved into Campus PM, a late night, weekend service provided by a joint effort of the University and the community's Mountain Line bus service.

1999 — MOUNTAINEER MANIACS

This athletic booster club was begun by students and continues to be student-run, with the support of Student Affairs and the Athletic Department. Hundreds of students have joined to cheer on the Mountaineers.

2000 — 21st BIRTHDAY LETTER

A card offering best wishes and tips for a safe celebration is sent to all students celebrating their 21st birthday.

2000 — SENIOR YEAR EXPERIENCE

A year-long series of celebrations and events, along with academic capstone courses, help our seniors prepare for the transition from college to career.

2001 — STUDENT RECREATION CENTER

The Student Recreation Center opened its doors in July 2001 and attracts thousands of students daily. The state of the art center features a climbing wall, weight and fitness centers, a recreational pool, a lap pool, running and walking tracks, basketball and other courts, a laundry, study lounges and more.

2002 — FACILITIES MASTER PLAN

A technology-based library opened in January 2002, and a new life sciences building opened in August 2002 for classes, further enhancing WVU's learning environment. A state-of-the-art Visitors Research Center also opened in 2002.

Assessment Strategies and Results

Michael J. Siegel
Policy Center on the First Year of College

Assessment has been a primary focus of higher education researchers, scholars, and practitioners for more than two decades. The assessment movement was prompted by a national call in the 1970s and 1980s for institutional accountability and confirmation that colleges and universities were meeting the needs of students and using resources effectively. In an era characterized by retrenchment, increased accountability to external publics, and growth in complex administrative structures and functions, the assessment enterprise has been fueled by a fundamental demand for educators to provide evidence of viability and ensure relevance of campus programs and services.

Nowhere has the application of assessment been more important than in the student affairs function in higher education. Traditionally, there has been much scrutiny by the higher education community of the relative value of campus social activities and other out-of-class experiences that are meant to support the academic mission of colleges and universities. Assessment has played a necessary and significant role in helping the profession document with empirical evidence the importance of the co-curriculum in helping students adjust to college as well as meet the academic demands of the curriculum.

This chapter will identify strategies for assessing campus activities and the co-curriculum in the first college year and make the case for an intentional commitment by colleges and universities to identify and use effective assessment strategies to improve campus activities. These characteristics will help practitioners identify assessment goals and initiatives that will aid in measuring outcomes, such as the impact of campus activities on first-year student satisfaction and retention. Campus activities and other co-curricular initiatives are critical components of the collegiate experience. Colleges and universities program and administer campus activities in large measure to facilitate the successful transition of first-year students into the campus environment and to provide a range of experiences that support, balance, and complement the academic endeavors of college students. Programming campus activities is a powerful way to transmit norms of behavior, values, rules, rituals, myths, stories, and other elements of campus culture to students.

At no time is the need for effective programming more evident than during the first year of college, the successful foundation of which has implications for the entire college experience. As Gardner, Siegel, and Cutright

(2001) point out, "The first months, weeks, and even days on campus are the time when students will make decisions about whether they seriously wish to pursue higher education and whether a particular college or university is the best place for them" (p. 3). The effective delivery of campus activities, programs, and services in the first year of college—and particularly in the first semester or term—is crucial to institutional efforts to improve satisfaction and retention among students. To determine whether or not campus activities positively impact satisfaction and retention, broad assessment is needed.

This chapter begins by making the case for an in-depth assessment of first-year students and activities. Next, it briefly examines research findings from a national survey on current practices in the co-curriculum. This section explores various first-year program areas, such as orientation and residence life, that have responsibility for planning and delivering initiatives for first-year students. These components of the college experience, which support the transition and socialization of first-year students into the campus environment, are key areas for targeted assessment of campus activities. Finally, strategies for effective assessment of campus activities are offered.

Making the Case for Assessment in the First-Year Co-Curriculum

In their seminal book on assessment for student affairs practitioners, Upcraft and Schuh (1996) suggest that assessment is a matter of survival for student affairs. With growing questions about accountability, higher education costs, student engagement, retention, and access, student affairs is at the center of the debate about whether or not colleges and universities are effective in their delivery of programs and services. While assessment in higher education has been, for many years, focused on learning outcomes and the impact of the curriculum on student learning and academic success, there has been a marked shift in the past decade toward assessment of student engagement and experiences outside the classroom. These co-curricular experiences are largely within the domain of student affairs, and further, within the domain of campus activities, the assessment of which is the focus of this chapter.

Assessment in the first year of college is increasingly targeted at the co-curriculum and focused on the academic and personal gains students make during college. Essentially, the purpose of this type of assessment has been to identify and document the extent to which various out-of-class experiences contribute to desired outcomes of college in the academic, personal, and social domains. Kuh and his colleagues elsewhere in this monograph define the co-curriculum broadly, suggesting that out-of-class experiences encompass the traditional co-curriculum—for example, leadership programs, student union work, and student government-which includes activities not traditionally linked to the classroom, and the non-traditional co-curriculum, which includes activities that occur outside the classroom but that may be linked to the classroom—for example, service-learning, on and off-campus internships, and campus honors programs. As they note, recent trends indicate that students are less involved in traditional forms of activity and are more involved in activities such as academic clubs, undergraduate research, on and off-campus work, service-learning, volunteer work, and other forms of community service.

Key to the proliferation of first-year assessment initiatives at many colleges and universities is the alarming national attrition rate of students from the first college year to the second. According to research conducted in 1997 by American College Testing (ACT), the national dropout rate from the first year to the second year was 47.4% for public, two-year institutions; 31.8% for private, two-year institutions; 32% for public, four-year institutions; and 29.9% for private, four-year institutions. To address the attrition issue, educators often turn to data that provide an indication of factors that predict student retention. Such factors include combined curricular and co-curricular initiatives, such as academic preparation of entering students, involvement in the academic and social life of the campus, faculty-to-student and student-to-student interaction, civic engagement, use of campus resources, participation in campus activities, and student engagement and motivation, among others.

Only with effective programming and planning is it possible to leverage campus activities to have an appreciable effect on the success and the satisfaction of first-year students. Just as planning and programming are vital to the dissemination of campus activities, assessment is the key component in determining how well campus activities, programs, and services are meeting their goals and performing successfully. In order to investigate the extent to which campus initiatives are effective, it is necessary to develop a campus-wide assessment plan structured around examining the desired outcomes and goals of activities planning.

First-year assessment is intended to lay the groundwork for continual institutional assessment that will be conducted throughout the remainder of the student experience. In addition, having data on first-year programs and services better positions institutions to develop longitudinal assessment initiatives and a more comprehensive picture of the student experience.

So where do practitioners turn for models of assessment to measure the impact of the co-curriculum on first-year students? To begin the process of developing goals and outcomes statements for assessment, practitioners will first want to consult current campus-based guidelines that outline the various goals and purposes of program areas. If none are available, or if existing guidelines are inadequate, assessment professionals can use as a benchmark established guidelines and standards that are published by professional higher education organizations. One of the most important and often-consulted set of standards is provided by the Council for the Advancement of Standards in Higher Education (1994). The Council, known as CAS, was established more than 20 years ago for the purpose of developing and promoting standards of professional practice in working with college students. The standards published by the organization are intended to guide higher education institutions and practitioners in both the delivery and assessment of multiple program areas found on college campuses. Focused on student leaning and personal development, particularly the field of student affairs, standards of practice are available for 28 functional areas.

Included are standards and guidelines for each functional area along with a description of its historical evolution and contextual setting. The standards can be an invaluable tool for helping beginning assessment practitioners establish goals and benchmarks for the assessment process.

The Importance of Context in First-Year Assessment

Like all methods of evaluation in social science research, assessment in higher education is organized around a complex system of principles, guidelines, beliefs, and terms. For assessment to have meaning, practitioners must interpret the system contextually within the frame of their own world view. That is, assessment practitioners must necessarily operationalize assessment concepts based on local campus environments and cultures, and in short they must recalibrate global assessment concepts to meet the needs of their constituents at the campus level.

Many of the outcomes and goals with which campus practitioners are concerned in the first college year (e.g., retention, student engagement, success, satisfaction, cognitive learning, and civic engagement and humanitarianism) exist in the abstract as concepts derived from national data and trends and fashioned into theoretical frameworks. Operationalizing concepts so that they have local and campus-based meaning is vitally important if practitioners are to understand how outcomes impact their campus. So, for example, if measuring student engagement is the priority for first-year assessment, the following question should be asked: "What does it mean to be an engaged student specifically as it relates to this campus?"

Though in large part similar, the assessment terms "objective" and "goal" more closely resemble flip sides of the same coin. In short, a goal, where assessment is concerned, is a broad and abstract

> "First-year assessment is intended to lay the groundwork for continual institutional assessment that will be conducted throughout the remainder of the student experience."

term. An objective, on the other hand, is a concrete and narrowly defined concept, often stemming from larger goals. Goals are usually comprised of smaller, discrete objectives, but the reverse is not necessarily true. What assessment practitioners in the first year are ultimately striving for is the development of statements that are measurable, and measurement is most effectively conducted at the level of objectives rather than goals. While the terms are used somewhat interchangeably in this chapter, it should be noted that there is a distinguishable difference between the two.

Terms such as student success, student engagement, and retention only have meaning for us in the contextual sense, defined locally by each campus, because what constitutes success on one campus may not be so for another campus. Before any campus program, activity, or service is assessed, key questions must be asked that help institutions put goals and objectives into context. Chief among the questions a practitioner might ask are

1. What matters in the first college year on this campus in terms of programs and services?
2. Are certain co-curricular structures, programs, policies, and modes of delivery of student activities more desirable than others? Similarly, to whom would such programs be more desirable? And how will we find out?
3. To what resources, data, and assessment-related research do we turn for guidance in the development of assessment initiatives to address student needs in the co-curriculum?
4. Given the academic mission of our campus, the populations our institution serves, and the institutional culture, how do we define student learning, success, engagement, humanitarianism, and other outcomes of the student experience?
5. Are there beliefs and views about campus activities for which we have anecdotal evidence but little or no empirical evidence?

It is very important for practitioners to first consider the extent to which student activities promote and encourage gains in student learning outcomes, and then frame the above questions in terms of their centrality to the academic mission of the institution. Assessment in student affairs has largely been concerned with student satisfaction and engagement in activities outside of the classroom, and there is a growing demand for student affairs professionals to restructure out-of-class activities so that they have more relevance to the academic mission of the institution. This, of course, entails coming to some agreement on campus about what it means for an activity to be related to the academic mission. Even though student activities are not necessarily developed for, or intended to be part of, the curriculum, their centrality to the academic enterprise is becoming more apparent. And as such, they are increasingly being evaluated in terms of how effective they are in facilitating student learning outcomes.

The National Landscape of First-Year Co-Curricular Practices

To frame the context of assessment of first-year student activities, national data examining the extent to which student activities are prevalent on college campuses are explored. The most comprehensive picture of the programs and services available to first-year students outside the classroom is provided by the Policy Center on the First Year of College, a national-level center with a mission to improve the first year of college through research, dissemination, conferences, consultation, and most importantly, assessment.

Supported by grants from The Atlantic Philanthropies and The Pew Charitable Trusts, the Policy Center conducted a national survey, called the National Survey of First-Year Co-Curricular Practices, in the fall of 2000. The project marked the first and only descriptive research study in American higher education that aims to look broadly at first-year co-curricular activities. This section of the chapter highlights findings from the study, and in doing so provides a context in which assessment strategies and techniques for campus activities can be better understood and explored.

The National Survey of First-Year Co-Curricular Practices

The Policy Center on the First Year of College, with input from a nationally known team of educational research experts and first-year program directors, developed and administered the survey, asking a broad range of questions about several areas of student life including admissions, orientation, student activities, athletics, Greek life, and residence life. A web link to the survey, imbedded in an e-mail invitation, was sent to 621 randomly selected chief student affairs officers representing a wide range of two-year and four-year institutions. Of the 568 individuals who successfully received the e-mail message, responses were obtained from 291—an overall response rate of 51%.

The findings from the survey are not intended to be prescriptive, diagnostic, or evaluative. Nor are they meant to highlight "best practices" in the first-year co-curriculum. They are intended, rather, to paint a descriptive picture of current practices in specific program areas in the first year. That is, the survey is an attempt to capture a snapshot of the co-curricular landscape at U.S. colleges and universities. While some findings are consistent with anecdotal evidence about the first year, other data appear to be in conflict with widely held beliefs about what happens to first-year students outside of the classroom. Following is a brief summary of selected findings, with implications for assessment. To narrow the discussion, the examination will focus on key areas of campus life where student activities play an important role, and for which assessment should be a priority. These include orientation, residence life, and Greek life.

A major issue impacting evaluation of the co-curriculum is the challenge institutions face in bringing resources and personnel to bear on the assessment process and galvanizing support for assessment-related initiatives. The first question on the survey asked whether or not there is a single individual or unit responsible for first-year co-curricular programs on campus (no distinction was made between the individual and the unit in this question). The institutions most likely to assign responsibility for first-year co-curricular programs to a single individual or office are baccalaureate-liberal arts colleges, with 70% indicating this type of arrangement. Following liberal arts institutions were the research-extensive universities, with 57% reporting that responsibility for program delivery is assigned to one person or campus unit. In contrast, only one in three two-year and research-intensive universities reported this type of arrangement.

Respondents answering "yes" to this question provided a number of specific titles and office designations. Generally, the responsibility for first-year programs is assigned to a larger student affairs division or sub-unit, such as academic advising, student development, or campus activities; however, approximately 10% of respondents indicated the existence of separate first-year offices or individuals such as "Deans of Freshmen," "First-Year Experience Directors/Coordinators," and "Directors of Retention."

Orientation. New student orientation is a cornerstone of the first-year experience and a key time period for exposing students to campus activities and acquainting them with the culture of campus life. The survey asked several questions about the organization, delivery, and evaluation of campus orientation, and found that nearly all institutions offer some type of orientation to college, with general reporting lines to the vice president for student affairs. Findings indicate two-year institutions are more likely to schedule an orientation of half a day or less; research universities one and a half to two days, and baccalaureate colleges more than two days. In addition the survey found the majority of institutions do some type of regular evaluation of orientation. Both staff and students frequently evaluate orientation, but staff are somewhat more likely to conduct an evaluation of orientation than are students. What is suggested here is that evaluation and assessment be ongoing components of a comprehensive orientation evaluation plan, involving significant numbers of students as well as other members of the campus community.

The degree to which an institution's orientation function is coupled with campus activities is largely a matter of institutional size and mission. Simply stated, co-curricular activities, and offices responsible for their coordination, are typically more tightly coupled at smaller institutions than at large institutions, where autonomous, yet related, units are likely to be more prevalent. One major issue that informs campus activities assessment relates to the content of orientation. That is, inquiry should be made into the types of activities first-year students are involved in during orientation, the relative value new students assign to orientation activities, and the degree to which orientation is social versus an introduction to the academic expectations of the college or university. In addition, campus activities and assessment professionals should use orientation to gather information about student expectations. Data can be compared later to actual experiences, providing an important snapshot of any discrepancies between college expectations and reality for first-year students.

An emerging trend in orientation is the inclusion of a greater number of academic activities. For both two-year and four-year institutions, the academic activities most likely to be included in orientation are small-group student and faculty sessions where academic programs are discussed. A large percentage of all institutional types report that faculty routinely meet with students during orientation. A smaller percentage of schools, however, indicate that faculty meet with family members or that faculty and students engage together in some type of service activities during orientation. As might be expected, such faculty and student service activities are most likely to occur during orientation at small, four-year, liberal arts institutions. Finally, four-year institutions are more likely than two-year institutions to offer special orientation sessions for student sub-populations, such as minority students, international students, and student athletes.

Residence Life. Residence life has been a vital part of the first-year experience throughout the history of American higher education. Campus residence halls have been one of the major vehicles for the delivery of first-year programs

and services as well as the conduit through which social and co-curricular domains of student life have been given attention.

Residence life plays a significant role in the lives of first-year students, academically as well as socially. For many entering college students, the first year marks the first time they have lived either on their own or away from their parents. While the experience can be quite rewarding and liberating for some, it can be terrifying and confining for others. The residence life function is a primary vehicle for the socialization of first-year students and a catalyst for helping students make the transition from high school to college. For that reason, effective campus activities programming related to the living and learning experience is crucial.

Linking special academic programs, such as learning communities and first-year seminars, and offering special academic services or programs such as honors programs, housing separated by major, foreign language, or international status, and tutoring or academic advising is undertaken by only a small percentage (approximately 30%) of American colleges and universities. In general, larger institutions are more likely than smaller institutions to design residential linkages

In terms of residence life and the assessment process, the survey asked respondents whether or not their institution had assessed particular residential life outcomes, specifically student satisfaction; residential versus non-residential retention rates; residential versus non-residential academic performance; residential versus non-residential social/personal development; and residential versus non-residential student involvement. Among the six variables, institutions in the aggregate were most likely to evaluate student satisfaction and its relationship to residence life—just over 85% of respondents reported evaluation of satisfaction. Within that percentage, master's institutions were most likely to conduct residential student satisfaction assessment. The second most commonly evaluated outcome was student retention. Approximately 40% of institutions evaluate retention as a function of residence life, and within that group, master's institutions again are more likely than other institutional types to conduct this type of assessment. Among the key findings that have implications for first-year campus activities and assessment are the following:

1. Residence halls that have restricted, or designated, first-year floors or wings are most likely to be found at the small, four-year, liberal arts institutions.
2. Although two-year campuses are less likely to have residence halls, approximately 20% of the two-year respondents do house some students on campus.
3. Residence life is linked to academic programs and structures in different ways. Less than one fourth of residential institutions offer residential learning communities, and just under one third link residence life with first-year seminars. Approximately one fourth have some honors housing, and approximately one of every three offers tutoring or academic advising in the residence hall.
4. Overall, the most common type of faculty involvement in residence life is faculty presentations in residence halls.

Greek Life. Thirty-two percent of the institutions represented in the study—all of them four-year schools—sponsor Greek social organizations that first-year students may join. But overall the percentage of first-year students who join Greek organizations is low. Approximately 60% of respondents indicated that no more than 10% of first-year students join Greek letter organizations.

Although Greek life affects only a fraction of the nation's first-year students, the impact it has on both the students and the larger college community is often dramatic. While philanthropy and service have largely been positive aspects of the Greek experience, other characteristics of Greek life have been more deleterious to the value of campus life. Nearly one third of respondents indicated that hazing had occurred on their campus during the past two years involving first-year Greek students. The process of rush can also be very disruptive to new students, academically as well as socially,

and devastating to students who do not receive a "bid" from their preferred fraternity or sorority. The potential for disruption is even greater when rush occurs during the first few weeks of the college experience, a time when new students are typically overwhelmed by multiple demands for their attention. In a more encouraging vein, research in the higher education literature has found that Greek affiliation is positively correlated with student retention and institutional satisfaction. The central issue for campuses to consider is whether Greek life supports or is a deterrent to the academic mission of an institution and whether the institution is able to effectively monitor and control the activities occurring within, and sponsored by, these organizations.

In sum, opportunities abound for first-year student involvement at all colleges and universities, regardless of size and function. Yet, first-year students are more likely to encounter specialized first-year activities—especially leadership and student government activities—at large research universities than at other types of institutions. That is, there is likely to be a greater proliferation of student activities designed for, and by, targeted groups of students at research universities than at smaller schools, given the diverse numbers and needs of students in attendance. Whether the scenario is problematic or fortuitous for assessment is largely contextual. There may be a greater abundance of assessment opportunities in more areas of campus life, but defining problems and developing a manageable and sensible assessment plan may be overwhelming.

The three areas discussed above, while considered key springboards to further involvement in the life of the campus, represent only a fraction of the campus activities in which students have the opportunity to participate during their first year of college. Other areas of campus life that might be the focus of assessment

"In sum, opportunities abound for first-year student involvement at all colleges and universities, regardless of size and function."

include, among other things, honor societies and ethnic and cultural centers; academic-based groups such as environmental clubs, science organizations, and language clubs; and a mix of other activities such as student-run businesses, performing arts groups, political organizations, recreation groups, service organizations, religious clubs, and club sports teams.

Nine Principles of Effective Assessment

After targeting areas of campus life for evaluation, how shall assessment be conducted and what principles should guide the process? To frame the discussion of student activities assessment in the first college year, some basic fundamentals and principles of assessment will be highlighted. One set of principles, developed by practitioners (Astin et al., 1992) invited to a meeting of the American Association for Higher Education Assessment Forum, serves as a benchmark in the field of higher education. The statements are widely accepted as principles of good practice in assessment. The principles, originally designed to address student learning related to the curriculum, have broad applicability and can be used to inform campus activities assessment.

1. The assessment of student learning begins with educational values.
2. Assessment is most effective when it reflects an understanding of learning as multidimensional, integrated, and revealed in performance over time.
3. Assessment works best when the programs it seeks to improve have clear, explicitly stated purposes.
4. Assessment requires attention to outcomes but also and equally to the experiences that lead to those outcomes.
5. Assessment works best when it is ongoing not episodic.
6. Assessment fosters wider improvement when representatives from across the educational community are involved.
7. Assessment makes a difference when it begins with issues of use and illuminates questions that people really care about.
8. Assessment is most likely to lead to improvement when it is part of a larger set of conditions that promote change.
9. Through assessment, educators meet responsibilities to students and to the public.

Effective assessment is not simply the strategic selection of instruments, surveys, questionnaires, or qualitative methodologies for the purposes of evaluation or program review, although such an endeavor is certainly an important part of the assessment process. Nor is assessment the write-up of progress reports, the conducting of research, or the simple documentation of statements, goals, and objectives about the delivery of campus programs and services. Assessment is most effective when it is a comprehensive or systematic combination of the two.

The Nine Principles Applied to the First-Year Co-Curriculum: Steps and Strategies

Central to the implementation of a campus assessment plan is the development of key statements of needs, goals, and aspirations. Assessment starts with an organizing set of principles and procedures, and practitioners should avoid "putting the cart before the horse," or selecting instruments and tools for assessment before doing a needs analysis and establishing goals. Before surveys can be administered and assessment methodologies employed, questions about the nature of what is to be studied, by whom, and for what purposes must be asked. Drawing on the work of Banta, Lund, Black, and Oblander (1996) and Upcraft and Schuh (1996), the following section outlines a series of nine strategies for conducting effective assessment of campus activities. What is offered in this section is a reframing of the above nine principles of effective assessment from the standpoint of the co-curriculum. That is, each of the principles will be restated in co-curricular terms, and the result will be a series of strategies and steps that will be useful as a guide for conducting assessment initiatives related to student activities in the first year of college.

Strategy 1: Define the purpose of campus activities assessment using clear and well-defined goals statements.

An institution or campus unit undertaking assessment of campus activities must first address a series of important questions, the purpose of which is to derive explicitly stated outcomes that will ultimately guide the assessment process. All assessment should start with this question in mind: "What is the basic purpose of conducting assessment?" From that answer all the other details of an assessment plan flow. Is the purpose to challenge widely held beliefs about student participation in, and satisfaction with, campus activities? Is the purpose to make the case for an investment of resources into new campus programs or activities, or to justify the continual existence of current programs or activities? Is there a concern that the institution is not doing enough to promote student involvement in the co-curriculum and is, therefore, in need of assessment data to find out what might attenuate the problem?

The answers that follow from the questions above must be informed by explicitly stated goals and outcomes. Whether it is the goal of an activities director to increase minority student participation in student leadership programs or examine the impact of Greek organization on first-year academic experiences, the foundation of assessment rests on developing clear objectives that are realistic, measurable, and appropriate for the application of any clearly defined assessment plan.

Strategy 2: Identify the problem areas or concerns on campus that need to be addressed by assessment.

A major step toward defining assessment goals is performing a needs analysis of the problem areas or concerns to be addressed. There are many goals of a needs assessment, the most important of which is to identify structures, programs, or activities on campus that need improvement or alteration in some way. Practitioners should keep in mind that not everything on campus can, or should, be fixed, improved, restructured, or changed in some way. It is therefore important to identify problems for which there is a significant amount of interest in addressing on campus, and for which assessment is likely to yield results that can be leveraged for change.

Within reason, institutions ultimately want to meet the needs of students. To understand student needs, it is necessary to identify patterns of student use of resources and facilities and their participation in campus activities. It should be noted, however, that mere use of facilities and participation in activities, services, and programs is not sufficient as an indicator of problem areas or concerns. Identifying problems must, therefore, include a combination of student participation and use of services, staff and administrator perceptions about student behavior, and institutional data collected on student needs. For instance, one such problem that assessment can help answer is the difference between perceived and actual barriers to student participation in campus activities or use of campus resources.

Strategy 3: Outline and document, using a data-audit process, what is already known about first-year students and the activities in which they engage.

The Policy Center on the First Year of College, in collaboration with the National Center for Higher Education Management Systems (NCHEMS) conducted during the 2001-02 academic year a pilot study of what is called the Data Audit and Analysis Project. An assessment tool called *The Data Audit Toolkit* (NCHEMS, 2002) was developed during the pilot study, and participating institutions were instructed to inventory current databases on campus that might contain data relevant to first-year student behaviors and attitudes as the first step in the delivery of assessment initiatives. The same principles are encouraged here for student activities practitioners.

The basic premise of a data audit is that institutions must find out what data they already possess before they seek more and other types. Taking an inventory of current assessment data on entering students will help institutions generate a picture of what is currently known about first-year students. In addition, it will help practitioners avoid duplication of efforts in data collection, which is typically a drain on resources. Institutions invariably want to develop a comprehensive understanding of their first-year students so that they can more effectively organize programming and activities around student needs. The data audit is a powerful mechanism for helping institutions understand more holistically the experiences of first-year students, and ultimately match student needs more effectively with institutional resources.

Whether an institution is conducting a self-study, gathering data and information for accreditation purposes, or embarking on a new assessment program for the first year of college, the data audit offers an intentional means by which institutions can locate and document existing data sources on campus, with the ultimate goal of improving the structure and flow of data.

Strategy 4: Determine what population, or which campus activities, will be targeted for assessment.

This strategy underscores the importance of focused assessment, or directing assessment measures at specific populations of program areas. A crucial element of the decision-making process is the development of a decision tree that ranks from highest to lowest priority those elements to be addressed. For instance, practitioners can start by making a list of possible assessment activities in the first year, which might include measuring student satisfaction with orientation, student use of campus resources and facilities, the impact of residence hall programs on student learning, or the use of student leadership programs by minority and international students, among others. Taking into consideration human and financial resources, as well as the priorities of those involved in the assessment process, practitioners will have to determine what can and should be assessed, and to what extent. It will be to the benefit of any student activities assessment plan to maximize what are likely to be limited available resources, so the streamlining of efforts to develop tightly defined and targeted projects will be of utmost importance.

While practitioners and interested constituent groups might consider broad assessment ideal, it may not be possible or even practical to assess all students who participate in or experience a particular program, activity, or intervention. This, of course, largely depends on the size of the institution or unit, as well as the scope of the assessment initiative and the attendant methodology. It must, therefore, be determined which individuals or groups of students will be assigned to which assessment interventions. If, for instance, one would like to measure student perceptions about the extent to which residence halls support and promote academic integration into the institution, he or she will need to determine whether it is necessary to survey all first-year students living in residence halls or whether it is more feasible to compare selected academic living and learning communities with floors or halls that are not organized around any particular theme.

Strategy 5: Identify individuals or groups that will be involved in the assessment process, from data collection to analysis.

It is important to determine which individuals or constituency groups on campus will take part in the assessment process, and whether their involvement is more appropriate to the development of the assessment plan, the actual administration of surveys and collection of data, or data analysis. If a student affairs professional is interested in learning about the level of engagement of first-year students in various orientation activities, then determining who will need to be involved in the data collection process and how many individuals will be needed to undertake the task is central to planning. In addition, decisions must be made about who will be responsible for analyzing the data and where the data will be stored. The scope of any assessment initiative will have ramifications for which groups or individuals will be involved in the assessment process.

The key factor in determining which individuals will be involved in the assessment process is the selection of the methodology, or methodologies, that will be used to gather student data. The assignment of individuals to conduct assessment and the selection of the methodology by which assessment will be conducted may occur concomitantly, as the selection of one is likely to be dependent on the selection of the other.

Strategy 6: Determine the most suitable and effective methodology(ies) for conducting assessment, given the contextual nature of activities targeted for assessment.

Given decisions about the purpose of assessment initiatives and the problems or concerns that need to be addressed by the institution, how will data be collected? Plans for institutional assessment should include selecting among a variety of evaluative methods, modes of inquiry, and processes for undertaking data collection. Selecting from among multiple methods is important in that it gives practitioners broad insight into the student experience and provides a comprehensive picture of behavior that is based on statistical data as well as qualitative information. The process of using more than one method to gather data is called "triangulation," and it provides a richer and more in-depth analysis of student use of campus resources and involvement in campus activities.

Typically, assessment methodology falls into one of two major social science traditions—quantitative and qualitative. Under the rubric of qualitative methodology, researchers study phenomena as they occur and exist in a natural state within a particular environment, ideally free of external manipulation. Theoretically, data collection and analysis are guided by an inductive process, whereby assessment questions are posed, data about people and programs are gathered, and themes are developed based on information that is collected. In contrast, quantitative methodology is guided by a deductive process, whereby theoretical assumptions, developed prior to data gathering, are tested using an assessment or evaluation tool (Patton, 2002). In terms of selection, you will have the option of choosing one or the other, or a combination of the two methodologies. You might decide to apply separate methodologies to different assessment initiatives or you may apply a combination of methodologies within the same initiative, which I refer to as a "hybrid study" (e.g., a survey administration followed up with focus group interviews related to the study or concerned with the same topic).

Strategy 7: Determine how data are to be collected and analyzed, and identify a central storehouse or collection point where data will be housed.

Once the methodological modes of inquiry are selected for the data collection process, the nature by which they will employed must then be addressed. If a qualitative design is a preferred approach, what types of qualitative questions will be asked of student participants and what type of interviews or focus groups will be conducted? Will a case study approach be desired, whereby the experiences of a small number of individuals are examined and analyzed? If a quantitative design is used, what survey instruments or questionnaires will be used and how will they be administered? Will the institution use national-level instruments or locally developed assessment tools? And if a combination of approaches are used in the assessment process, how much attention will be given to each and who will be responsible for conducting the various assessment interventions. Finally, who, or what office, will be responsible for serving as the storehouse for the data, and in what format will it be kept?

These and other questions address the data collection and storage component of assessment, and they must be answered in an effort to determine the parameters of the data collection process and to ascertain the manageability of the overall assessment initiative. Student affairs and student activities practitioners will want to consider the extent to which the data collected will be integrated with other campus databases and coded so that retrieval of records and data analysis can be effectively undertaken. (The data audit process

"Typically, assessment methodology falls into one of two major social science traditions—quantitative and qualitative."

outlined in Strategy #3 is designed to assist practitioners in this endeavor).

Strategy 8: Determine how information from data analyses will be disseminated.

Once data are gathered and an alyses are performed, how will the assessment findings be documented and shared within the institutional community? In other words, what is the best strategy for the dissemination of findings and results from the assessment initiatives that are undertaken? Certain individuals (i.e., directors of programs and other mid-level unit directors on campus) might be concerned with the two or three most salient and important findings related to their programming needs. Other individuals—perhaps the president and other senior administrators—might not want or need access to lengthy reports or tables of information and will instead require an executive summary briefly outlining major findings. Still others who might have either a greater capacity or interest in data (e.g., institutional researchers or assessment directors) might want to read full reports or perhaps have access to raw data and databases. And what about reporting to constituents external to the college or university? If institutions want to share information and findings with parents, members of the press or other media entities, or community organizations, reporting structures and formats must be tailored accordingly.

Strategy 9: Identify ways in which assessment findings can be used to leverage change on campus.

Ultimately, the end game of assessment is change. Whether findings reaffirm empirically what has always been assumed on campus anecdotally or whether they reveal fundamental weaknesses in the most esteemed and prized campus programs or activities, assessment is typically organized to leverage change in some way. Institutions undertake assessment because they want to be more informed in making decisions about whether, and to what extent, changes need to be made to their programs, policies, and services. Campus activities assessment should follow the same principle.

To identify ways to leverage change on campus, institutions must revisit their purposes for conducting activities and determine how the findings can be used to frame solutions to identified problems. Typical questions might include

1. What types of changes are we willing to make, even if drastic, in our unit or area if the findings yield unfavorable information?
2. What are explicit steps that we need to take to move from findings to action?
3. What individuals or constituent groups on campus were interested in the findings in the first place and would want to know outcomes of the assessment?
4. Which key faculty will we need to enlist in the change process so that we maximize the academic merit of our programs and services?
5. What are some ways in which we can collaborate with other departments to ensure broad investment in the change process?

In sum, reporting results and findings is only the first step in the change process. Indeed, having results but no particular outlet to make them known or to be used in some way is not an efficient use of campus data. Practitioners must develop useful methods of both reporting data and ensuring its use in the change process.

Conclusion

The degree to which students are successful in making the transition from high school to college will in large measure influence whether they are successful in making the subsequent transition from the first year of college to the second year. To be sure, the first days, weeks, and months of the first year of college are critical, for it is a time when students begin to develop behaviors, attitudes, and opinions about college that will likely be sustained throughout the entire collegiate experience. At the individual level, student success is a function of several interrelated components, including academic preparation, social adjustment, and cognitive maturity. At the institutional level, student success is largely a function of the effective delivery of campus academic programs, student support services, and campus activities, among others.

The co-curriculum plays a vital role in the success of college students throughout their entire collegiate experience, but has its maximum potential impact during the first college year. The degree to which institutions take responsibility for assuring that co-curricular initiatives intentionally support student learning and socialization affects the impact of these initiatives on student success. And the degree to which co-curricular initiatives support the academic mission of a campus will directly impact the likelihood that co-curricular units will be supported and perceived essential to the overall success of students.

Generally, first-year programs are one of a number of responsibilities given to student affairs divisions, and resources are often limited. In addition, many assessment pursuits in the first year are marked by a failure to develop a coherent set of goals and strategies, which often results in duplication of efforts, confusion over administrative responsibilities, and wasted resources. Although there is no one best way to assess first-year campus activities, the most important aspect to consider is the relationship campus activities have to the academic mission of the institution. Documenting the centrality of the academic mission in the programming and delivery of campus activities will be a significant undertaking for student affairs and campus activities assessment practitioners in the future.

References

American College Testing. (1998, April 1). *National college dropout and graduation rates, 1997.* Retrieved May 30, 2002, from http://www.act.org/news/releases/1998/04-01b98.html

Astin, A. W., Banta, T. W., Cross, K. P., El-Khawas, E., Ewell, P. T., Hutchings, P., et al. (1992). *Assessment forum: 9 principles of good practice for assessing student learning.* Washington, DC: American Association for Higher Education.

Banta, T. W., Lund, J. P., Black, K. E., & Oblander, F. W. (1996). *Assessment in practice: Putting principles to work on college campuses.* San Francisco: Jossey-Bass.

Council for the Advancement of Standards in Higher Education. (1994, November 18). *History of CAS.* Retrieved September 20, 2002 from http://www.cas.edu/historya.cfm

Gardner, J. N., Siegel, M. J., & Cutright, M. (2001, Fall). Focusing on the first-year student. *AGB Priorities,* 17.

National Center for Higher Education Management Systems. (2002). *The data audit toolkit.* Denver: National Center for Higher Education Management Systems.

National Survey of First-Year Co-Curricular Practices. (2000). Brevard, NC: Policy Center on the First Year of College. Retrieved December 2, 2002 from http://www.brevard.edu/fyc/survey/curricular

Patton, M. (2002). *Qualitative evaluation and research methods* (3rd edition). Newbury Park, CA: Sage.

Upcraft, M. L., & Schuh, J. H. (1996). *Assessment in student affairs: A guide for practitioners.* San Francisco: Jossey-Bass.

Other Suggested Readings

Angelo, T. A., & Cross, K. P. (1993). *Classroom assessment techniques: A handbook for college teachers* (2nd ed.) San Francisco: Jossey-Bass.

Astin, A. W. (1991). *Assessment for excellence: The philosophy and practice of assessment and evaluation in higher education.* New York: Macmillan.

Gardner, J. N., Barefoot, B. O., & Swing, R. L. (2001). *Guidelines for evaluating the first-year experience* (2nd ed.). Columbia, SC: University of South Carolina, National Resource Center for The First-Year Experience and Students in Transition.

Kuh, G. D. (2000, May 18). Tools for assessing the first-year student experience. [First-Year Assessment Listserv (FYA-List) Contribution]. Retrieved December 2, 2002 from http://www.brevard.edu/fye/listserv/remarks/kuh.htm

Kuh, G. D., & Whitt, E. J. (1988). *The invisible tapestry: Culture in American colleges and universities.* ASHE-ERIC Higher Education Reports, No. 1. Washington, DC: Association for the Study of Higher Education.

Lincoln, Y. S., & Guba, E. G. (1985). *Naturalistic inquiry*. Beverly Hills, CA: Sage.

Merriam, S. B. (1988). *Case study research in education: A qualitative approach*. San Francisco: Jossey-Bass.

Palomba, C. A., & Banta, T. W. (1999). *Assessment essentials: Planning, implementing, and improving assessment in higher education*. San Francisco: Jossey-Bass.

Schechter, S. (2002, August 8). Internet Resources for Higher Education Outcomes Assessment. Retrieved September 15, 2002 from http://www2.acs.ncsu.edu/UPA/assmt/resource.htm

Schilling, K. M., & Schilling, K. L. (1999). Increasing expectations for student effort. *About Campus, 4*(2), 4-10.

Swing, R. L. (2001). *Resource notebook on first-year assessment instruments*. Brevard, NC: Policy Center on the First Year of College.

Connecting Academic and Student Affairs: A Synthesis for Engaged Learning and Retention

Carolyn Haynes
Dennis C. Roberts
Miami University

As the new millennium unfolds, the pressures on first-year undergraduate students and higher education institutions that must attract and retain them continue to mount. High school populations and graduation rates are steadily rising, thus potentially augmenting the numbers of all types of students eligible for college, including minorities and females. With this possible increase in the number and variety of college students, the competition for admission to four-year institutions-particularly those with strong reputations-intensifies. Prospective students are keenly aware that the better the college degree, the greater the earning capacity of the graduate. The U.S. Department of Labor estimates that over a working lifetime, a college graduate with a bachelor's degree will earn $600,000 more than a high school graduate. An advanced degree will bring $800,000 more, while a professional graduate degree in medicine, law, or business will result in an additional $1.3 million (Greene, 1998). Degrees from the most reputable institutions yield even greater results.

To attract a large pool of qualified applicants, universities and colleges fiercely compete for top spots in U.S. News & World Report's annual college rankings. Even a minor jump in this ranking can boost a school's applicant pool

sharply. Such a competitive and hierarchical educational system mirrors the economic marketplace, in which "small differences in performance (or even small differences in the credentials used to predict performance) translate into extremely large differences in reward" (Frank, 2001, p. 5). Participants in this winner-take-all market face strong incentives to invest in performance improvement, thereby increasing their chances of coming out on the winning side. Consequently, universities are spending more and more to recruit and retain the best first-year students, and tuition costs soar.

Higher tuition rates as well as our winner-take-all society put greater stress on entering college students who are concerned about their ability to pay for college and to secure a return on their investment. Thus, rather than being concerned with developing a philosophy of life or political or civic awareness, the first-year students of the new millennium not only experience more depression and anxiety and place more emphasis on securing good grades than in past decades, but they also are more committed to materialistic values (Astin, 1998). As a result, they seek technical, scientific, and literate knowledge and leadership skills required to excel in an increasingly global and insecure economy (Cooperative Institutional Research Program, 2001). As noted in Chapter 8 of this monograph, the insistence on a monetary return for attending college has also filtered into the legislature and general public, who more than ever are demanding that institutions of higher learning prove academic excellence and a high-quality education in the face of more rigorous accreditation criteria and procedures, and increased regulation.

Equally dramatic as the evolution of the concerns and attitude of entering students is the change in the role of the faculty. Beyond performing the traditional functions of teaching, research, and service, faculty must increasingly augment their contact with students as mentors outside the classroom, demonstrate new competencies in technology, attract external funds for research and teaching, serve as liaisons for alumni fundraising, engage in cross-disciplinary endeavors, and infuse their research and teaching with real-world applications-all within universities whose numbers of full-time faculty have been diminishing in recent years (Rhoades, 2000).

As the 21st century advances, colleges and universities interested in improving the experience of their first-year students face a host of challenges and changes: increased competition for a diverse student body, highly organized and career-minded first-year students, a more technologically and socially complex global environment, a faculty with tremendous demands on its time, and a skeptical public concerned with rising tuition costs. The chapters in this book suggest that there is no shortage of thoughtful and ingenious ideas for how to address many of the issues that face educators wanting to improve the experiences and profile of entering students. The challenge is not identifying solutions; rather, the difficulty lies in choosing the best option. In other words, rarely do educators lack ideas, they lack the ability to discern which ideas would be most useful within their context and how to effect lasting and purposeful change. The final chapter proposes a process for generating a unique vision for a campus-wide, first-year experience by referencing some of the dominant themes and points from the preceding chapters. We used this process in our own work, and we provide the outcome as an example of a comprehensive strategy. Any strategy that is likely to be effective must be informed by the best traditions and theories across the nation and suited to the unique needs and purposes of your campus community. Moreover, whereas separate individual campus activities programs for first-year students can and do help to address many of the myriad problems listed above, a more systemic and lasting impact on recruiting and retaining first-year students can be made when the entire campus-faculty, staff, administrators, and students-collectively come to the same understanding of what the first-year experience should be on their campus and create a coherent set of programs that reinforce that shared vision.

A Process for Change

The process of changing a university's focus to first-year students' experiences is complex and idiosyncratic. Experience suggests that effective change does not happen when an institution merely copies the programming and plans of another institution. Nor does it happen when an institution takes a band-aid approach and tries to initiate one new program to address a complicated and interrelated set of problems or when an institution creates an ambitiously long laundry list of ideas that may look impressive in a report but are never fully implemented. Although change is often driven by external factors (e.g., low yield for high-ability and multicultural students, poor retention rate for first-year students, or a perceived slipping of academic standards), significant change can only happen internally-that is, when the members of the community are willing to accept mutual responsibility to re-envision the way they perceive the first-year experience and their role and relationships within it. This point is accentuated in *Leadership Reconsidered: Engaging Higher Education in Social Change* (Astin & Astin, 2000) in which the authors argue that if vitality in learning is to be achieved, fundamental questions relating to mutual responsibility must be addressed:

- What has to be changed about the nature of teaching?
- What must faculty do?
- What must students do?
- What must student affairs staff do?

In essence, *Leadership Reconsidered* proposes that fundamental and transformative change entails a wholesale cultural shift in which key stakeholders come together to rethink the way they see themselves, the way they see others, and the way they relate to others. At the same time, those seeking change must be cognizant of their institution's entelechy. Entelechy, from the Greek *enteles*, means complete or full, which in turn derives from *telos*, or goal. According to Engell (2001), an entelechy "demands we envision how to fulfill the potential of the whole by coordinating and giving proper weight to a set of varied goals and the goods they seek to achieve" (p. 44). For each university, this process entails a particular inflection or emphasis. As Gray puts it, "The single most serious problem of our universities is their failure to adhere steadily to their own purposes" (as cited in Axtell, 1998, pp. 213-24). Thus, the type of learning environment one creates depends on the college or university culture, the nature of faculty and staff in that culture, the demographics and preparation of students, and the creativity of planners who seek to fuse the interests and needs of those involved in the community with the learning mission espoused by the college or university.

Effective transformative change will not only help to coalesce and motivate all of the key agents on campus, but it will also improve the retention rates of students. Levitz, Noel, and Richter (1999) have noted that the "success of an institution and the success of its students are inseparable" (p. 31). Institutions that seriously commit to this credo and involve every person in this effort-from the president to the faculty to the support staff-are much more likely to reduce the dropout rate of their students; and because attrition rates are greatest in the first year of college, it is crucial that emphasis is placed on special affective and cognitive needs of entering college students. Indeed, as Dennis (1998) notes,

"Research indicates that the first six weeks of the semester are the most critical for retaining first year students as they struggle to adapt to a new environment and academic challenges" (p. 81). To prevent students from experiencing those feelings of disappointment, failure, and confusion that lead a student to drop out of college, the holistic needs of the student must be addressed. Research indicates that attrition is determined not only by a student's relative intellectual ability but even more so by a number of key affective variables such as study habits, academic confidence, desire to finish college, attitude toward educators, self-reliance, and openness (Levitz, Noel, & Richter, 1999). Thus, one program or activity conducted by one office with a singular focus is not enough to meet this challenge. A comprehensive and coordinated effort that involves the entire campus is essential in addressing the complex and varied needs of incoming students and in ensuring a successful and completed undergraduate experience.

Although improving the first-year experience is an ambitious proposition, this type of substantial change in a university or college should not happen all at once-nor should it necessarily involve a one-time radical transformation in which all of the traditional programming and practices are discarded and new ones suddenly mandated. Not only should it be viewed by everyone involved as an ongoing and evolutionary process (which they can help to shape and reshape), but it should also be made manageable and feasible. Beginning by revising or piloting a few quality programs that really make a difference to first-year students and faculty is far preferable to instituting an array of mediocre programs or taking on one major initiative in which most key stakeholders do not feel invested. Indeed, incremental and successful steps can sometimes help

> "Effective transformative change will not only help to coalesce and motivate all of the key agents on campus, but it will also improve the retention rates of students."

a group shift its thinking and thereby make possible a more radical transformation in the future. As faculty, staff, and students witness successful small changes, they may be more willing to take responsibility for larger ones. Key to enabling this shift is creating a system of open and regular communication. Because a university consists of many units with very different ways of perceiving the world and often little interaction with one another, it is imperative that before and during a change, all of those involved are kept abreast of developments, given frequent opportunities to offer feedback, and taken seriously when they do offer feedback.

A commitment to improving the first-year experience is significant not only for the faculty and staff who must rethink their own roles and relationships with others, but also for the students. As Gardner (2001) puts it, "The first year of college is one of life's most crucial and memorable transitions. The degree to which students achieve success navigating this watershed year exerts an enormous influence on their academic progress, career pursuits, and social endeavors" (p. 1). The following steps have been found to be logical and incremental points along the way toward achieving a shared commitment to enhancing the first-year experience. Although these steps are listed in a linear fashion, they may not always happen consecutively, and they should be modified to suit the needs of one's particular context.

Create an Integrated Academic and Student Affairs Committee

Because the university is often fragmented into different divisions and departments, it is important to pursue active collaboration with various parts of the institution from the very beginning of the change process. One way to do this is to create a comprehensive task force or committee, with representation from those units with the largest stake in the first-year experience. Some key stakeholders whose concerns are most directly influenced by first-year students and who have the greatest influence on them include admission and recruitment staff, first-year instructional staff in core or liberal arts courses,

residence hall or commuter center staff who deal primarily with first-year students, academic advising staff, representatives from student clubs and organizations who are eager to have new members, and administrators who will have to perfect support services and systems to accommodate any recommended changes resulting from the committee's work. In addition, alumni and community members can also be critical in forming a planning team. If representatives of these units are not available to serve on the actual committee, it is important that committee members seek out their input in other ways-through interviews, conversations, surveys, or an invitation to review preliminary drafts of the committee report. All those on the committee should understand that their roles are not only to represent the stakes of their constituents, but also to facilitate effective communication-that is, to take information back to their constituents, seek feedback on that information, refine it, and then return to the committee with those newly refined ideas. A spirit of inclusive and open collaboration is crucial to effecting change.

In order to model this spirit of collaboration, it may also be advisable for the committee to have co-chairs, one from student affairs and the other from academic affairs. The co-chairs must model this open exchange of ideas, worldviews, and respect and demonstrate a willingness to synthesize perspectives. Coming from separate divisions, the authors of this chapter found the experience of co-chairing a first-year-experience committee to be an eye-opening and critical means to creating systemic change. Both academic and student affairs staff tend to perceive the world in different ways. Their vocabularies, assumptions about learning, and priorities can also vary, and each division tends to harbor hidden prejudices, fears, and stereotypes about the other. For example, academic affairs staff often believe that student affairs staff sometimes distract students from serious intellectual and academic inquiry and coddle them, thereby feeding into students' narcissistic proclivities. Conversely, student affairs personnel often express frustration at faculty, who they feel focus exclusively on cognitive development to the neglect of more holistic concerns, such as interpersonal, intrapersonal, physical, and spiritual development. The co-chairs can ensure that all of the committee members gain a better understanding of and empathy for the positions of those from divisions different from their own, thereby paving the way for a more open system of communication and a true integration of ideas and perspectives. Moreover, they can help committee members overcome the harmful "zero-sum-gain" mindset (the idea that if I compromise on one issue, I am necessarily losing power, control, and resources). If the co-chairs are willing to look critically at their own units and division, to listen carefully to the perspective of their fellow chair, and to make changes in the way they perceive the world and function in it, then they set a powerful tone of collaboration for others on the committee and across the university to follow.

Review Professional Literature

Like the co-chairs, each of the committee members should pursue their work as collaborative members of a learning team. All should be learners, conceptualizers, and gatherers of critical information. To start the process of inquiry, the committee should explore, research, and generate theoretical concepts that underlie how the college or university perceives learning. As this process of discovery unfolds, the committee should formulate a set of founding assumptions about first-year students and their learning. If there are faculty members or staff on the campus who pursue the study of student development or teaching pedagogy, they should be included as members or consultants to the planning committee. Consulting these experts not only demonstrates respect for their work but also allows easy and quick access to information that would otherwise have to be gleaned from publications or consultations with experts elsewhere.

Although there are many definitions and theories about learning, one that appeals to many in both academic and student affairs capacities is the "Powerful Partnerships" model (1998), compiled through the collaboration of

American Association for Higher Education, American College Personnel Association, and National Association of Student Personnel Administrators. This model includes a set of principles designed to stimulate high-quality learning. These principles hold that learning is fundamentally about making and maintaining connections between in-class and out-of-class experiences as well as among students and faculty. Students' learning can be enhanced when they are actively involved in the search for meaning, receive continual constructive feedback and engage in self-reflection, are encouraged to integrate new information with old, and are immersed in a challenging learning environment. "Powerful Partnerships" offers an idealized view of learning as a collaborative, contextual, developmental, and cumulative process. Underlying this definition of learning is the assumption that learning can happen in any context and is made more profound if connections are made throughout these different contexts.

Reinforcing the notion of learning as fundamentally collaborative is important not only because it can help to unify faculty, staff, students, and even alumni in their striving for deeper learning in all experiences, but also because it works against the traditional academic emphasis on competition in intellectual inquiry. Whether one uses or revises the "Powerful Partnerships" model or another of the many excellent models that exist, what is important is to identify or develop a compelling model for enhancement, one that is derived from the unique understanding of learning in the specific campus environment and that can be used to stimulate the creative thinking of the planning team. Such a model will help committee members decide what to include in the first-year experience and how to modify existing components of the first-year program.

Conduct an Internal Analysis

Every campus has a first-year program. At some campuses, it is implicit rather than explicit. The first-year planning committee should seek to expose the implicit first-year courses, activities, and other components already in existence so that they can deliberate on whether the implicit assumptions and practices of this existing program are defensible in the context of research and theory. Conducting an inventory and creating a list of existing components of your first-year program—beginning with the initial recruitment and marketing efforts of your university and ending with the transition into the sophomore college year—can be an excellent early step in the process. Committee members can deepen their awareness and understanding of these existing activities and practices as well as their strengths and current obstacles through interviews, focus groups, questionnaires, and other research methods. In addition, specific and critical analyses should be performed (or recent studies used) to discover how students on the campus think and relate to others as well as how they perceive themselves and their role in learning.

The analysis of how students see learning and how they interact with others may lead to new insights about what is required to foster productive learning. Student development theory clearly indicates that students' affective development heavily influences their ability to pursue rigorous intellectual learning. As Baxter Magolda (1999) has found in her longitudinal study of adult learners, learning is a slowly evolving and developmental process. To achieve "self-authorship" (the ability to define one's own views rather than to blindly accept others'), one must gain "simultaneously an ability to construct knowledge in a contextual world, an ability to construct an internal identity separate from external influences, and an ability to engage in relationships without losing one's internal identity" (p. 12). In other words, cognition is necessarily intertwined with the intrapersonal and interpersonal dimensions of learning. Thus, to pay attention to affective or social development is not to "dumb down" the intellectual experience, it is simply to acknowledge that, without giving attention to natural developmental transitions, students will not be freed for productive and purposeful learning.

Beyond understanding the way students learn on your campus, it is important to think about students' attitudes toward academic study

and effort. In a recent study that focused on student expectations about learning at several Midwest universities, Schilling and Schilling (1999) discovered that "most incoming students report expecting to spend thirty or forty hours a week in academic pursuits, including attending classes" (p. 4). In other words, they expect to spend about an hour a day outside of class for every hour in class. Faculty, however, expect students to spend two to three times that much. Even more surprisingly, by the spring semester of the first year, most students were devoting much less time (20 or fewer hours a week) on academic study than the amount that they had originally set for themselves, thereby widening the gap between faculty and student expectations for student effort even further.

These findings underscore the importance of balance between first-year students' curricular and co-curricular lives. Students need help deciding how to spend their time, energy, and their intellectual and interpersonal resources. The relationship among these various choices is especially important; students need to have a model for how their choices will influence their learning and eventual career and personal experiences. As Arminio and Loflin have shown in Chapter 3, purposeful involvement in co-curricular activities and organizations can help to deepen student learning, advance student intellectual development, and ensure their completion of college. Similarly, King and Wooten point out in Chapter 4 that students who are part of a campus community and take part in campus activities (such as orientation, residence hall events, and campus celebrations) are more satisfied with college and tend to persist to graduation. Finally, Kuh, Palmer, and Kish in Chapter 1 provide evidence that students engaged in purposeful out-of-class experiences reap tangible educational rewards.

The greater threat to academic excellence and devotion than over-involvement in co-curricular activities is an over-indulgence in certain types of social experiences. The problems of alcohol and other drug abuse are legendary and intractable in many collegiate settings; this problem and West Virginia University's creative response, which involved the collaboration of student and academic affairs, is described by Gray, Lang, and Collins in Chapter 7. Although higher education administrators are not responsible for the choices students make about social life after class hours and off the geographic boundaries of the campus, it is clear that the choices many students make have a negative impact on their learning. To begin addressing this, a comprehensive plan to enhance first-year students' engagement must take into account such things as peer influence, students' perceptions (or misperceptions) of what is expected related to drinking and other forms of socializing, and what qualifies as acceptable entertainment on weeknights and late-night on weekends.

In addition to helping students set realistic expectations about academic learning and effort, it is also important to help faculty and student affairs staff redefine and better communicate their own expectations about learning to students and to understand the changing nature of students in today's higher education institutions. In Chapter 2, Schroeder explains the changes among students that impact the campus and those who serve them. Faculty and staff will be more effective in achieving their goals if they are well informed about these dynamics. Unlike many faculty and staff members who went to college to identify a philosophy of life, felt alienated from traditional authorities and establishments, and developed an ironic cynicism on life, today's students are "incredibly industrious. They like to study and socialize in groups. They create and join organizations with great enthusiasm. . . . They feel no compelling need to rebel. Not even a hint of one. They not only defer to authority; they admire it. 'Alienation' is a word one almost never hears from them. They regard the universe as beneficent, orderly and meaningful" (Brooks, 2001, p. 54). Moreover, they have grown up influenced by MTV more than by J. D. Salinger. Thus, they respond well to visual and audio stimulation and a quicker pace of communication. They also are much more candid in communication and are more comfortable with overt sexuality and the exploration of difference than previous generations of students. If faculty do not know that MTV influences many students' worldviews, opportunities to connect are lost.

The changing demographics and attitudes of students dictate that new pedagogies be explored in teaching. Service- and problem-based learning, collaborative learning, interdisciplinary teaching, and technology-enhanced learning (see Chapter 5 for exciting ideas on distance learning) are all possible ways of connecting to this more industrious, social, and pragmatic generation of first-year college students. What makes these innovative pedagogies particularly promising is that they typically address the cognitive and affective developmental needs of students and they encourage faculty and students to collaborate with others around them, including faculty from other departments, members of the community, as well as student affairs staff. Learning done in any classroom setting can be deepened and made more relevant to students' lives if out-of-class experiences (e.g., study groups in the residence halls, service experiences, field trips) that connect to the in-class learning are created.

Benchmark with Other Institutions

Studying the existing practices, attitudes, assumptions, and patterns of the current students, staff, and faculty of one's own institution is critical to developing an effective first-year program. Yet, in addition to conducting this type of internal reflection and analysis, it is important to look outward at what other similar and successful institutions have done to enhance the first-year experience. One way to do this is through benchmarking, the process of identifying, learning, adapting, and implementing outstanding practices and processes from outside organizations in order to help an organization

"If faculty do not know that MTV influences many students' worldviews, opportunities to connect are lost."

improve its performance. For some, however, benchmarking means figuring out "How we compare in the pecking-order of comparable institutions." Whereas that type of benchmarking may be useful for evaluative purposes, a first-year planning committee needs to focus on exploring peer and aspirational institutions with strong first-year programs, rather than other measures of status. Thus, it is advisable to search broadly for institutions with innovative and effective practices in this area and then to involve key stakeholders on campus to help adapt these practices to their own context.

Where at all possible, committee members should be funded to visit other campuses to be able to benchmark. Literature survey, web analysis, and telephone conferences prove useful when it comes to making the important decisions of how to enhance first-year student learning, but nothing compares to a face-to-face interaction with others who have already trod the same path. If conducted with the right spirit, benchmarking can be an eye-opening experience and a means of overcoming resistance to change. Inviting a skeptic to visit another university that has implemented a successful first-year program can help create better "buy-in" and thus speed along the process of organizational change. Moreover, by venturing outside one's own sector, fresh, breakthrough ideas as well as an appreciation for what one's own institution does well are obtained.

Create a Provisional Model

Once all of the information has been collected from the review of professional literature, the internal analysis, and the external benchmarking process, the committee can turn its attention to creating a model for the first-year experience that builds on the best internal and external practices and that is uniquely suited to the local campus culture. As the committee develops the model, these questions should be considered:

♦ Does each component of the first-year program (e.g., course, activity, program, or opportunity) currently offered or planned promote the definition of learning to which the committee has agreed?

♦ Are the developmental needs of first-year students being recognized and accommodated?

♦ Can existing efforts be modified in ways to complement the emerging notions of what the ideal learning environment would entail? If possibilities exist, how can those who are responsible for these existing components join in the refinement and change effort?

♦ Are there programs that can or should be eliminated?

♦ Do the proposed new initiatives respond to the critical issues identified in the external and internal research phases?

♦ Are there adequate resources to support the recommended changes? If resources exist, are there enough so that each of the initiatives can become exemplary marks of quality? If not, how might you secure the resources?

♦ Can other proposals, for which there are no resources, be "sold" to those who will have to change or will have to provide resources in order for the first-year initiatives to be successful?

♦ Is there enough "buy-in" from key stakeholders (e.g., faculty, upper-class students, staff, administration)? If not, how can this support be ensured?

These questions and areas of concern are not static and finite. In fact, as planning proceeds, new issues will emerge and take prominence above others. The critical factor is that the co-chairs and the rest of the committee must see potential obstacles as opportunities to forge new relationships and innovations.

Ensure Continuous Improvement Through Assessment

In Chapter 8, Siegel points out that one powerful way to leverage change and improvement in any program is through assessment. Assessment, according to Siegel, entails a series of beneficial steps that include defining the purpose and goals of a program, identifying concerns or problems associated with that program, gathering data and information that address those concerns or questions, sharing findings, and using findings to create improvement. Thus, it is imperative that as the committee is developing or revising a first-year program, they simultaneously generate a clear means of assessing the effectiveness of the new comprehensive plan as well as the individual program initiatives to enhance first-year students' experiences.

Assessment should be formulated to determine whether there is both an individual impact on students as well as a systemic or environmental change that complements the vision of the planning team. Key stakeholders from student and academic affairs should be involved in conceptualizing and collecting the assessment and evaluation information. The stakeholders must be able to be critical and analytical of themselves while at the same time offering insight and assistance to colleagues elsewhere in the institution who are striving to achieve the purposes of the plan.

Disseminate and Incorporate New and Revised Ideas

Throughout the planning process, the committee should share the emerging model with all of the stakeholders interviewed or surveyed. The committee members must become "charismatic listeners" who absorb feedback from others so carefully that, even if the advocated change is not adopted (or the advocated status quo is not maintained), it is undeniable that the feedback was heard. Where at all possible, revise the emerging document on a regular basis and share drafts with key change agents for additional feedback. In fact, it is best if the committee views the plan as a living document until all those involved have signed on to its tenets.

When criticisms emerge—even harsh criticisms—it is important to remember that any change that is significant is going to meet with resistance. Because change often entails rethinking one's habits, values and attitudes, it is necessarily going to meet with some resistance. Thus, not only is resistance something that one should not avoid, it should be met with empathy and interest. The opinions of the resisters will offer committee members valuable insights into the feasibility of the present proposed changes and possibly provide some ideas for

how to improve the plan so that it can be implemented more successfully.

Seek Endorsement While Building Grassroots Support

Heifetz (2002) argues that what often stops institutional change from occurring is the failure on the part of leaders to make distinctions between technical challenges (those which ask us to apply current know-how and can be decided by authorities) and adaptive challenges (those which require us to learn new ways and which must be done by the people within the program). The model advanced in this chapter demands adaptive rather than technical leadership. Although adaptive leadership underscores the importance of "bottom-up" decision-making (that is, involving all of those key change-agents—students, faculty, and staff—in the process), it also does not ignore the formal hierarchy of the university. Even the highest officials of the university must be kept abreast of the deliberations of the first-year planning committee throughout the process. Once the committee agrees to a comprehensive plan, the endorsement of institutional positional leaders should be sought and their advocacy made public. Endorsement is primarily a way of reinforcing the good grassroots work that should have been done through the committee's analysis and planning.

Making it Work: Process to Action

This chapter has been as much about the process of stimulating change as it has been a model for the future trends of working with first-year students. The reason for this particular emphasis is our discovery that, while we sought to create change, our ability to exercise flexible and inclusive leadership was much more important than having prescribed models of the first-year experience. As noted earlier, the first-year model that each campus generates should necessarily vary. The following paragraphs describe the outcome of the work of the Miami University's First-Year Experience (FYE) Committee, a plan now in the process of implementation.

The external and internal analyses yielded some fascinating findings. Miami already offers an impressive array of first-year initiatives—including a time-honored summer reading program, an expanding honors program, theme living-learning communities, residentially based courses and advising, as well as many successful leadership development and involvement opportunities in student organizations. Yet, some concern was raised that the many extra-curricular and co-curricular opportunities offered to first-year students have distracted them from focusing sufficiently on academic learning. In addition, concerns were expressed that first-year courses were not as demanding or challenging as they could be.

After exploring the professional literature, the FYE Committee generated a unifying theme or model-entitled "Choice Matters"—which promotes an integrated vision of learning for first-year students at Miami. This theme advances intellectual challenge by supporting explicit and purposeful connections among parts of the curriculum and between the curriculum and other aspects of the collegiate experience. To achieve this vision, students must be challenged to deepen learning in all facets of their lives—in their courses as well as their other collegiate experiences. They must learn to make purposeful choices about which experiences they will pursue, choices that are in keeping with their educational goals and that simultaneously encourage them to grow in new ways.

The "Choice Matters" initiative is committed to helping entering students to do the following:

♦ Set high expectations about learning for themselves and others
♦ Make purposeful decisions and focused use of time and resources
♦ Take risks to promote learning in a diverse and complicated world
♦ Work with others to deepen their understanding of self
♦ Integrate and reflect critically on knowledge gained from diverse experiences.

Both student and academic affairs are launching several progressive elements to help students learn the importance of making good choices, taking purposeful risks, and working to achieve balance and connection in their learning experience. Some of the specific projects include

♦ *Promotional Materials and Information.* Entering students are greeted at orientation with a newsletter, speeches, skits, as well as written brochures that reinforce the importance of the "Choice Matters" initiative. Faculty members are also given a brochure on "Choice Matters" and suggestions for how they can reinforce these themes in the classroom. A web site on the FYE at Miami is being created.

♦ *"Learning Goals" Worksheet.* During the four days before class begins as well as the first week of classes, students will work with student leaders and resident assistants to complete a set of "provisional goals" using a "Learning Goals" worksheet. The worksheet will be used to demonstrate how to make discerning and purposeful choices about academic and co-curricular involvement. "Choice Matters" workshops in residence halls and with commuting students will reinforce the importance of the "Learning Goals" during the first few weeks of the semester. Student discussions will be stimulated by *Finding Forrester*, a film depicting a young male and his mentor struggling with issues of identify and choice. Viewing of the film is complemented by a web site including segment clips, an electronic discussion board, and other interactive elements.

♦ *Summer Reading Program Discussion.* All students meet with a faculty member to discuss the summer reading selection on the day before classes begin. During that discussion, faculty facilitators will emphasize the theme of choices in the book and ask students to reflect on their own choices.

♦ *Mega Fair.* A major involvement and service fair will bring all organizations open to new student participation together for new students to see. All service, multicultural, Greek, and other clubs and organizations will be invited to participate. Students will be exposed simultaneously to the array of involvement opportunities at Miami. The groups and organizations participating in Mega Fair will be encouraged to present themselves as part of the holistic Miami experience and that each and every one of them has something to contribute to students' educational attainment. Students will be encouraged to prepare by targeting specific types of involvement they wish to pursue. Students will be urged to select their involvements with academics as their first priority and with co-curricular involvement complementing classes in purposeful ways.

♦ *Developmental Advising in the Residence Hall.* First-Year Advisors (professional staff advisors in the residence halls and commuter center) will integrate the "Learning Goals" worksheet in advising appointments. Students will be helped to understand how to make their own independent decisions, free of excessive or unthinking peer influence. They will also be helped to learn to "let go" of ideas that can undermine good decision making and appropriate balance while at Miami. Of particular importance are reducing the sense of competition and undue pressure to perform, understanding that making decisions is a natural part of one's existence, and realizing that mistakes are not irreparable and new courses of action can be taken. Students will be encouraged to make careful involvement decisions during the "red zone" of the first few weeks of college. Upperclass students will be encouraged to be conscientious role models, and all will be encouraged to accept the mutual accountability so critical to establishing a healthy learning environment.

♦ *Student Organization Intervention.* Student organizations will be encouraged to increase their focus and purpose in campus event and activity scheduling. They will be particularly encouraged to promote balance, focus, and reflection in students' experiences. The staff advisors working with these organizations will urge appropriate scheduling of events, event posting on the University calendar, fewer sponsored events, and greater collaboration with other organizations, thereby enhancing the quality and reducing the costs of these co-curricular events.

The above strategies were created by an energetic, imaginative, and risk-taking group committed to a compelling and common goal—enhancing Miami students' first-year experience. The initiatives to which they committed the University were the outcome of thoughtful homework assignments, charismatic listening, coalition building, and respect accorded to all those who could possibly contribute. This example stands as testament to the fact that the process principles provided for your use can, indeed, achieve lasting and deep change. This is not a cookbook approach, but one that requires any institution serious about change to commit to comprehensive and systemic change. Finally, and perhaps most important, the process and the product helped the creators of this first-year initiative to grow in their respect for each other and in their commitment to collaborative work in the future.

References

Astin, A. W. (1998). The changing American college student: Thirty-year trends, 1966-1996. *The Review of Higher Education. 21*(2), 115-135.

Astin, A. W., & Astin, H. (2000). *Leadership reconsidered: Engaging higher education in social change.* Battle Creek, MI: W. K. Kellogg Foundation.

Axtell, J. (1998). *The pleasures of academe: A celebration and defense of higher education.* Lincoln: University of Nebraska Press.

Baxter Magolda, M. B. (1999). *Creating contexts for learning and self-authorship.* Nashville: Vanderbilt University Press.

Brooks, D. (2001, April). The organization did. *The Atlantic Monthly*, pp. 40-54.

Cooperative Institutional Research Program. (2001) Los Angeles: Higher Education Research Institute, UCLA.

Dennis, M. J. (1998). *A practical guide to enrollment and retention management in higher education*. Westport, CT: Bergin & Garvey.

Engell, J. (2001). The idea of organic growth in higher education. In M. E. Devlin, & J. W. Myerson (Eds.), *Forum futures: Exploring the future of higher education, 2000 papers*. (pp. 43-64). San Francisco: Jossey-Bass.

Frank, R. (2001). Higher education: The ultimate winner-take-all market? In M. E. Devlin, & J. W. Myerson (Eds.), *Forum futures: Exploring the future of higher education, 2000 papers*. (pp. 3-12). San Francisco: Jossey-Bass.

Gardner, J. N. (2001, Fall). Focusing on the first-year student. *Priorities, 17*, 1-10.

Greene, H. R. (1998). *The select: Realities of life and learning in America's elite college*. New York: HarperCollins.

Heifetz, R. A. (2002). *Leadership on the line: Staying alive through the dangers of leading*. Boston: Harvard Business School Press.

Levitz, R. S., Noel, L., & Richter, B. J. (1999). Strategic moves for retention success. In G. H. Gaither (Ed.), *Promising practices in recruitment, remediation, and retention*. (pp. 31-50). San Francisco: Jossey-Bass.

Powerful partnerships: A shared responsibility for learning. (1998, June 2). Joint Report from the American Association for Higher Education, American College Personnel Association, and National Association of Student Personnel Administrators.

Rhoades, G. (2000). The changing role of faculty. In J. Losc, & B. L. Fife (Eds.), *Higher education in transition: The challenges of the new millennium*. (pp. 29-50). Westport, Connecticut: Bergin & Garvey.

Schilling, K. M., & Schilling, K. L. (1999, May/June). Increasing expectations for student effort. *About Campus*, 4-10.

About the Contributors

Roxanne Argo, communications manager for the National Association for Campus Activities (NACA), has a varied background in fundraising, public relations, advertising, and integrated communications. Argo worked for NACA from 1995 to 1997 facilitating internal fund-raising campaigns and returned in 1999 to focus on corporate sponsorship initiatives. She assumed the duties of her current position in 2001. In addition to working with NACA, Argo has been public relations director and development director for two non-profit organizations. She also served as account executive for one of the Carolina's largest advertising agencies, managing an integrated communications and strategic marketing plan for a global client. A native of Arkansas, Argo received a bachelor's degree in communications from Arkansas State University and is currently pursuing a master's degree in mass communication at the University of South Carolina.

Jan Arminio is an associate professor in the department of counseling at Shippensburg University of Pennsylvania, leading the college student personnel graduate program there. Prior to becoming a faculty member she served in student affairs for 17 years in the areas of residence life, student activities, college unions, judicial affairs, and multicultural programs. Arminio's scholarship focuses on student affairs practice in higher education and on multicultural education.

Mary L. Collins is special assistant to the vice president for student affairs at West Virginia University, where her responsibilities include communications, development, student government, and the creation and implementation of innovative programs and services. As a representative of WVU, she has made several professional presentations nationally and has published articles in higher education journals and magazines. Her efforts have been recognized with membership in the Leadership Monongalia Class of 2002-03, with the Richard T. Feller Outstanding Alumni Award for Distinguished Service to Students in 2001, and with the Outstanding New Professional Award, presented by the West Virginia Association of Student Personnel Administrators in 1999. She is a member of National Association of Student Personnel Administrators and West Virginia Association of Student Personnel Administrators, and serves as chair or member of several WVU committees and organizations. Prior to her work at WVU, Collins was a freelance writer whose work was featured in several national Catholic publications. She earned bachelor's and master's degrees from WVU.

Zav Dadabhoy is the director of student activities at the Metropolitan State College of Denver. Before his current appointment, he worked at Longwood University in Farmville, Virginia as a student development educator. His research interests are technology and how higher education could view it as a strategic asset, enrollment management, the role of environmental variables in student decisions to persist, student learning as an organizational mission and as an imperative for student affairs' units, and student experiences at urban commuter campuses. He has numerous national conference presentations and publications to his credit. Dadabhoy has a doctorate in educational leadership and innovation from the University of Colorado and a master's degree in sociology from the University of Wisconsin-Milwaukee.

Alan B. Davis was appointed executive director of National Association for Campus Activities (NACA) in 1996. Prior to joining NACA, he worked at Tulane University for 21 years, serving in a variety of positions in student and auxiliary services. While at Tulane, Davis also held a variety of leadership positions in the Association of College and University Housing Officers-International and the National Association of College Auxiliary Services (NACAS), eventually serving as president-elect of NACAS. A native of Long Island, Davis received bachelor's and master's degrees from Stetson University in Florida and completed the Management Development Program of the Institute for Educational Management at the Harvard University Graduate School of Education.

Jonathan C. Dooley is assistant dean of student development at Marquette University. He has 10 years of experience as an educator working with leadership programs, campus activities, student union programs, and residence life. His participation in a U.S. Department of Education grant to develop an application guide for the Social Change Model of Leadership Development fueled his passion for educating college and high school students to become more effective citizen leaders with the ability to initiate and sustain change efforts. Dooley has

served in a variety of leadership roles with the National Association for Campus Activities (NACA) and currently serves on its board of directors. He has also served as a vice-chair for the American College Personnel Association's Commission IV, and presented at a number of regional and national conferences for NACA, Association of College-Unions International, and other professional associations. Dooley has a bachelor's degree from St. Norbert College and an M.Ed. in counseling psychology (college student personnel administration) from James Madison University.

Kenneth D. Gray is vice president for student affairs at West Virginia University. In 2001 he was given the WVU Outstanding Alumni Award, and in 2002 he was awarded the Richard T. Feller Outstanding Alumni Award for Distinguished Service to Students. In 1969, he received his J.D. from West Virginia University's College of Law and entered active duty in the U.S. Army Judge Advocate General's Corps. He served in various assignments during his military career, culminating with his promotion to Major General and service as the Assistant Judge Advocate General of the Army from 1993 to 1997. His military awards include the U.S. Army Distinguished Service Medal, the Legion of Merit, Bronze Star, two awards of the Meritorious Service Medal, Army Commendation Medal, and Army Achievement Medal. He received the Justicia Officium Award, which is the highest award given by the College of Law at West Virginia University, and received the National Bar Association's 1998 Gertrude E. Rush Distinguished Service Award for outstanding leadership and devoted service. Gray received a bachelor's degree from West Virginia State College in 1966.

Carolyn Haynes became a faculty member and director of the Windate Writing Center in the School of Interdisciplinary Studies at Miami University in 1993 immediately after receiving a doctorate in American Literature from the University of California, San Diego. Along with publishing a number of articles, she is author of *Divine Destiny: Gender and Race in Nineteenth-Century Protestantism* (1998, University Press of Mississippi) and editor and author of *Innovations in Interdisciplinary Teaching* (2002, Greenwood Press). Currently, she is president of the Association for Integrative Studies, a national organization devoted to advancing interdisciplinary scholarship and teaching in higher education, and consultant-evaluator for North Central Association for Colleges and Schools.

Mary Stuart Hunter is the director of the National Resource Center for The First-Year Experience and Students in Transition at the University of South Carolina. Her work centers on providing educators with resources to develop personal and professional skills while creating and refining innovative programs designed to increase student success. In addition to her administrative and teaching responsibilities, she conducts workshops on the first-year experience, first-year seminars, and teaching. Hunter has published on the first-year experience, first-year seminars, and academic advising, and she edited a monograph on instructor training. Beyond the university, she serves on the national advisory boards of the Policy Center on the First Year of College, the National Society of Collegiate Scholars, the Columbia Pastoral Counseling Center, and sits on the Council of Advisers for the Network of Colleges and Universities Committed to the Elimination of Drug and Alcohol Abuse. She was honored in 2001 as the Outstanding Alumnae of the Year by USC's Student Personnel/Higher Education department program.

Nancy S. King is vice president for student success and enrollment services and professor of English at Kennesaw State University in Kennesaw, Georgia. Previously, King was associate vice president in student affairs, director of the CAPS Center, and the coordinator of the New Student Experience program at KSU. King is active in numerous professional organizations and has held leadership roles in many associations. She has published in the field of academic advising and first-year seminar programs and serves frequently as a consultant to colleges and universities in the area of advising, first-year experience programs, and student success. King has made presentations on these topics at state, regional, national, and international conferences. She has also published and presented on the topic of collaboration between student affairs and academic affairs. In 1999, King received the Outstanding First-Year Student Advocate award from the National Resource Center for The First-Year Experience and Students in Transition and Houghton Mifflin Company; in 2000 she received the Virginia N. Gordon Award for Excellence in the Field of Advising from the National Academic Advising Association (NACADA); and in 2001 she received the Pacesetter Award from NACADA. She has a bachelor's degree in English and psychology from Mercer University and master's and doctoral degrees in English from Georgia State University.

Kelly Kish is a doctoral student in higher education administration with a minor in inquiry methodology at Indiana University. Currently, she works with the Center for Postsecondary Research and Planning as a project associate with the College Student Experiences Questionnaire Research Program. Her research interests include undergraduate socialization, academic and student affairs collaboration, and assessment in higher education. She received a bachelor's degree in government and politics from the University of Maryland and a master's degree in higher education and student affairs from Indiana University.

George Kuh is Chancellor's Professor of Higher Education at Indiana University in Bloomington. He directs the College Student Experiences Questionnaire Research Program and the National Survey of Student Engagement funded by Lumina Foundation for Education and The Pew Charitable Trusts and co-sponsored by The Carnegie Foundation for the Advancement of Teaching. His contributions in the areas of student engagement, assessment, institutional improvement, and college and university cultures have been recognized with awards from the American College Personnel Association, Association of Institutional Research, Association for the Study of Higher Education, Council of Independent Colleges, and National Association of Student Personnel Administrators.

Gerald E. Lang is provost and vice president for academic affairs and research at West Virginia University. As provost, he serves as the chief academic and operating officer for all of the institution's policies, programs, and budget and capital planning efforts excluding those in the health sciences. Lang came to WVU in 1976 as an assistant professor of biology. He was appointed as assistant dean for research and graduate studies in 1984 and then dean of the Eberly College of Arts and Sciences in 1986 before being named provost in 1995. As dean, he oversaw a $25 million fundraising initiative that led to the naming of the college. Lang spent three years at Dartmouth College as a postdoctoral fellow. As a scientist, he was an active researcher with consistent competitive funding from National Science Foundation and other federal agencies throughout his career. He has published over 50 scientific papers and given numerous presentations. He was recognized as a Distinguished Alumnus from Western Illinois University, where he received a bachelor's degree. He received a master's degree from the University of Wyoming, and a doctorate from Rutgers.

Stephen E. Loflin is the executive director of the National Society of Collegiate Scholars, a national non-profit honor society offering lifetime membership and opportunities for scholarship, leadership, and service to high-achieving first- and second-year college students. He has served as residence coordinator at the University of North Florida and also as director of student life at George Washington University and director of student programs at Georgetown University, both in Washington, D.C. He was a resident director on the Spring 1995 Semester at Sea program. Originally from South Carolina, Loflin received a bachelor's degree in business administration with an emphasis in marketing from the University of South Carolina and a master's degree in higher education administration under the direction of Dr. Melvene Hardee at Florida State University.

Megan Palmer is a higher education doctoral candidate at Indiana University with a minor in social foundations of education. She currently works at the National Survey of Student Engagement as a project associate. Prior to returning to graduate school, Palmer worked with TRIO programs at the University of Kansas. Her professional experiences also include work in residence life and leadership development programs. Her main research interests include the partnership between secondary and postsecondary education, college choice, early intervention programs, access and equity in higher education, and parent involvement in secondary and postsecondary education. Palmer holds a bachelor's degree in speech communication and sociology from the University of St. Thomas in St. Paul, Minnesota and a master's degree in student affairs in higher education from Colorado State University.

Dennis C. Roberts is assistant vice president for student affairs at Miami University in Oxford, Ohio. He is also an assistant professor in the educational leadership department at the university. Roberts is the author of numerous articles and chapters in books, as well as the editor for *Student Leadership Programs in Higher Education* (1982), the first book advocating and providing an explicit model for leadership development in higher education, and *Designing Campus Activities to Foster a Sense of Community* (1989). He held several leadership positions in the American College Personnel Association, including serving as its president in 1985-86. Roberts currently serves on the board of directors of the LeaderShape Institute and is the founding convener of the International Leadership Association's Leadership Educators' section. His scholarship and practice are committed to understanding leadership, leadership development, community, and student affairs work as a catalyst for deeper learning. He has a bachelor's degree in music and an M.Ed. in student personnel administration from Colorado State University, and a Ph.D. in college student personnel from the University of Maryland.

Charles C. Schroeder has served as the chief student affairs officer at Mercer University, Saint Louis University, Georgia Institute of Technology, and the University of Missouri-Columbia during the past 23 years. In 2001, he became a professor of higher education in the educational leadership and policy analysis department at the University of Missouri-Columbia. He has assumed various leadership roles in the American College Personnel Association, serving as president in 1986 and 1993 and as executive editor of *About Campus: Enriching the Student Learning*

128

Experience. Schroeder has written more than 60 articles and published a book in 1994 with Phyllis Mable titled *Realizing the Educational Potential of Residence Halls*. He received bachelor's and master's degrees from Austin College and a doctorate from Oregon State University.

Kathy M. Shellogg, associate vice president for student life and campus community at Nebraska Wesleyan University, has been a leadership educator for 15 years. Working with college students, young professionals, volunteer organizations, and communities, she has sought to educate and develop citizen leaders who understand the process of leadership. She has facilitated the development of several leadership programs on a variety of campuses through the generous support of the W.K Kellogg Foundation and the U.S. Department of Education's Eisenhower Grant Program. Shellogg was a founding board member of the American College Personnel Association (ACPA)'s Educational Leadership Foundation, a presenter at many regional National Association for Campus Activities (NACA) conferences, the chair of ACPA's Commission IV, and a participant in a number of the earliest National Leadership Symposiums sponsored by NACA. Educational Foundation, Kellogg Foundation, the Interassocation Leadership Project and the University of Maryland at College Park. Shellogg has a bachelor's degree from Wittenberg University and a master's degree in psychological counseling from the University of Notre Dame.

Michael J. Siegel serves as research associate with the Policy Center on the First Year of College, supported by grants from The Atlantic Philanthropies and The Pew Charitable Trusts and located in Brevard, North Carolina. He is responsible for a wide range of projects and research initiatives aimed at improving the first college year. His research interests include the learning experiences of new college and university presidents, first-year student expectations and engagement, and the study of colleges and universities as culture-bearing organizations. Siegel recently published a book called *Primer on Assessment of the First College Year* (2003). He holds a doctorate in higher education and a minor in anthropology from Indiana University, where he also

served as project manager for the College Student Experiences Questionnaire. He also has a master's degree in counseling from Georgia State University and a bachelor's degree in psychology from Wake Forest University.

Tracy L. Skipper is editorial projects coordinator for the National Resource Center for The First-Year Experience and Students in Transition at the University of South Carolina. Prior to her work at the Center, she served as director of residence life and judicial affairs at Shorter College in Rome, Georgia, where her duties included teaching in the college's first-year seminar program and serving as an academic advisor for first-year students. She also served as director of student activities and residence life at Wesleyan College. Skipper has taught in the first-year English program at USC and currently teaches University 101. She holds a bachelor's degree in psychology from USC, a master's degree in higher education from Florida State University, and a master's degree in American literature from USC. She is currently pursuing a doctorate in composition and rhetoric and has a research interest in the teaching of writing in first-year seminar courses.

Brian M. Wooten is the assistant director of student life at Kennesaw State University in Kennesaw, Georgia. He has been involved in various professional organizations and has held leadership roles with the National Association for Campus Activities (NACA). Currently, he serves as the NACA South Regional Coordinator. Other leadership roles in NACA include Regional Conference Chair 2000-01, Associate Member Relations Coordinator 1998-99, and Associate Member Contact for NACA South 1997-98. Wooten has been honored with numerous awards including the 1999 C. Shaw Smith New Professional Award presented by NACA as well as the 1997 New Professional award for the Southeast Region. At Kennesaw State University he has been named the KSU Outstanding Advisor and recognized by the African American Student Alliance as the 1998 Staff Supporter of the Year. Wooten received a bachelor's degree from Furman University and a master's degree in public affairs from Kennesaw State University.

About the Sponsors

Located in Columbia, South Carolina, the National Association for Campus Activities has served as the nation's largest professional organization for campus activities for more than 40 years, with programs and services designed to reflect the field's increased responsibilities for student leadership development as well as entertainment programming. NACA links the higher education and entertainment communities in a business and learning partnership, creating educational and business opportunities for student and professional members.

The mission of the National Resource Center for The First-Year Experience and Students in Transition at the University of South Carolina is to build and sustain a vibrant campus-based and international educational community committed to the success of first-year college students and all students in transition. We achieve this mission by providing opportunities for the exchange of practical and theory-based information and ideas through the convening of conferences, teleconferences, institutes, and workshops; publishing monographs, a peer-reviewed journal, a newsletter, guides, and books; generating and supporting research and scholarship; hosting visiting scholars; and administering a web site and electronic listservs.

Additional Titles on Promising Practices in the First College Year from the National Resource Center for The First-Year Experience & Students in Transition

Monograph 35. *2000 National Survey of First-Year Seminar Programs: Continuing Innovations in the Collegiate Curriculum.* This volume reviews national data on first-year seminars in nearly 750 regionally accredited colleges and universities in the United States. Information is offered on both the structure and content of these courses, with a discussion of how the seminar has changed over the last decade. Brief descriptions of courses representing the five most common seminar types are also provided. Data and course descriptions can be used to design, refine, or build support for the first-year seminar on a variety of campuses. 128 pages. ISBN 1-889271-39-X.

Monograph 34. *Service-Learning and The First-Year Experience: Preparing Students for Personal Success and Civic Responsibility.* Edward Zlotkowski, *Editor. Produced in association with Campus Compact.* This monograph combines a research-based argument for the value of service-learning in the first year of college with a practical discussion of the issues related to implementation. Readers will find program and course models from a variety of disciplines, curricular structures, and institutional types. Connecting service-learning to the broader issues of the first college year, this monograph allows readers to examine where and how learning best takes place. 167 pages. ISBN 1-889271-38-1.

Monograph 26. *Learning Communities: New Structures, New Partnerships for Learning.* Jodi H. Levine, *Editor.* Learning communities have become one of the most widely used structures for achieving both academic and social integration of new students. This monograph describes various successful models, links theory with examples of good practice, and describes how learning communities can facilitate faculty development. In addition, chapter authors outline strategies for dealing with logistical concerns and provide comprehensive resource listings and recommendations for building learning community programs. 180 pages. ISBN 1-889271-27-6.

Monograph 5. *Residence Life Programs and The First-Year Experience.* William J. Zeller, Dorothy S. Fidler, and Betsy O. Barefoot, *Editors. Published jointly with the Association of Colleges and University Housing Offices-International.* This monograph presents research and innovative programming ideas for improving the first-year residential experience. Chapter topics include the role of residence life in recruitment and orientation, assignment issues, promoting diversity, working with paraprofessional staff, safety and security, living-learning programs, and assessment. 144 pages. ISBN 1-889271-04-7.

Strengthening First-Year Student Learning at Doctoral/Research-Extensive Universities: Examples of Current Practice. Marc Cutright. *Published by the Policy Center on the First Year of College.* This monograph is a selection of 25 narratives submitted by Carnegie Doctoral/Research-Extensive Universities to a web-based database created by the Policy Center on the First Year of College. The monograph highlights a variety of efforts gaining strength at research universities, including learning communities, disciplined-based first-year seminars, and Supplemental Instruction. 107 pages. ISBN 0-9726527-1-X.

Learning Interdependence: A Case Study of the International/Intercultural Education of First-Year College Students. David J. Bachner, Laurence J. Malone, and Mary C. Snider. Challenging the notion that study abroad programs are best suited for "mature" students, faculty and administrators at Hartwick College designed an intercultural, interdisciplinary course for first-year students, spanning an entire academic year. The book includes information on program development and student outcomes, with an appendix featuring syllabi from six courses based on the model. 203 pages. ISBN 1-889271-35-7.

Use the order form on the next page to order any of these titles from the National Resource Center.

Use this form to order additional copies of this monograph or to order other titles from the National Resource Center for The First-Year Experience & Students in Transition.

Prices advertised in this publication are subject to change.

Item	Quantity	Price	Total
Monograph 36. *Involvement in Campus Activities & Retention of First-Year Students*		$30.00	
Monograph 35. *2000 National Survey of First-Year Seminar Programs*		$30.00	
Monograph 34. *Service-Learning and The First-Year Experience*		$35.00	
Monograph 26. *Learning Communities*		$30.00	
Monograph 5. *Residence Life Programs and The First-Year Experience*		$35.00	
Strengthening First-Year Student Learning at Doctoral/Research-Extensive Universities: Examples of Current Practice		$25.00	
Learning Interdependence		$30.00	
		Shipping and Handling	
		Total	

*Call for shipping charges on this item.

Shipping Charges:	Order Amount	Shipping Cost
U.S.	$0 - $50	$ 6.50 US
	$50 - $150	$10.00 US
	over $150	$15.00 US

Customers outside the U.S. will be billed exact shipping charges plus a $5.00 processing fee. Fax or e-mail us to obtain a shipping estimate. Be sure to include a list of items you plan to purchase and to specify your preference for Air Mail or UPS delivery.

Name _____   **Department** _____

Institution _____   **Telephone** _____

Mailing Address _____

City _____ **State/Province** _____ **Postal Code** _____

E-mail Address _____

Select your option payable to the University of South Carolina:

☐ **Check Enclosed**   ☐ **Institutional Purchase Order**   **Purchase Order No.** _____

Credit Card: ☐ VISA   ☐ ⬤   ☐ 🗖   **Expiration Date** _____

Card No. _____

Name of Cardholder _____

Signature _____

Mail this form to: National Resource Center for The First-Year Experience & Students in Transition, University of South Carolina, 1629 Pendleton Street, Columbia, SC 29208. Phone (803) 777-6229. FAX (803) 777-4699. E-mail burtonp@gwm.sc.edu Federal ID 57-6001153.